A GEOGRAPHIC DICTIONARY OF MASSACHUSETTS

By
HENRY GANNETT

CLEARFIELD

Reprinted for
Clearfield Company, Inc. by
Genealogical Publishing Co., Inc.
Baltimore, Maryland
1999

Originally published: Washington, D.C., 1894
as U.S. Geological Survey, Bulletin No. 116
Reprinted: Genealogical Publishing Co., Inc.
Baltimore, 1978
From a volume in the George Peabody Branch,
Enoch Pratt Free Library,
Baltimore, Maryland
Library of Congress Catalogue Card Number 78-59121
International Standard Book Number 0-8063-0818-4
Made in the United States of America

UNITED STATES GEOLOGICAL SURVEY
J. W. POWELL, DIRECTOR

A

GEOGRAPHIC DICTIONARY

OF

MASSACHUSETTS

BY

HENRY GANNETT

WASHINGTON
GOVERNMENT PRINTING OFFICE
1894

LETTER OF TRANSMITTAL.

DEPARTMENT OF THE INTERIOR,
U. S. GEOLOGICAL SURVEY, DIVISION OF GEOGRAPHY,
Washington, D. C., January 15, 1894.

SIR: I have the honor to transmit herewith a geographic dictionary of Massachusetts.

Very respectfully,

HENRY GANNETT,
Chief Topographer.

Hon. J. W. POWELL,
Director U. S. Geological Survey.

A GEOGRAPHIC DICTIONARY OF MASSACHUSETTS.

The Geographic Dictionary of Massachusetts, which constitutes this bulletin, is designed to aid in finding any geographic feature upon the atlas sheets of that State which are published by the U. S. Geological Survey. It contains all the names given upon the sheets, and is limited to them. Under each name is a brief statement showing the feature it designates and its location, and opposite to it the name of the atlas sheet, or sheets, upon which it is to be found.

The atlas sheets upon which the State is represented are the result of a survey made at the joint expense of the U. S. Geological Survey and the Commonwealth of Massachusetts. The scale upon which they are published is 1:62500; that is, 62,500 inches upon the ground, or very nearly one mile, is represented by one inch upon the map. Relief, or the variation of elevation, is represented by contour lines, or lines of equal elevation above mean sea level. These contour lines are at vertical intervals of 20 feet; that is, each successive contour indicates a level 20 feet higher than the one below it. Upon the map all water bodies—bays, ponds, rivers, etc.—are represented in blue; the contour lines representing the relief, together with the figures representing absolute elevations, are printed in brown; while the lettering and all symbols of the works of man are printed in black.

The area of the State is represented upon 54 sheets, each sheet comprising 15 minutes of latitude by 15 minutes of longitude. The territory covered by each sheet is, therefore, about 17½ miles from north to south, and about 13 miles from east to west, and its area is about 225 square miles. Of these sheets 29 only lie entirely or virtually within the State, the others comprising portions of the adjacent States of New Hampshire, Vermont, New York, Rhode Island and Connecticut. The following is a list of the sheets, showing the names assigned to them and their limits in latitude and longitude:

Sheets.	Limits.			
	In latitude.		In longitude.	
	° ′	° ′	° ′	° ′
Newburyport	42 45 to	43 00	70 45 to	71 00
Haverhill	42 45	43 00	71 00	71 15
Gloucester	42 30	42 45	70 30	70 45
Salem	42 30	42 45	70 45	71 00
Lawrence	42 30	42 45	71 00	71 15
Lowell	42 30	42 45	71 15	71 30
Groton	42 30	42 45	71 30	71 45

A GEOGRAPHIC DICTIONARY OF MASSACHUSETTS. [BULL. 116.

Sheets.	Limits.			
	In latitude.		In°longitude.	
	° ′	° ′	° ′	° ′
Fitchburg	42 30	42 45	71 45	72 00
Winchendon	42 30	42 45	72 00	72 15
Warwick	42 30	42 45	72 15	72 30
Greenfield	42 30	42 45	72 30	72 45
Hawley	42 30	42 45	72 45	73 00
Greylock	42 30	42 45	73 00	73 15
Berlin	42 30	42 45	73 15	73 30
Boston Bay	42 15	42 30	70 45	71 00
Boston	42 15	42 30	71 00	71 15
Framingham	42 15	42 30	71 15	71 30
Marlboro	42 15	42 30	71 30	71 45
Worcester	42 15	42 30	71 45	72 00
Barre	42 15	42 30	72 00	72 15
Belchertown	42 15	42 30	72 15	72 30
Northampton	42 15	42 30	72 30	72 45
Chesterfield	42 15	42 30	72 45	73 00
Becket	42 15	42 30	73 00	73 15
Pittsfield	42 15	42 30	73 15	73 30
Provincetown	42 00	42 15	70 00	70 15
Duxbury	42 00	42 15	70 30	70 45
Abington	42 00	42 15	70 45	71 00
Dedham	42 00	42 15	71 00	71 15
Franklin	42 00	42 15	71 15	71 30
Blackstone	42 00	42 15	71 30	71 45
Webster	42 00	42 15	71 45	72 00
Brookfield	42 00	42 15	72 00	72 15
Palmer	42 00	42 15	72 15	72 30
Springfield	42 00	42 15	72 30	72 45
Granville	42 00	42 15	72 45	73 00
Sandisfield	42 00	42 15	73 00	73 15
Sheffield	42 00	42 15	73 15	73 30
Wellfleet	41 45	42 00	69 55	70 10
Plymouth	41 45	42 00	70 30	70 45
Middleboro	41 45	42 00	70 45	71 00
Taunton	41 45	42 00	71 00	71 15
Providence	41 45	42 00	71 15	71 30
Chatham	41 30	41 45	69 45	70 00
Yarmouth	41 30	41 45	70 00	70 15
Barnstable	41 32	41 47	70 15	70 30
Falmouth	41 30	41 45	70 39	70 45
New Bedford	41 30	41 45	70 45	71 00
Fall River	41 30	41 45	71 00	71 15
Nantucket	41 13	41 28	69 57	70 12
Muskeget	41 15	41 30	70 15	70 30
Marthas Vineyard	41 15	41 30	70 30	70 45
Gay Head	41 15	41 30	70 45	71 00
Sakonnet	41 15	41 30	71 00	71 15

The spelling of the names conforms to the decisions of the United States Board on Geographic Names.

Massachusetts is one of the original thirteen States. It was the sixth to ratify the Constitution, which it did on February 6, 1788. The boundary lines between Massachusetts and adjacent States are somewhat irregular. They were established, in the main, during colonial days as the result of compromises between conflicting claims for jurisdiction among the colonies. The lines were surveyed and marked also in early days, when methods of surveying were much cruder than at present. Both of these facts serve to account for their irregularity.

The eastern part of the north boundary is a line traced at a distance of 3 miles from the main course of the Merrimac River and parallel to its windings. As run and marked it consists of a series of straight lines broken by angles generally parallel to the river. At a point three miles north of Pawtucket Falls it ceases to run parallel to the river, and thence it was designed to run due west. This was the result of a compromise between the colonies of Massachusetts Bay and New Hampshire, thus settled by a decree of the king. The line westward from that point was run under instructions from the governor of New Hampshire, who furnished to the surveyor as the magnetic variation an amount largely in excess of the fact. The line was run accordingly, and consequently is directed considerably north of west.

The west boundary of the State is the result of an agreement made with the New York colony, and the south boundary is similarly the result of compromises and conventions between the colony and State of Massachusetts and its neighbors, Connecticut and Rhode Island. These boundaries are so irregular that it is impossible to describe them otherwise than by means of a map or by a detailed statement of courses and distances.

The total area of the State is 8,315 square miles, of which it is estimated that 275 square miles are water surface, consisting of landlocked bays, ponds, and rivers, leaving as the land area 8,040 square miles.

The State is divided into fourteen counties, and these are subdivided into towns and cities, of which there are 352. The following table presents a list of the counties, with the number of towns and cities in each and the area of each county:

County.	Towns and cities.	Area.
		Sq. miles.
Barnstable	15	434
Berkshire	32	942
Bristol	20	589
Dukes	6	110
Essex	35	554
Franklin	26	730
Hampden	22	604
Hampshire	23	620
Middlesex	54	840
Nantucket	1	51
Norfolk	27	433
Plymouth	27	722
Suffolk	4	51
Worcester	59	1,635
Total	352	8,315

A GEOGRAPHIC DICTIONARY OF MASSACHUSETTS.

Atlas sheets.

Abbott; brook in west part of Chester, about 4 miles long, tributary to west branch of Westfield River............... Chesterfield.
Abbott; hill in west part of Chester; elevation, 1,455 feet.... Chesterfield.
Abbott Run; stream in North Attleboro and Attleboro, Mass.; and in Rhode Island................................... Providence.
Abington; town in Plymouth County; area, 11 square miles.. Abington.
Abner; pond in southern part of Plymouth.................... Plymouth.
Abram; hill in Tyngsboro; elevation, 280 feet................. Lowell.
Accord; pond in western part of South Scituate............. Abington.
Acton; town in Middlesex County; area, 21 square miles.... { Framingham. Lowell.
Acton Center; village in Acton .... Framingham.
Acushnet; town in southeastern part of Bristol County; area, 19 square miles .... New Bedford.
Acushnet; village in town of same name at head of New Bedford Harbor... New Bedford.
Acushnet; river, outlet of New Bedford Reservoir in Acushnet, flowing into New Bedford Harbor..................... New Bedford.
Acushnet Cedar; swamp in northern part of New Bedford.... New Bedford.
Acushnet Station; railway station in New Bedford........... New Bedford.
Adams; town in northern part of Berkshire County; area 23 square miles .... Greylock.
Adams; village in southern part of town of same name....... Greylock.
Adams; mountain in Rowe; altitude 1,900 feet .... Hawley.
Adamsville; village in town of Coleraine .... Greenfield.
Addition; hill in Marlboro; elevation 440 feet................ Marlboro.
Agassiz Rock; hill in town of Manchester.................... Salem.
Agawam; town in Hampden County; area 28 square miles.... Springfield.
Agawam; village in town of same name...................... Springfield.
Agawam; village in Wareham............................... Plymouth.
Agawam; brook in Stockbridge, flowing into Konkapot Brook .... Pittsfield.
Agawam; lake on boundary between Great Barrington and Stockbridge... Pittsfield.
Agawam; river tributary to Wareham River, draining parts of Wareham and Plymouth .... Plymouth.
Alum; hill in southeastern part of Sheffield; elevation, 1,099 feet... Sheffield.
Alden; hill in Lakeville; elevation, 178 feet .... Middleboro.
Aldrich Mills; village in northwest part of Granby .... Northampton.
Alexander; hill in Northfield; elevation, 1,220 feet........... Warwick.
Alford; town in southwestern part of Berkshire County; area, 10 square miles. { Pittsfield. Sheffield.
Alford; village in town of same name........................ Sheffield.

11

Atlas sheets.

Allen; brook in Shelburne and Greenfield, tributary to Green River .... Greenfield.
Allen; harbor on southern coast of Harwich .... Yarmouth.
Allen; hill in Barre; elevation, 1,225 feet. .... Barre.
Allen; point at northeast extremity of Chatham .... Chatham.
Allen; pond in southern part of Dartmouth .... { New Bedford. / Fall River.
Allerton; point on northeast coast of Hull..................... Boston Bay.
Allston; village in Boston on Boston and Albany R. R .... Boston.
Almshouse Station; village on Salem and Lawrence R. R. in Tewksbury .... Lawrence.
Altar Rock; hills in Nantucket............................... Nantucket.
Alum; pond in northwest part of Sturbridge................... Brookfield.
Ames; pond in southern part of Stoughton..................... Dedham.
Amesbury; town in Essex County; area, 14 square miles...... Newburyport.
Amesbury; village in town of Amesbury .... Newburyport.
Amherst; town in northern part of Hampshire County; area, 26 square miles. { Belchertown. / Northampton.
Amherst; village in town of same name .... Northampton.
Amos; point at southern extremity of Chatham................ Chatham.
Andover; town in Essex County; area, 33 square miles .... Lawrence.
Andover; principal village in town of same name on Boston and Maine R. R. .... Lawrence.
Andrews; pond in Harwich................................... Yarmouth.
Angelica; point at southeastern extremity of Mattapoisett.... New Bedford.
Annasnappet; brook in Plympton and Carver .... Middleboro.
Annawon Rock; hill in Rehoboth .... Taunton.
Annisquam; village in northern part of Gloucester on Annisquam Harbor... Gloucester.
Annisquam; harbor on northern coast of Gloucester.......... Gloucester.
Annursnack; hill in Concord................................ Framingham.
Anthony; creek tributary to Hoosic River in eastern part of Adams .... Greylock.
Apple; island south of Winthrop............................. Boston Bay.
Apponaganset; village in eastern part of Dartmouth......... New Bedford.
Apponaganset; harbor on eastern coast of Dartmouth; also called Apponaganset Bay .... New Bedford.
Apponaganset; river in Dartmouth, flowing into Apponaganset harbor... New Bedford.
Ararat, Mount; hill in Millbury; altitude, 700 feet............ Webster.
Archelaus; hill in West Newbury; elevation, 240 feet......... Newburyport.
Archer; pond in Wrentham................................... Franklin.
Arlington; town in Middlesex county; area, 5 square miles.. Boston.
Arlington; village in town of same name .... Boston.
Arlington Heights; village in town of same name........... Boston.
Arthurs Seat; hill in Deerfield; elevation, 927 feet........... Greenfield.
Artichoke; river in West Newbury........................... Newburyport.
Arbajona; river between Mystic Lakes and ponds at head of Willow Brook in Winchester................................ Boston.
Asbury Grove; village in southwestern part of Hamilton.... Salem.
Ash; swamp in Townsend .... Fitchburg.
Ashby; town in Middlesex County; area, 23 square miles..... Fitchburg.
Ashby; village in town of same name .... Fitchburg.
Ashburnham; town in Worcester County; area, 42 square miles .... Fitchburg.

GANNETT.] A GEOGRAPHIC DICTIONARY OF MASSACHUSETTS. 13

	Atlas sheets.
Ashburnham; village in town of same name	Fitchburg.
Ashburnham Junction; station in town of Ashburnham	Fitchburg.
Ashfield; town in Franklin County; area, 70 square miles	{ Chesterfield. Hawley.
Ashland; town in Middlesex County; area, 13 square miles	{ Framingham. Franklin.
Ashland; village in town of same name	Framingham.
Ashley; brook, outlet of Ashley Lake in Washington, flowing into Housatonic River	Becket.
Ashley Falls; village in southern part of Sheffield on Housatonic River	Sheffield.
Ashley; lake near central part of Washington	Becket.
Ashley; mountain in southwestern part of Mount Washington, Berkshire County	Sheffield.
Ashley; pond in Holyoke	Springfield.
Ashleyhill; brook in southern part of Mount Washington, tributary to Lee Pond Brook	Sheffield.
Ashleyville; village in West Springfield	Springfield.
Ashmore; lake in eastern part of Hinsdale	Becket.
Ashod; village in west part of Duxbury	Abington.
Ashuela; brook in Gill and Bernardston, flowing into Connecticut River	Warwick.
Ashumet; pond on boundary line between Falmouth and Mashpee	Falmouth.
Asnebumskit; brook in Holden	Worcester.
Asnebumskit; hill in Paxton; elevation, 1,400 feet	Worcester.
Asneconick; pond in Hubbardston	Worcester.
Assabet; brook tributary to Assabet River in Harvard and Stow	Marlboro.
Assabet; hill in Northboro; elevation, 454 feet	Marlboro.
Assabet; river, tributary to Concord River in eastern part of the State	Framingham.
Assawompsett; pond in Lakeville	Middleboro.
Assinippi; village in west part of South Scituate	Abington.
Assonet; village in Freetown	Taunton.
Assonet; bay in Freetown and Berkley	Taunton.
Assonet; river tributary to Taunton River in Lakeville	Taunton.
Assonet Neck; in town of Berkley	Taunton.
Asylum Station; station in northwestern part of Danvers, on Salem and Lawrence R. R.	Salem.
Athol; town in Worcester County; area, 35 square miles	{ Winchendon. Warwick.
Athol; village in town of same name	Winchendon.
Athol Center; village in town of Athol	Winchendon.
Atlantic Station; station in Quincy on Old Colony R. R.	Boston.
Attleboro; town in Bristol County; area, 28 square miles	Providence.
Attleboro; village in town of same name	Providence.
Auburn; town in Worcester County	Webster.
Auburn; village in town of same name	Webster.
Auburndale; village in Newton	Boston.
Auburnville; village in southwest part of Whitman	Abington.
Aucoot; cove in southern coast of Marion	New Bedford.
Averic Lake; in Stockbridge	Pittsfield.
Avery; brook tributary to West Brook	{ Hawley. Northampton.
Avon; town in Norfolk County; area, 4 square miles	Dedham.

	Atlas sheets.
Ayer; town in Middlesex County; area, 12 square miles.......	Groton.
Ayers; village on boundary between Haverhill and Methuen..	Haverhill.
Ayers; village in town of Lowell................................	Lowell.
Ayers; hill in Haverhill; elevation, 339 feet...................	Haverhill.
Ayers Junction; village in town of Ayer.......................	Groton.
Babcock; brook in Princeton...................................	Worcester.
Babery; hill in Townsend; elevation, 688 feet................	Groton.
Babery Hill; brook in Townsend, tributary to Squannacook River..	Groton.
Babylon; hill in Burlington; elevation, 240 feet................	Boston.
Bachelder; brook in northern part of Rowley, tributary to Mill River..	Salem.
Bachelor; brook flowing westerly through Grandy and South Hadley into Connecticut River.	{ Belchertown, Northampton.
Back; river in northwestern part of Bourne, flowing into Buzzards Bay...	Falmouth.
Baddacook; brook in Groton...................................	Groton.
Baddacook; pond in Groton....................................	Groton.
Bad Luck; brook in Rehoboth.................................	Taunton.
Bad Luck; mountain in Granville; altitude, 1,220 feet........	Granville.
Bad Luck; pond in Douglas....................................	{ Webster. Blackstone.
Bad Luck; swamp in Rehoboth................................	Taunton.
Bailey; brook in Gardner and Winchendon, tributary to Otter River..	Winchendon.
Baiting; brook in Framingham.................................	Framingham.
Baker; brook in town of Gardner...............................	Fitchburg.
Baker; brook in Fitchburg and Leominster....................	Fitchburg.
Baker; island about 2 miles south of Manchester Harbor.....	Salem.
Baker; hill in north part of Hingham...........................	Abington.
Baker; pond on boundary line between Brewster and Orleans..	Wellfleet.
Baker; pond in Dennis...	Yarmouth.
Bald; hill in Douglas; elevation, 700 feet......................	Blackstone.
Bald; hill in northeastern part of Beverly; elevation, 110 feet.	Salem.
Bald; hill in southwestern part of Northampton; elevation, 840 feet...	Northampton.
Bald; hill in Wrentham; elevation, 400 feet...................	Franklin.
Bald; hill on boundary line between Boylston and Northboro.	Marlboro.
Bald; hill in Westminster; elevation, 1,220 feet...............	Fitchburg.
Bald; mountain in western part of Clarksburg................	Greylock.
Bald; mountain in Charlemont; altitude, 1,375 feet...........	Hawley.
Bald; mountain in Shelbourne; altitude, 1,690 feet...........	Greenfield.
Bald; mountain in Bernardston; altitude, 1,167 feet..........	Greenfield.
Bald; mountain in Monson; altitude, 860 feet.................	Palmer.
Baldhead; hill in Lenox; elevation, 1,583 feet.................	Pittsfield.
Bald Pate; hill in Georgetown; elevation, 340 feet...........	Lawrence.
Bald Pate; hill in Newton; elevation, 300 feet................	Boston.
Bald Pate; pond in northeastern part of Boxford.............	{ Lawrence. Salem.
Baldwin; pond in Wayland	Framingham.
Baldwinville; village in Templeton	Winchendon.
Ball Mountain; hill in Leyden; elevation, 1,197 feet.........	Greenfield.
Ballard; hill in Ashland; elevation, 360 feet...................	Framingham.
Ballard; hill in Lancaster; elevation, 465 feet	Marlboro.

A GEOGRAPHIC DICTIONARY OF MASSACHUSETTS. 15

	Atlas sheets.
Ballard; hill in Leicester; elevation, 920 feet	Webster.
Ballardville; village in Andover	Lawrence.
Ballville; village in Bolton, on Old Colony R. R	Marlboro.
Bancroft; brook in Pepperell, tributary to Robinson Brook	Groton.
Bancroft; hill in town of Gardner; elevation, 1,280 feet	Fitchburg.
Bancroft Station; village in northeastern part of Becket	Becket.
Ban Hill; pond in town of Harvard	Marlboro.
Banner; hill in Ashland; elevation, 320 feet	Framingham.
Baptist; village in Holyoke	Springfield.
Barber; hill in Gardner; elevation, 1,140 feet	Fitchburg.
Barber; hill in Warwick; elevation, 1,000 feet	Warwick.
Bardwell Ferry; village in town of Shelbourne	Greenfield.
Bardwell; ferry on Deerfield River in Shelbourne	Greenfield.
Bardwell; village in Belchertown	Palmer.
Barker; hill in Townsend; elevation, 781 feet	Groton.
Barkerville; village in Pittsfield	Pittsfield.
Barley Neck; peninsula on east coast of Orleans	Wellfleet.
Barnard; hill in Gill; elevation, 420 feet	Warwick.
Barnes; hill in Northboro	Marlboro.
Barnes; mountain in Tolland; altitude, 580 feet	Granville.
Barney; point in Wareham, on east side of Wareham River	Falmouth.
Barneyville; village in town of Swansea	Providence.
Barnstable; seacoast town in Barnstable County; area, 71 square miles	Barnstable.
Barnstable; village in town of same name	Barnstable.
Barnstable; harbor of Barnstable, opening into Cape Cod Bay	Barnstable.
Barr; rocks near the northeast shore of Scituate	Abington.
Barre; town in Worcester County; area, 57 square miles	Barre.
Barre; principal village in town of Barre	Barre.
Barre Falls; village in town of Barre	Barre.
Barre Plains; village in town of Barre on Ware River branch Boston and Albany R. R	Barre.
Barrett Junction; village in Belchertown on New London Northern and Springfield, Athol and North Eastern branch Boston and Albany R. R	Palmer.
Barrows; brook in Plympton and Kingston, tributary to Jones River Brook	Middleboro.
Barrowsville; village in Norton on Attleboro branch Old Colony R. R	Taunton.
Bartholomew; hill in western part of Ipswich; elevation 180 feet	Salem.
Bartholomew; pond in southern part of Peabody	Salem.
Bartlett; brook in Middleboro and Halifax	Middleboro.
Bartlett; brook in Methuen and Dracut	Lawrence.
Bartlett; hill in Shrewsbury; elevation, 673 feet	Marlboro.
Bartlett; pond in Northboro	Marlboro.
Bartlett; pond in Plymouth	Plymouth.
Bashan; hill in northwest part of Worthington	Chesterfield.
Bashbish; falls on Lee Pond Brook in western part of Mount Washington; elevation, 200 feet	Sheffield.
Bashbish; mountain in western part of Mount Washington; altitude, about 1,960 feet	
Basin; pond in southern part of Washington	Becket.

Atlas sheets.

Basin Pond; brook in southern part of Washington and northern part of Lee... Becket.
Basle; brook in Hawley, flowing into King Brook............ Hawley.
Bass; creek flowing into north side of Barnstable Harbor..... Barnstable.
Bass; point on southwest coast of Nahant.................... Boston Bay.
Bass; pond in Springfield..................................... Springfield.
Bass; reservoir in Warwick.................................... Warwick.
Bass; river flowing south through Beverly, into Beverly Harbor.. Salem.
Bass; river in southeastern part of Marshfield, tributary to Green Harbor.. Duxbury.
Bass Hole; harbor at mouth of Chase Garden Creek .... Yarmouth.
Bass Rocks; point on eastern coast of Gloucester............. Gloucester.
Bassett; brook in northern part of Kingston, flowing into Blackwater Pond.. Duxbury.
Bassett; island in eastern part of Buzzards Bay, between Red Brook and Pocasset Harbor................................... Falmouth.
Bassing; harbor lying north of Chatham..................... Chatham.
Bateman; pond in Concord................................... Framingham.
Batcheller; hill in North Brookfield; elevation, 920 feet....... Barre.
Battlecock; hill in east part of Chesterfield................... Chesterfield.
Batts; hill in Salisbury; elevation, 160 feet................... Newburyport.
Bay State; village on Mill River.............................. Northampton.
Bay View; village in northeastern part of Gloucester......... Gloucester.
Beach; hill in Blandford; elevation, 1,500 feet................ Granville.
Beach; hill, summit of Taconic Ridge in Hancock; altitude, 2,340 feet... Berlin.
Beach; hill on western boundary of Orange; elevation, 1,120 feet... Warwick.
Beach; point, the eastern extremity of Sandy Beach.......... Barnstable.
Beach Bluff Station; village in northeast part of Swampscott. Boston Bay.
Beachmont; village on southeast coast of Revere............. Boston Bay.
Beachwood; village in south part of Cohasset................ Abington.
Beal; cove on east side of Weymouth Back River in northwest part of Hingham.. Abington.
Beal Ledge; hills in Dighton; elevation, 140 feet............. Taunton.
Beaman; hill in Gardner; elevation, 1,200 feet................ Fitchburg.
Bean; railroad crossing in eastern part of Rowley............ Salem.
Bean Porridge; hill in town of Westminster.................. Fitchburg.
Bear; hill in Waltham; elevation, 340 feet.................... Framingham.
Bear; hill in Topsfield; elevation about 140 feet.............. Salem.
Bear; hill in Reading; elevation, 220 feet..................... Lawrence.
Bear; hill in Westford; elevation, 340 feet.................... Lowell.
Bear; hill in Quincy; elevation, 500 feet...................... Dedham.
Bear; pond in south part of Nahant .... Boston Bay.
Bear; river in Conway, tributary to Deerfield River........... Greenfield.
Bear; hill in Merrimac; elevation, 240 feet.................... Haverhill.
Bear; hill in town of Milford; elevation, 440 feet .... Blackstone.
Bear; hill in Hopkinton; elevation, 560 feet .... Blackstone.
Bear; hill in Stoneham; elevation, 320 feet .... Boston.
Bear Meadow; brook in New Hampshire and town of Ashburnham, Mass., tributary to Millers River................ Fitchburg.
Bear Meadow; brook in Methuen............................ Lawrence.
Bear Meadow; brook in Reading............................. Lawrence.

	Atlas sheets.
Bear; mountain in Wendell; elevation, 1,280 feet	Warwick.
Bear; mountain in northeastern part of Great Barrington, altitude, 1,865 feet.	Pittsfield. Sheffield.
Bearden; brook in Montgomery	Granville.
Beaver; creek in northern part of Clarksburg, tributary to north branch of Hoosic River	Greylock.
Beaver; brook in East Bridgewater	Abington.
Beaver; brook in Bridgewater, flowing into Spring Brook	Middleboro.
Beaver; brook in Lexington and Waltham, tributary to Charles River	Boston.
Beaver; brook in eastern part of Williamsburg, tributary to Mill River	Northampton.
Beaver; brook in Royalston, flowing into Lawrence Brook	Winchendon.
Beaver; brook in Littleton and Westford	Lowell.
Beaver; brook in Royalston, flowing into Lawrence Brook	Winchendon.
Beaver; brook in Chelmsford	Lowell.
Beaver; brook in Harvard and Littletown	Groton.
Beaver; brook in Boxboro	Marlboro.
Beaver; brook in West Newbury and Newbury	Newburyport.
Beaver; brook in Enfield and Ware	Palmer. Belchertown.
Beaver; brook in Danvers, tributary to Crane River	Salem.
Beaver; pond in northern part of Beverly	Salem.
Beaver; pond in Lincoln	Framingham.
Beaver; pond in Franklin	Franklin.
Beaver; pond in Bellingham	Franklin.
Beaver Brook; village and railway station on the Salem and Lawrence R. R. in northwestern part of Danvers	Salem.
Beaver Meadow; village in Leyden	Greenfield.
Beaverdam; brook in Lynnfield, 2 miles long, tributary to Saugus River	Lawrence.
Beaverdam; brook in Ashland, Framingham, Sherborn, and Natick	Framingham.
Beaverdam; brook in Carver, 3 miles long, tributary to Weweantic River	Middleboro.
Beaverdam; pond in Wareham	Plymouth.
Beaverdam; pond in Plymouth	Plymouth.
Beck; pond in southeastern part of Hamilton	Salem.
Becket; town in eastern part of Berkshire County; area, 48 square miles	Becket.
Becket; mountain in western part of Becket; altitude, 2,200 feet	Becket.
Becket Center; village and post-office in Becket	Becket.
Bedford; town in Middlesex County; area, 15 square miles	Framingham. Lowell.
Bedford; village in Bedford on Boston and Lowell R. R.	Framingham
Bedford Station; village in Bedford on Boston and Lowell R. R.	Framingham
Bedlam; brook in Blandford, Hampden County, 2 miles long, and tributary to Pebble Brook	Granville.
Bee; hill in Leominster	Marlboro.
Beech; hill in south part of Rockland	Abington.
Beech; hill on boundary line between Gardner and Westminster; elevation, 1,160 feet	Fitchburg.

Bull. 116——2

18 A GEOGRAPHIC DICTIONARY OF MASSACHUSETTS. [BULL. 116.

Atlas sheets.

Beech; hill in Salisbury, Essex County; elevation, 200 feet ... Newburyport.
Beech Hill Meadows; name applied to small tract in south part of Rockland .... Abington.
Beer Mountain; hill in Northfield; altitude, 940 feet .... Warwick.
Beer Plain; in western part of Northfield, on New London Northern R. R .... Warwick.
Belchertown; town in Hampshire County; area, 54 square miles. { Belchertown. Palmer.
Belchertown; village in town of same name, on New London Northern R. R .... Belchertown
Bell; brook in Oakham, New Braintree and Barre, 3 miles long. Barre.
Belle; inlet on northwest boundary of Winthrop .... Boston Bay.
Belleville; village in eastern part of New Bedford .... New Bedford.
Bellevue; hill in Boston; elevation 320 feet .... Boston.
Bellingham; town in Norfolk county; area 19 square miles ... Franklin.
Bellingham; village in town of same name .... Franklin.
Bellows; hill in Carlisle; elevation 260 feet .... Lowell.
Bellows; hill in Shelburne; elevation 920 feet .... Greenfield.
Belmont; town in Middlesex County; area 5 square miles..... Boston.
Belmont; village in town of same name, on Massachusetts Central R. R .... Boston.
Benjamin; hill in Winchendon .... Winchendon.
Bennett; brook in Northfield .... Warwick.
Bennett; brook in Harvard, Ayer and Littleton; 4 miles long .. Groton.
Bennett Neck; narrow, irregularly shaped island in northern part of Buzzards Bay about five-eighths of a mile long, and trending north and south .... Falmouth.
Benson; pond in Middleboro .... Middleboro.
Benton; hill in northern part of Becket; elevation 1,740 feet.. Becket.
Berkley; town in Bristol county; area 17 square miles .... Taunton.
Berkley; village in town of same name .... Taunton.
Berkley; bridge across Taunton River, in Berkley and Taunton. Taunton.
Berkshire; village in southeastern part of Lanesboro .... Greylock.
Berlin; town in Worcester county; area 14 square miles .... Marlboro.
Berlin; village in town of same name .... Marlboro.
Bernardston; town in Franklin county; area 22 square miles... Greenfield.
Bernardston; village in town of same name, on Connecticut River .... Greenfield.
Beverly; seaboard town in southeastern part of Essex county; area 20 square miles .... Salem.
Beverly; village in southern part of town of same name, on Beverly Harbor .... Salem.
Beverly; cove in southern coast of town of Beverly .... Salem.
Beverly; harbor, an arm of the sea indenting southeastern coast of Essex County, between Beverly and Salem .... Salem.
Beverly; reservoir on a hill about 160 feet high in northern part of Beverly .... Salem.
Beverly Farms; village in southeastern part of Beverly .... Salem.
Bickford; hill in town of Gardner; elevation, 1,260 feet .... Fitchburg.
Big; brook in Hampden and Wilbraham, 3 miles long, flowing into Scantic Brook .... Palmer.
Big Sandy; pond in Yarmouth .... Yarmouth.
Bigelow; brook in Phillipston and Petersham .... Winchendon.
Billerica; town in Middlesex County; area, 27 square miles.. { Lowell. Lawrence.

	Atlas sheets.
Billerica; village in town of same name on Boston and Lowell R. R.; Billerica branch	Lowell.
Billerica; station on Boston and Lowell R. R., in Billerica	Lawrence.
Billerica Spring; station in Bedford, on Boston and Lowell R. R.; Billerica branch	Lowell.
Billings; pond in Sharon	Dedham.
Billingsgate; island on west shore, at entrance to Wellfleet Harbor, in Cape Cod Bay	Wellfleet.
Billingsgate; light-house on southeast extremity of Billingsgate Island, in Cape Cod Bay	Wellfleet.
Billington Sea; pond in northern part of Plymouth, which was discovered by Billington, of the Mayflower, for whom it was named	Plymouth.
Birch; brook in Norton and Rehoboth, tributary to Three Mile River; is 4 miles long	Taunton.
Birch; hill in Stow; elevation 380 feet	Marlboro.
Birch; hill in Winchendon	Winchendon
Bird Island; light-house on Bird Island, in Buzzards Bay, at east entrance of Sippican Harbor	Falmouth.
Birch; pond in Saugus and Lynn; Essex County	{ Boston. Boston Bay.
Birds; hill in Needham; elevation, 220 feet	Boston.
Bishop and Clerks; a 4-second order flashing white light in tower, on Bishop and Clerks Ledge, 2¼ miles south-southeast from Point Gammon. Lantern 59 feet above sea level; visible 13 miles	Barnstable.
Bixby; reservoir in Townsend	Groton.
Black; brook in East Bridgewater	Abington.
Black; brook tributary to Ipswich River, in Hamilton	Salem.
Black; brook in Middleboro and Rochester, tributary to Great Quitticas Pond; is 5 miles long	Middleboro.
Black; brook in town of Easton	Dedham.
Black; brook in Dunstable, tributary to Salmon river	Lowell.
Black; brook in Blandford and Montgomery, 4 miles long, tributary to Westfield River	Granville.
Black; brook in West Springfield, tributary to Westfield River, and 4 miles long	Springfield.
Black; creek in Quincy	Boston Bay.
Black; pond in northern part of South Scituate	Abington.
Black; pond in Plymouth	Plymouth.
Black; pond in Granville	Granville.
Black; pond in Harvard	Groton.
Black Betty; brook in Brockton and West Bridgewater, flowing into West Meadow Brook. Is 3 miles long	Dedham.
Black Pond; hill in northern part of South Scituate	Abington.
Black Pond; swamp in the northern part of South Scituate	Abington.
Black Rock; island north of Cohasset	Boston Bay.
Black Rock; creek in Salisbury	Newburyport
Blackburn; village in Ashburnham	Fitchburg.
Blackfish; creek in Wellfleet, flowing into Wellfleet Harbor	Wellfleet.
Blackington; village in northeastern part of Williamstown, on the Hoosic River	Greylock.
Blackmore; pond in Wareham	Middleboro.
Black Point; pond in town of Chilmark, Marthas Vineyard	Marthas Vineyard.
Blackstone; village in town of the same name	Blackstone.

Atlas sheets.

Blackstone; town in Worcester county; area 17 square miles. Blackstone.
Blackstone; river in southern part of the State, tributary to { Blackstone.
Providence River. { Webster.
Blackwater; pond in northeastern part of Kingston........... Duxbury.
Blake; hill in southwest part of Sturbridge; elevation 1,060 feet... Brookfield.
Blake; hill in Westford; elevation 360 feet................... Lowell.
Blanchard; hill in northern part of Brookfield; elevation 800 feet... Brookfield.
Blanchard; hill in Dunstable; elevation 360 feet............... Groton.
Blanchardville; village in town of Palmer, on Boston and Albany R. R... Palmer.
Blandford; town in Hampton county; area 55 square miles.... Granville.
Blandford; village in town of Blandford...................... Granville.
Blankenships; cove in Sippican Harbor, between Sippican Neck and Planting Island, on southern coast of Marion.... Falmouth.
Blair; pond in Blandford...................................... Granville.
Blish; point in northern part of Barnstable, extending into Barnstable Harbor... Barnstable.
Bliss; brook in Rehoboth..................................... Providence.
Block; brook in West Springfield, tributary to Westfield River, 3 miles long... Springfield.
Blodgett Mill; brook in Warren and Brimfield, tributary to Chicopee River .... Palmer.
Blood; hill on boundary between Ashby and Ashburnham..... Fitchburg.
Blood; pond in Charlton and Dudley.......................... Webster.
Bloody; brook tributary to Mill River, in southern part of Deerfield .... Northampton.
Bloody; brook in Methuen and Lawrence, tributary to Spickett River .... Lawrence.
Bloody; pond in Plymouth..................................... Plymouth.
Blue, Mount; hill in north part of South Scituate .... Abington.
Blue Hills; range of hills in Dedham, Milton, and Quincy. Altitude from 300 to 600 feet .... Dedham.
Blueberry Peak; hill in Charlemont. Elevation 1,695 feet... Hawley.
Bluefield; brook in New Hampshire and town of Ashburnham, 3 miles long... Fitchburg.
Bluefish; marshy brook in eastern part of Duxbury .... Duxbury.
Bluefish; point extending into Katama Bay, on coast of Edgartown, Marthas Vineyard .... Marthas Vineyard.
Boat Meadow; river in town of Eastham, flowing into Cape Cod Bay... Wellfleet.
Boggistere; brook in Sherborn and Millis...................... Franklin.
Bolster; hill in Warwick; elevation, 1,160 feet................ Warwick.
Bolton; town in Worcester County; area, 19 square milese.... Marlboro.
Bolton; village in town of same name .... Marlboro.
Bolton Cedar; swamp in southeastern part of Freetown on { Middleboro.
line of New Bedford. { New Bedford.
Bond; hill in Millbury; elevation, 520 feet .... Webster.
Bond; village in Palmer....................................... Palmer.
Bonney; hill in central part of Hanson .... Abington.
Boon; hill in Stow; elevation, 360 feet .... Marlboro.
Boon; pond in Stow... Marlboro.
Boot; pond in Plymouth .... Plymouth.

GANNETT.] A GEOGRAPHIC DICTIONARY OF MASSACHUSETTS 21

Atlas sheets.

Booth; hill in west part of Scituate .... Abington.
Borden; brook in Blandford and Granville, tributary to Westfield Little River; four miles long........................... Granville.
Boston; city in Suffolk County; area, 42 square miles .... Boston.
Boston and Albany; a railroad running westward from Boston to Albany, N. Y., with numerous branches and feeders.
Boston and Lowell; part of the Boston and Maine R. R. system.
Boston and Maine; railroad running northward and westward from Boston and, with its many branches, covering nearly all of northeastern Massachusetts.
Boston and Providence; railroad system in southeastern Massachusetts, connecting Boston with Providence, Fall River, New Bedford, and other points.
Boston Bay; a subdivision of Massachusetts Bay, situated at its western end and included between Nahant Head and Strawberry Point. Between these limits it is 11 miles wide and makes into the land for a distance of 4 miles .... Boston Bay.
Boston; brook in Andover, North Andover, and Middleton, tributary to Ipswich River, and is 8 miles long................ Lawrence.
Boston; harbor between Deer Island and Point Allerton; is 3¼ miles wide.. Boston.
Boston; hill on eastern boundary of Shrewsbury; elevation, 560 feet... Marlboro.
Boston; hill in North Andover; elevation, 380 feet............ Lawrence.
Boston; light-house, on Little Brewster Island .... Boston Bay.
Boston, Salem and Nashua; a part of the Boston and Maine R. R. system.
Bottomless; pond in Sudbury................................... Framingham.
Bottomly; pond in town of Paxton............................. Worcester.
Bound; brook in southeast part of Cohasset .... Abington.
Bound; pond in southeastern part of Hamilton, having an outlet into Chebacco Lake....................................... Salem.
Bound Brook; island in Wellfleet and Truro................... Wellfleet.
Bourne; town in Barnstable County, on eastern shore of Buzzards Bay; area, 44 square miles. { Falmouth. Plymouth.
Bourne; cove, an arm of Buzzards Bay, extending about one-half-mile northwestwardly into the southern coast of Wareham .... Falmouth.
Bourne; hill in southeast of Sandwich village; elevation about 280 feet... Barnstable.
Bourne; hill in southern part of Wareham, between Crooked River and the bay; elevation about 100 feet .... Falmouth.
Bourne Neck; low neck of land between Cohasset Narrows and Monumet River, in Bourne .... Falmouth.
Bournedale; village in Bourne .... Plymouth.
Bow; brook in Shirley and Lancaster, 1 mile long .... Groton.
Bowen; pond (salt) in southern part of Falmouth, opening into Vineyard Sound... Falmouth.
Bowenville; village in northern part of city of Fall River, on Franklin River... Fall River.
Bower; brook in Harvard and Bolton .... { Groton. Marlboro.
Bowerman; creek, tributary to Hoosic River in southeastern part of North Adams .... Greylock.

	Atlas sheets.
Bowman; pond in southern part of Falmouth	Falmouth.
Boxboro; town in Middlesex County; area 12 square miles	Marlboro. / Framingham.
Boxboro; village in town of same name	Marlboro.
Boxford; town in central part of Essex County; area 24 square miles	Lawrence. / Salem.
Boxford; village in southern part of Boxford	Salem.
Boxford; railway station in eastern part of Boxford	Salem.
Boyce; brook in Royalston	Winchendon.
Boylston; town in Worcester County; area 20 square miles	Marlboro. / Worcester.
Boylston; part of the city of Boston, Suffolk County	Boston.
Boylston; village in town of Boylston, on Massachusetts Central R. R.	Marlboro.
Boylston Center; village in town of Boylston	Marlboro.
Boylston Common; village in West Boylston on Fitchburg and Worcester R. R.	Worcester.
Bozrah; brook in Charlemont and Hawley, tributary to Deerfield River; is 3 miles long	Hawley.
Brace; cove on eastern coast of East Point, in Gloucester	Gloucester.
Bradford; town in Essex County; area 7 square miles	Haverhill. / Lawrence.
Bradford; village in town of same name, Boston and Maine R. R.	
Bradford Branch; brook tributary to East Branch of Mill River, in Williamsburg	Northampton.
Bragg; hill in town of Granby; elevation, 520 feet	Palmer.
Braggville; village in Holliston	Franklin.
Braintree; town in Norfolk County; area, 15 square miles	Dedham. / Abington.
Braley Station; railway station in southeastern part of Freetown	New Bedford.
Branch, The; stream in east part of Chesterfield	Chesterfield.
Branch; creek, tributary to North River in northeastern part of Marshfield	Duxbury.
Brandy Brow; hill on boundary between Haverhill and Merrimac; elevation, 238 feet	Haverhill.
Brant; hill in Berkley	Taunton.
Brant; island in Nasketucket Bay, south of Mattapoisett Neck	New Bedford.
Brant Point; light-house on north coast of Nantucket at entrance to Nantucket Harbor	Nantucket.
Brant Rocks; small rocky islet near eastern shore of Marshfield	Duxbury.
Brayton; point on southern coast of Somerset in Mount Hope Bay	Fall River.
Braytonville; village in northwestern part of North Adams on Hoosic River	Greylock.
Bread and Cheese; brook tributary to East Branch of Westport River in northern part of Westport	Fall River.
Breakneck; right branch of Quineboag River, in Sturbridge	Brookfield,
Breakneck; hill in southwest part of Westhampton	Chesterfield.
Breakneck; hill in Freetown; elevation, 120 feet	Taunton.
Breed; hill on an island northeast of East Boston; elevation 140 feet	Boston.
Breed; island northwest of Winthrop	Boston Bay.

GANNETT.] **A GEOGRAPHIC DICTIONARY OF MASSACHUSETTS.** 23

	Atlas sheets.
Breed; pond near central part of Lynn	Boston Bay.
Brewster; town in Barnstable County; area, 27 square miles	{ Yarmouth. Wellfleet.
Brewster; village in town of same name	Wellfleet.
Briar; pond in Harwich	Yarmouth.
Bridge; brook in Sudbury	Framingham.
Bridge; creek flowing from Great Marshes into Barnstable Harbor	Barnstable.
Bridge Meadow; brook in Tyngsboro and Westford; 4 miles long	Lowell.
Bridgewater; town in Plymouth County; area 29 square miles.	{ Middleboro. Abington. Taunton.
Bridgewater; village in town of same name on Old Colony R. R.	Middleboro.
Briggs; pond in Harwich	Yarmouth.
Briggsville; village in town of Attleboro	Providence.
Briggsville; village in southern part of Clarksburg	Greylock.
Brigham; hill in town of Grafton; elevation, 600 feet	Blackstone.
Brighton; village in Boston, on Boston and Albany R. R.	Boston.
Brightwood; village in Springfield, on Connecticut River R. R.	Springfield
Brimfield; town in Hampden County; area, 35 square miles..	{ Brookfield. Palmer.
Brimfield; principal village in town of same name	Brookfield.
Brimstone; hill in Ware; elevation, 860 feet	Belchertown.
Brimstone; hill in Shelburne; elevation, 840 feet	Greenfield.
Britaniaville; village in Taunton, on main line of Old Colony R. R.	Taunton.
Broad; brook in Belchertown and Ludlow; 5 miles long	Palmer.
Broad; brook, tributary to Mill River, in southwestern part of Hatfield	Northampton
Broad; brook in Southampton and Holyoke	Springfield.
Broad; cove in Dighton, opening into Taunton River	Taunton.
Broad; cove opening into Hingham Harbor, on coast of Hingham	Abington.
Broad; creek in Nantucket	Muskeget.
Broad Creek; branch of North River, in northeastern part of Marshfield	Duxbury.
Broad; hill in Natick; elevation, 300 feet	Framingham.
Broad Meadow; brook in Worcester and Millbury	Webster.
Broad Meadow; brook in Marlboro and Southboro	Marlboro.
Brockton; city in Plymouth County; area, 21 square miles	Dedham.
Brockton; village in Brockton, on Old Colony R. R.	Dedham.
Brockton; reservoir in Stoughton	Dedham.
Brockton Heights; village in town of Brockton	Dedham.
Bromps; pond in Plymouth	Plymouth.
Bronson; brook in north part of Worthington	Chesterfield.
Brook; pond on boundary of Oakham, New Braintree, North Brookfield and Spencer	Barre.
Brook; village in Templeton	Winchendon.
Brookfield; town in Worcester County; area, 26 square miles..	Brookfield.
Brookline; village in town of same name, on Boston and Albany R. R., Brookline branch	Boston.
Brookline; town in Norfolk County; area, 7 square miles	Boston.

	Atlas sheets.
Brookside; station in Westford, on Stony Brook R. R.	Lowell.
Brown; brook in Webster, tributary to Lake Chaubunagungamaug	Webster.
Brown; hill in town of Ayer; elevation, 442 feet	Groton.
Brown; hill in Ashburnham; elevation, 1,320 feet	Fitchburg.
Brown; hill in Fitchburg; elevation, 1,180 feet	Fitchburg.
Brown; pond in south part of Peabody	Boston Bay.
Brown; pond at southern point of boundary line between Salem and Peabody	Salem.
Brown; pond on western boundary of Templeton	Winchendon.
Brown Loaf; hill in Groton; elevation, 448 feet	Groton.
Browning; pond in Spencer	Worcester.
Brush; hill in Sherborn; elevation, 400 feet	Framingham.
Brush; hill in western part of New Marlboro; elevation about 1,420 feet	Sheffield.
Brush; mountain in Northfield, on the New London Northern R. R.; elevation, 1,580 feet	Warwick.
Brush; valley in Warwick	Warwick.
Bryant Neck; in Freetown	Taunton.
Bryantville; village in western part of Pembroke	Abington.
Buck; hill in town of North Brookfield; elevation, 880 feet	Barre.
Buck; hill in Lexington; elevation, 200 feet	Boston.
Buck; river tributary to Farmington River, flowing southeasterly through Sandisfield	Sandisfield.
Buckland; town in Franklin County; area, 21 square miles	Hawley.
Buckland; village in town of same name	Hawley.
Buckland Four Corners; village in town of Buckland	Hawley.
Buckman; brook in Athol, flowing into Millers River; 2 miles long	Winchendon.
Buckmaster; pond in Dedham, Norfolk County	Dedham.
Buddock; brook in Buckland, tributary to Clesson Brook	Hawley.
Buel; lake, containing 344 acres, on boundary line between Monterey and New Marlboro	Sheffield.
Bull; brook tributary to Rowley River, in northern part of Ipswich	Salem.
Bullardville; village in town of Winchendon	Winchendon.
Bumkin; island west of Hull, in Boston Bay	Boston Bay.
Bummet; brook in Shrewsbury and Northboro; 2 miles long	Marlboro.
Bump; hill in Dracut; elevation, 160 feet	Lowell.
Bungay; river in Attleboro and North Attleboro	Providence.
Bungy; hill in Montgomery; elevation, 1,400	Granville.
Bunyan; mountain in town of Monson; altitude, 780 feet	Palmer.
Burbank; pond in Woburn	Boston.
Burges; pond in Westford	Lowell.
Burkville; village in Conway	Greenfield.
Burlington; town in Middlesex County; area, 13 square miles	Boston.
Burlington; village in town of same name	Lawrence.
Burn; hill in Westford; elevation, 340 feet	Lowell.
Burn; hill in Dracut; elevation, 260 feet	Lowell.
Burncoat; brook in Leicester; 1 mile long	Webster.
Burncoat; pond in Leicester and Spencer	Webster.
Burnett; pond in north part of Chesterfield	Chesterfield.
Burnshirt; river in Templeton, Hubbardston and Barre	Barre.

A GEOGRAPHIC DICTIONARY OF MASSACHUSETTS. 25

	Atlas sheets.
Burnt Plain; swamp near central part of South Scituate	Abington.
Burnt Swamp; corner in State boundary in Wrentham, Norfolk.	Franklin.
Burrill; hill in western part of Lynn	Boston Bay.
Burrow; brook in Oakham and Barre; 3 miles long	Barre.
Burtts Crossing; station on Salem and Lowell R. R	Lawrence.
Bush; hill in Merrimac; elevation, 260 feet	Haverhill.
Bush; hill in central part of Ipswich; elevation, 140 feet	Salem
Bush; mountain in Leverett; elevation, 1,260 feet	Belchertown.
Bushnell; mountain in southern part of Egremont, on the line of Sheffield; altitude, 1,868 feet	Sheffield.
Bute; brook in Lakeville, tributary to Assawompsett pond	Middleboro.
Butler; point at extreme southern end of Sippican Neck, in town of Marion	Falmouth.
Butlerville; village in town of Wilbraham	Palmer.
Buttonwood; brook in Dartmouth, flowing into Apponagansett Harbor	New Bedford.
Buttonwood; hill in east part of South Scituate	Abington.
Buxton; brook, tributary to West Brook, in northeastern part of Williamstown	Greylock.
Byfield; village in Newbury on Boston and Maine R. R., Newburyport branch	Newburyport.
Buzzards; bay on southern coast of Massachusetts, between the mainland on the west, Cape Cod on the east, and Elizabeth Islands on the south. It is about 20 miles long, with an average width of about 5 miles and has deep water throughout.	Gay Head. New Bedford. Falmouth.
Cadwell; creek in Enfield, Pelham, and Belchertown flowing into Swift River; 3 miles long	Belchertown.
Cady; brook tributary to Quineboag River in Charlton and Southbridge.	{ Webster. Brookfield.
Cady; small pond in Groton	Groton.
Cahoon Hollow; life-saving station on east coast of Wellfleet	Wellfleet.
Calves Pasture; pond north of Barnstable, connecting with Barnstable Harbor	Barnstable.
Cambridge; city in Middlesex County; area, 7 square miles	Boston.
Cambridgeport; village in city of Cambridge	Boston.
Campello; village in Brockton on Old Colony R. R	Dedham.
Canapitsett Gut; passage between the islands of Nashawena and Cuttyhunk, Gosnold	Gay Head.
Candlewood; hill in Blackstone; elevation 300 feet	Blackstone.
Canesto; brook in Hubbardston and Barre; is 7 miles long	Barre.
Canesto; brook in Templeton and Hubbardston	Winchendon.
Canoe; river in Bristol County, tributary to Taunton River	{ Taunton. Dedham.
Cannonville; village in southern part of Mattapoisett	New Bedford.
Cannonville; village in western part of New Bedford	New Bedford.
Canton; town in Norfolk County; area, 19 square miles	Dedham.
Canton; village in town of same name on Boston and Providence R. R., Stoughton branch	Dedham.
Canton Junction; village in town of Canton at junction of Boston and Providence R. R. and Stoughton branch	Dedham.
Cape; pond in Rockport	Gloucester.

	Atlas sheets.
Cape Cod; a peninsula forming the southeastern part of Massachusetts and constituting the southern and eastern limits of Cape Cod Bay; its surface is, in the main, low and sandy and dotted with numerous ponds. Politically it constitutes Barnstable County.	Provincetown. Wellfleet. Chatham. Yarmouth. Barnstable.
Cape Cod; bay having the peninsula of Cape Cod on the east and south, and the mainland of Massachusetts on the west.	Plymouth. Barnstable. Yarmouth. Wellfleet. Provincetown.
Cape Poge; light-house on Cape Poge, Chappaquiddick Island, in Edgartown, Marthas Vineyard	Marthas Vineyard.
Cape Poge; bay on coast of Chappaquiddick Island in Edgartown, Marthas Vineyard, opening into Edgartown Harbor	Marthas Vineyard.
Captain; hill on a peninsula in southeastern part of Duxbury; elevation, about 200 feet	Duxbury.
Carlisle; town in Middlesex County; area, 16 square miles	Lowell.
Carlisle; village in town of same name	Lowell.
Carlisle Station; village on Framingham and Lowell R. R., in town of Carlisle	Lowell.
Carmel; hill in Andover; elevation, 240 feet	Lawrence.
Carpenter; brook in Rehoboth	Providence.
Carpenter; hill in Charlton; elevation, 865 feet	Webster.
Carr; island in Merrimac River	Newburyport.
Carter; hill in Leominster; elevation, 700 feet	Fitchburg.
Carver; town in Plymouth County; area, 40 square miles	Plymouth. Middleboro.
Carver; village in town of same name	Middleboro.
Caryville; village in Bellingham, on New York and New England R. R., Woonsocket division	Franklin.
Castle; hill in eastern part of Ipswich; elevation, about 140 feet	Salem.
Castle; hill in Saugus; elevation, 280 feet	Boston.
Castle; hill in Medfield; elevation, 240 feet	Franklin.
Castle Neck; a low, sandy peninsula on eastern extremity of Ipswich	Salem. Gloucester.
Castle Neck; marshy river in eastern part of Essex County, tributary to Essex River	Salem.
Catacoonamug; brook in Lunenburg; 3 miles long	Groton.
Catamount; hill in Coleraine; elevation, 1,220 feet	Greenfield.
Cataumet; village in southwestern part of Bourne	Falmouth.
Cataumet; harbor on the western shore of Falmouth	Falmouth.
Cattle; pond in Plymouth	Plymouth.
Cedar; mountain on line between New York and Mount Washington; altitude, about 1,820 feet	Sheffield.
Cedar; point on eastern coast of Scituate	Duxbury.
Cedar; cove on southern coast of Gardeners Neck, Swansea	Fall River.
Cedar; hill in western part of Lynn	Boston Bay.
Cedar; hill in Waltham; elevation, 240 feet	Boston.
Cedar; pond draining into Quineboag River in Sturbridge	Brookfield.
Cedar; pond in Wareham	Plymouth.
Cedar; pond in the southwestern part of Peabody, drained by Goldthwait Brook	Salem.
Cedar; pond in western part of Wenham	Salem.

A GEOGRAPHIC DICTIONARY OF MASSACHUSETTS. 27

	Atlas sheets.
Cedar; pond in Orleans	Wellfleet.
Cedar; pond in Dennis	Yarmouth.
Cedar; pond in Lakeville	Middleboro.
Cedar; pond in north part of Lynn	Boston Bay.
Cedar; pond in Boxford	Lawrence.
Cedar; pond in northwestern Falmouth	Falmouth.
Cedar; swamp in town of Gardner	Fitchburg.
Cedar; swamp in central part of Mattapoisett	New Bedford
Cedar Swamp; mountain in town of Monson; altitude, 1,100 feet	Palmer.
Cedar Swamp; brook in Middleboro and Rochester	Middleboro.
Cedar Meadow; pond in Leicester	Webster.
Cedar Swamp; pond in Webster	Marlboro.
Cedar Swamp; pond in Milford	Blackstone.
Cedar Swamp; river in Lakeville	Middleboro.
Cedar Tree Neck; point on coast of Tisbury, Marthas Vineyard	Gay Head.
Center; pond near central part of Becket	Becket.
Center; creek in Upton, tributary to West River	Blackstone.
Center Hill; point on coast of Plymouth	Plymouth.
Center Hill; pond in Plymouth	Plymouth.
Centerville; village in south part of Barnstable	Barnstable.
Centerville; village in town of Uxbridge	Blackstone.
Central; village in central part of Westport	Fall River.
Central; station on Boston and Providence R. R., in city of Boston	Boston.
Centralville; village in Lowell	Lowell.
Chaffinville; village in Holden, on Boston, Barre and Gardner R. R.	Worcester.
Chamberlain; mountain in eastern part of Brimfield; altitude, 1,020 feet	Brookfield.
Chandler; island in entrance to Hingham Harbor	Boston Bay
Chandler; pond in Boston	Boston.
Chapin; pond in Ludlow	Palmer.
Chaplinville; village in southeastern part of Rowley	Salem.
Chappaquiddick; island which forms part of Edgartown, Marthas Vineyard	Marthas Vineyard.
Chappaquonsett; pond in Tisbury, Marthas Vineyard	Marthas Vineyard.
Charge; pond in southern part of Plymouth	Plymouth.
Charlemont; town in Franklin County; area, 24 square miles	Hawley.
Charlemont; village in town of Charlemont	Hawley.
Charles; small brook tributary to the Quineboag River in Brimfield	Brookfield.
Charles; river in Middlesex and Norfolk counties; is about 40 miles long and flows into Boston Harbor.	{ Framingham. Blackstone. Boston.
Charles River; village in Needham	Framingham.
Charlestown; part of the city of Boston, on north bank of Charles River	Boston.
Charlton; town in Worcester County; area, 46 square miles	{ Webster. Brookfield.
Charlton; village in town of same name	Webster.
Charlton City; village in town of Charlton	Webster.

	Atlas sheets.
Charlton Depot; village in town of Charlton, on Boston and Albany R. R.	Webster.
Charltonville; village in northern part of Plymouth	Plymouth.
Chartley; brook in Attleboro	Taunton.
Chase Garden; brook on boundary between Dennis and Yarmouth, Barnstable County	Yarmouth.
Cheese Cake; creek in Newton, tributary to Charles River; 3 miles long	Boston.
Chelmsford; town in Middlesex County; area, 24 square miles.	Lowell.
Chelmsford Center; village in town of Chelmsford, on Framingham and Lowell R. R.	Lowell.
Chelsea; city in Suffolk County; area, 3 square miles	Boston.
Chelsea; creek in southeast part of Saugus	Boston Bay.
Chene; brook in Orange	Warwick.
Cherry; hill in southern part of Wenham; elevation, 160 feet	Salem.
Cherry; brook in Weston	Framingham.
Cherry Brook; station on Massachusetts Central R. R. in Weston	Framingham.
Cherry Valley; village in Leicester	Webster.
Cheshire; town in northern part of Berkshire County; area, 28 square miles	Greylock.
Cheshire; village in central part of town of same name	Greylock.
Cheshire; branch of Fitchburg R. R., running from South Ashburnham northwestward into New Hampshire.	
Chaseville; village in Dudley, on New York and New England R. R., Southbridge branch	Webster.
Chatham; seacoast town on Cape Cod, Barnstable County; Indian name, Monomoy; area, 17 square miles.	{ Yarmouth. Chatham.
Chatham; principal village in Chatham, Barnstable County; lies on the bluff facing Chatham Harbor	Chatham.
Chatham; harbor of Chatham Village, separating the main land from Nauset Beach	Chatham.
Chatham lights; two iron towers, 100 feet apart, in Chatham Village, with fourth-order, fixed, white lights; lanterns 80 feet above sea level; visible 14 miles	Chatham.
Chatham Port; village in Chatham	Chatham.
Chaubungungamaug; lake in Webster	Webster.
Chauncey; pond in Webster	Marlboro.
Cheapside; village in town of Deerfield, on Fitchburg R. R.	Greenfield.
Chebacco; lake in Essex County, on the boundary line between Hamilton and Essex	Salem.
Cheesboro; creek, tributary to Hoosic River, in northeastern part of Adams	Greylock.
Cheshire Harbor; village in northern part of Cheshire	Greylock.
Chester; town in Hampden County; area, 38 square miles	{ Chesterfield. Granville.
Chester; principal village in town of same name, on Boston and Albany R. R.	Chesterfield.
Chester Center; village in Chester, on Boston and Albany R. R.	Chesterfield.
Chesterfield; town in Hampshire County; area, 32 square miles.	Chesterfield.
Chesterfield Hollow; village in west part of Chesterfield	Chesterfield.
Chestnut; hill in Orange	Warwick.
Chestnut; hill in Montague; elevation, 1,460 feet	Warwick.
Chestnut; hill in Warwick; elevation, 1,020 feet	Warwick.
Chestnut; hill in northern part of Hatfield, on line of Franklin County; elevation, about 760 feet	Northampton

A GEOGRAPHIC DICTIONARY OF MASSACHUSETTS.

	Atlas sheets.
Chestnut; hill in Athol	Winchendon.
Chestnut; hill in Tolland	Granville.
Chestnut; hill in Newton; elevation, 280 feet	Boston.
Chestnut; hill in town of Grafton; elevation, 660 feet	Blackstone.
Chestnut; hill in Chelmsford; elevation, 360 feet	Lowell.
Chestnut; hills in Groton; elevation, 400 to 560 feet	Groton.
Chesnut Hill; reservoir in Newton and Boston	Boston.
Chickabut; hill in Quincy; elevation, 500 feet	Dedham.
Chickley; river in Charlemont, Hawley and Savoy, tributary to Deerfield River	Hawley.
Chicopee; town in Hampden County; area, 26 square miles	Springfield.
Chicopee; village in town of same name, on Connecticut River R. R.	Springfield.
Chicopee; mountain in Monson; altitude, 800 feet	Palmer.
Chicopee; river; left branch of Connecticut River, in central part of State.	{ Palmer. { Springfield.
Chicopee Falls; village in town of Chicopee	Springfield.
Child; river in Barnstable County, draining John Pond into Waquoit Bay	Falmouth.
Child; brook in south part of Cummington	Chesterfield.
Chilmark; town in Dukes County; area, 21 square miles	{ Marthas Vineyard. { Gay Head.
Chilmark; village in town of same name; on Marthas Vineyard.	Gay Head.
Chilmark; pond in town of Chilmark; on Marthas Vineyard.	{ Gay Head. { Marthas Vineyard.
Chochechiwick; river in North Andover, connecting Great Pond with Merrimac River	Lawrence.
Chockalog; pond in Uxbridge	Blackstone.
Christian; hill on southern boundary of Dracut; elevation, 300 feet	Lowell.
Christian; hill in Coleraine; elevation, 1,500 feet	{ Hawley. { Greenfield.
Christian; hill in central part of Great Barrington; elevation, about 940 feet	Sheffield.
Chubb; island south of Manchester, at west entrance to Manchester Harbor	Salem.
Church; hill in northeastern part of Otis; elevation, 1,845 feet.	Sandisfield.
Church; hill in Templeton; elevation, 1,160 feet	Winchendon.
City Mills; village in Norfolk, on New York and New England R. R., main line	Franklin.
City Point; eastern point of South Boston	Boston.
Clam; brook in Westfield, 3 miles long	Springfield.
Clam; river; tributary to Farmington River, flowing southerly through Sandisfield	Sandisfield.
Clam Pudding; pond in Plymouth	Plymouth.
Clam Shell; pond in town of Clinton	Marlboro.
Clapp; pond in western part of Washington	Becket.
Clapp; pond in Provincetown	Provincetown.
Clarendon; hill in northern part of Somerville	Boston.
Clarendon Hills; village in Hyde Park on Boston and Providence R. R.	Boston.
Clark; brook in Buckland and Ashfield	Hawley.
Clark; cove, arm of Buzzards Bay projecting into the southern part of Bristol County between Clark Neck and Dartmouth.	New Bedford.

	Atlas sheets.
Clark; island on eastern side of entrance to Duxbury Bay	Duxbury.
Clark; point on southern coast of New Bedford between Clark Cove and New Bedford Harbor	New Bedford.
Clark; reservoir in Sutton	{ Blackstone. Webster.
Clark Point; a fifth order, fixed white light on southern extremity of New Bedford at west entrance to New Bedford Harbor; lantern 68 feet above sea level and visible 13 miles.	New Bedford.
Clarksburg; town in Berkshire County; area, 13 square miles.	Greylock.
Clay Pit; brook in Lowell, two miles long, flowing into Merrimac River	Lowell.
Clear; pond in Carver	Plymouth.
Clear; pond in northern part of Plymouth	Plymouth.
Clear; pond in Lakeville	Middleboro.
Clear Run; brook in Seekonk and Rehoboth, 2 miles long	Providence.
Clematis; brook in Waltham and Belmont, 4 miles long; flows into Beaver Brook	Boston.
Clesson; brook in Buckland and Hawley; flows into Deerfield River	Hawley.
Clew; pond in Plymouth	Plymouth.
Cliff; pond in Brewster	Wellfleet.
Clifton Heights; village in Brockton	Dedham.
Clifton Station; village in southeast part of Marblehead	Boston Bay.
Cliftondale; village in Saugus on south branch of Boston and Maine R. R.	Boston.
Clinton; town in Worcester County; area, 7 square miles	Marlboro.
Clinton; village in town of same name	Markboro.
Clinton Mill; pond in town of Clinton	Marlboro.
Coatue; beach on coast of Nantucket	Nantucket.
Coatue; point at southern extremity of Coatue Beach in Nantucket Harbor	Nantucket.
Cobb; pond in Brewster	Wellfleet.
Cobber; brook in Merrimac	Haverhill.
Cobble; mountain in Granville and Russell; altitude, 1,220 feet.	Granville.
Cobbler; brook in Merrimac; flows into Merrimac River	Newburyport.
Cocassett; pond in Foxboro	Franklin.
Cochesett; village in West Bridgewater	Dedham.
Cochituate; village in Wayland	Framingham.
Cochituate; lake in Wayland, Framingham, and Natick	Framingham.
Cochituate; reservoir in Natick	Framingham.
Cochituate; railroad station in Framingham on Saxonville branch of Boston and Albany R. R.	Framingham.
Cochran; pond in Blandford	Granville.
Coffin; beach about 2 miles long in northern part of Gloucester on Annisquam Harbor	Gloucester.
Cohasse; brook, right-hand branch of Quineboag River in Southbridge	Brookfield.
Cohasset; town in Norfolk County; area, 13 square miles	{ Boston Bay. Abington.
Cohasset; village in east part of Cohasset	Abington.
Cohasset; cove opening into Cohasset Harbor on east coast of Cohasset	Abington.
Cohasset; harbor of irregular shape on east coast of Cohasset.	Abington.
Cohasset Narrows; channel connecting with Buzzards Bay and separating Wareham from Sandwich	Falmouth.

A GEOGRAPHIC DICTIONARY OF MASSACHUSETTS. 31

	Atlas sheets.
Colburn; reservoir in Leominster	Fitchburg.
Colchester; brook in Plympton and Halifax, tributary to Wenatuxet River, 4¼ miles long	Middleboro.
Cold; brook in Sudbury, 1¼ miles long	Framingham.
Cold; village in Oakham	Barre.
Cold; hill in western part of Granby; elevation, 380 feet	Northampton.
Cold; river in Charlemont and Florida, tributary to Deerfield River.	{ Greylock. Hawley.
Cold Harbor; brook in Boylston and Northboro, 3 miles long.	Marlboro.
Cold Spring; brook in Ashland and Hopkinton	Franklin.
Cold Spring; brook in Harvard, 2 miles long	Groton.
Cold Spring; brook in town of Sutton	Blackstone.
Cold Spring; brook in Newton, tributary to Charles River	Boston.
Cold Spring; brook in Ashland	Framingham.
Cold Springs; village in southern part of Otis on Farmington River	Sandisfield.
Coleman; hill in eastern part of Scituate; elevation, 100 feet.	Duxbury.
Coleraine; town in Franklin County; area, 41 square miles	{ Greenfield. Hawley.
Coleraine Center; village in town of same name	Greenfield.
Coles; river in Dighton, Rehoboth, and Swansea	{ Fall River. Taunton.
Coles Branch; small tributary to west branch of Westfield River in Middlefield	Becket.
Coles Station; railway station in southwestern part of Swansea	Fall River.
College; pond in Plymouth	Plymouth.
Colley; hill in northern part of Worcester County; elevation, 980 feet	Brookfield.
Collins; cove in the northeastern coast of Salem	Salem.
Collins Depot; village in Ludlow on Springfield, Athol, and northeastern branch of Boston and Albany R. R.	Palmer.
Colonel; mountain in northeastern corner of town of Palmer; altitude, 1,740 feet	Brookfield.
Commercial; point of Dorchester which extends into Dorchester Bay	Boston.
Concord; town in Middlesex County; area, 26 square miles	Framingham.
Concord; village in Concord on Fitchburg R. R.	Framingham.
Concord; river, right branch of Merrimac River in eastern part of State.	{ Framingham. Lowell.
Cone; brook in Richmond	Pittsfield.
Congamuck; ponds in Southwick	Granville.
Connecticut; river which heads in Canada, forms boundary between New Hampshire and Vermont, crosses Massachusetts and Connecticut, and flows into Long Island Sound.	{ Warwick. Greenfield. Northampton. Springfield.
Connecticut River; railroad forming part of the Boston and Maine railroad system which traverses the State from north to south, following the general course of the Connecticut River.	
Conscience; hills in Westford and Tyringham	Lowell.
Conspiracy; island in Taunton River in Berkley	Taunton.
Constitution; hill in central part of Lanesboro; elevation, 1,500 feet	Greylock.

32   A GEOGRAPHIC DICTIONARY OF MASSACHUSETTS. [BULL. 116.

	Atlas sheets.
Conway; town in southwestern part of Franklin County; area, 57 square miles.	{ Chesterfield. Northampton. Greenfield.
Conway; village in town of same name	Greenfield.
Conway Depot; railway station in town of Conway on New Haven and Northampton R. R.	Greenfield.
Cook; mountain in town of Brimfield; altitude, 1,000 feet	Palmer.
Cook; pond in northern part of Plymouth	Plymouth.
Cook; pond in southwestern part of Fall River	Fall River.
Cooley; brook in Buckland and Hawley, 1½ miles long	Hawley.
Cooleyville; village in New Salem	Belchertown.
Coolidge; hill in Gardner; elevation, 1,160 feet	Fitchburg.
Coon; hill in Charlemont	Hawley.
Coonemossett; pond in northern part of Falmouth, having an outlet into Great Pond	Falmouth.
Cooper; pond in Carver	Middleboro.
Copaum; pond in Nantucket	Nantucket.
Copecut; hill in eastern part of Fall River; elevation, 355 feet.	Fall River.
Copecut; river, tributary to Shingle Island River, in eastern part of Fall River	Fall River.
Copper Works; village in Norton	Taunton.
Cordaville; village in town of Southboro, on Boston and Albany R. R.	Marlboro.
Corey; hill in Brookline; elevation, 300 feet	Boston.
Cotley; river n Taunton and Berkley; tributary to Taunton River	Taunton.
Cottage City; town in Dukes County; area, 8 square miles	Marthas Vineyard.
Cottage City; village in town of Cottage City, Marthas Vineyard	Marthas Vineyard.
Cottsville; village in northeastern part of Pittsfield	Becket.
Cotuit; river on southwest boundary of Barnstable	Barnstable.
Cotuit; village in west part of Barnstable	Barnstable.
Cotuit; ponds in Barnstable	Barnstable.
Cotuit Highlands; name applied to high land lying south of Cotuitport, in southwest part of Barnstable	Barnstable.
Cotuitport; village on Osterville Harbor, on southwest coast of Barnstable	Barnstable.
Couch; brook in Bernardston, 3 miles long; tributary to Fall River	Greenfield.
Course; brook in Sherborn and Natick; 3 miles long; flows into Cochituate Reservoir	Framingham.
Cove; village in southern part of Beverly	Salem.
Cow; creek in Sandwich, emptying into Cape Cod Bay	Barnstable.
Cow; pond in Groton.	
Cow Pond; brook in Groton	Groton.
Cow Pond; meadows in Groton	Groton.
Cowdrey; hill in Stoneham; elevation, 200 feet	Boston.
Coweset; brook in Stoughton, Brockton, and West Bridgewater; 8 miles long	Dedham.
Cox; pond in eastern part of Wenham	Salem.
Coy; brook in North Brookfield	{ Brookfield. Barre.
Coy; hill in West Brookfield; elevation, 1,100 feet	Barre.
Crafts; hill in Holyoke; elevation, 560 feet	Springfield.

A GEOGRAPHIC DICTIONARY OF MASSACHUSETTS.

	Atlas sheets.
Crag; mountain in Northfield; elevation, 1,560 feet	Warwick.
Craigville; village in southern part of Barnstable	Barnstable.
Cranberry; river, small tributary to Quoboag River, in Spencer.	Brookfield.
Cranberry; pond in Montague	Greenfield.
Cranberry; pond in Lancaster	Groton.
Cranberry; pond in Lakeville	Middleboro.
Cranberry; pond in central part of Duxbury, drained by South River	Duxbury.
Cranberry; pond in south part of Braintree	Abington.
Cranberry Meadow; pond in Spencer	Brookfield.
Cranberry Pond; brook in Montague, 3 miles long, tributary to Connecticut River	Greenfield.
Crane; river in Danvers, formed by Crane and Beaver brooks, and emptying into Beverly Harbor	Salem.
Crane; pond in West Stockbridge	Pittsfield.
Crane; brook tributary to Crane River, in southern part of Danvers	Salem.
Crane; hill in eastern part of Washington; elevation, 1,780 feet.	Becket.
Crane; hill in Marlboro; elevation, 544 feet	Marlboro.
Crane Neck; hill in West Newbury; elevation, 234 feet	Newburyport.
Crane Station; village in Norton, on Mansfield branch of Old Colony R. R.	Taunton.
Creek; brook in Haverhill, 2¼ miles long, flows into Merrimac River	Haverhill.
Creek; pond in Haverhill	Haverhill.
Crescent; beach on southern coast of Gloucester between Magnolia Point and Normans Woe	Gloucester.
Crescent Beach Station; village on southeast coast of Revere.	Boston Bay.
Cricket; hill in southeastern part of Conway; elevation, 1,180 feet.	{ Greenfield. Northampton.
Crockerville; village in Fitchburg, on Fitchburg R. R.	Fitchburg.
Cromeset; point on southeastern end of Cromeset Neck, projecting into Buzzards Bay	Falmouth.
Cromeset Neck; peninsula extending from the coast of Wareham into Buzzards Bay, between Weweantic River and Mark Cove	Falmouth.
Crooked; pond in Falmouth	Falmouth.
Crooked; pond in southern part of Boxford	Salem.
Crooked; pond in Plymouth	Plymouth.
Crooked; pond in Plainfield	Hawley.
Crooked; river emptying into Wareham River, in Wareham	Falmouth.
Crooked Spring; brook in Chelmsford, 1¼ miles long	Lowell.
Croskaty; pond in Nantucket	Nantucket.
Cross; island in Annisquam Harbor, northwest of Gloucester	Gloucester.
Crow; hill in Templeton; elevation, 1,160 feet	Winchendon.
Crow; island in New Bedford Harbor between Fair Haven and New Bedford	New Bedford.
Crow; point on north coast of Hingham	Boston Bay.
Crow; point on eastern coast of Scituate, south of Scituate Harbor	Duxbury.
Crow; pond in Barnstable	Chatham.
Crowfoot; brook in Chicopee, 3 miles long, tributary to Chicopee River	Springfield.

	Atlas sheets.
Crow Hill; brook in Templeton, 2 miles long, flows into Trout River	Winchendon.
Crystal; pond in Wakefield	Boston.
Crystal; lake in town of Gardner	Fitchburg.
Crystal; lake near coast in south part of Barnstable	Barnstable.
Crystal; lake in Newton	Boston.
Crystal; pond in Melrose	Boston.
Cub; hill in west part of Westhampton	Chesterfield.
Cuggins; brook in Boxboro and Acton, 2 miles long	Framingham.
Cumberland Mills; village in Attleboro	Providence.
Cummingsville; village in Woburn	Boston.
Cummington; town in Hampshire County; area, 23 square miles	Chesterfield.
Curtis; hill in Charlton; elevation, 960 feet	Webster.
Curtis; point on southern coast of Beverly	Salem.
Curtis; pond in Greenwich	Belchertown.
Curtis; pond in Worcester	Webster.
Curtisville; village in Stockbridge	Pittsfield.
Cushing; pond south of central part of Hingham	Abington.
Cut River; marshy passage between Duxbury Bay and Green Harbor, in Marshfield	Duxbury.
Cutler; pond in southern part of Hamilton	Salem.
Cuttyhunk; harbor on Cuttyhunk Island	Gay Head.
Cuttyhunk; one of the Elizabeth Islands, Gosnold	Gay Head.
Cuttyhunk; light-house on coast of Cuttyhunk Island, Gosnold	Gay Head.
Cuttyhunk; pond on Cuttyhunk Island, opening into Cuttyhunk Harbor, Gosnold	Gay Head.
Date; hill in northern part of Danvers; elevation, 140 feet	Salem.
Dalton; town in central part of Berkshire County; area, 22 square miles	Becket.
Dalton; village in central part of Dalton	Becket.
Dam Lot; brook in Raynham, tributary to Taunton River	Taunton.
Damson; brook in Middleboro; 1 mile long, tributary to Bartlett Brook	Middleboro.
Dan; mountain in northwest part of Sturbridge	Brookfield.
Dana; town in Worcester County; area, 19 square miles	Belchertown.
Dana; village in town of same name	Barre.
Danforth; brook in Hardwick, 4 miles long	Barre.
Daniel; mountain in Douglass; altitude, 785 feet	Webster.
Daniel; brook in Pittsfield and Lanesboro	Pittsfield.
Danvers; town in southern part of Essex County; area, 14 square miles	Salem.
Danvers; village in southeastern part of Danvers	Salem.
Danvers Center; village in southern part of Danvers	Salem.
Danversport; village in southeastern part of Danvers	Salem.
Darby; mountain in northeastern part of Mount Washington; altitude, 2,020 feet	Sheffield.
Darby; pond in northern part of Plymouth	Plymouth.
Dark; brook in Auburn; 3 miles long	Webster.
Dartmouth; seaboard town in southern part of Bristol County, area 66 square miles	Fall River. New Bedford.
Dartmouth; village in southwestern part of Dartmouth	Fall River.
Davis; pond in Greenwich	Belchertown.
Davis; village in town of Rowe	Hawley.

A GEOGRAPHIC DICTIONARY OF MASSACHUSETTS. 35

Atlas sheets.

Davis Neck; island off northern coast of Gloucester .... Gloucester.
Davis Neck; peninsula in southern part of Falmouth, between Green Pond and Bowen Pond .... Falmouth.
Day; brook in central part of Chester .... Chesterfield.
Day; hill in eastern part of Williamsburg .... Northampton.
Dayville; village in Chester.................................. Chesterfield.
Dead; hill in Bradford; elevation, 280 feet................... Lawrence.
Dead; pond in Hardwick....................................... Barre.
Dead Branch; stream in Chesterfield.......................... Chesterfield.
Dead; swamp in Townsend...................................... Groton.
Dead; swamp in Raynham .... Taunton.
Dead; pond in Townsend .... Groton.
Dead; pond in Lunenburg...................................... Groton.
Dead Neck; narrow strip of land between Osterville Harbor and Nantucket Island in southwest part of Barnstable..... Barnstable.
Dean; pond near coast in Mashpee............................. Barnstable.
Dedham; town in Norfolk County; area, 23 square miles..... { Dedham. / Boston.
Dedham; village in town of same name, on Dedham branch of Boston and Albany R. R. { Dedham. / Boston.
Deep; brook in Chelmsford, 2 miles long...................... Lowell.
Deep; point on shore of Snipatuit Pond, Rochester............ Middleboro.
Deep; pond in Falmouth .... Falmouth.
Deep; pond, in northern part of Bourne .... Falmouth.
Deep Bottom; creek in Tisbury, Marthas Vineyard, tributary to Great Tisbury Pond .... Marthas Vineyard.
Deep Hole; harbor at west entrance of Osterville Harbor in southwest part of Barnstable .... Barnstable.
Deer; pond in southern part of Plymouth..................... Plymouth.
Deer; hill in southeast part of Huntington .... Chesterfield.
Deer; hill in southwest part of Plainfield .... Chesterfield.
Deer Island; granite beacon in the shape of a pyramid, south of Deer Island... Boston Bay.
Deerfield; town in Franklin County; area, 36 square miles..... Greenfield.
Deerfield; village in town of same name, on New Haven and Northampton R. R.. Greenfield.
Deerfield; swamp in western part of Dartmouth .... Fall River.
Demond; pond in Rutland..................................... Worcester.
Den Stream; brook in Middlefield, tributary to middle branch of Westfield River .... Chesterfield.
Denison; lake in Winchendon .... Winchendon.
Dennis; town in Barnstable County; area, 23 square miles.... { Yarmouth. / Wellfleet.
Dennis; village in town of same name........................ Yarmouth.
Dennis; pond south of Yarmouthport in town of Yarmouth... Barnstable.
Dennisport; village in town of Dennis....................... Yarmouth.
Denny; hill in Leicester; elevation, 960 feet.................. Webster.
Dennyville; village in town of Barre .... Barre.
Devereux Station; village in eastern part of Marblehead..... Boston Bay.
Devils Cavern; cave on line between Granby and Amherst.... Northampton.
Devol; pond in western part of Westport .... Fall River.
Dickinson Branch; brook in Granville, 4 miles long.......... Granville.
Dighton; town in Bristol County; area, 23 square miles....... Taunton.

Atlas sheets.

Dighton; village in town of same name on main line Old Colony R. R. .... Taunton.
Dighton Rock; small island in Taunton River .... Taunton.
Dimmick; pond in Springfield .... Palmer.
Dock; creek in north part of Sandwich, emptying into Cape Cod Bay .... Barnstable.
Dock; pond in southern part of Plymouth .... Plymouth.
Dodgeville; village in Attleboro .... Providence.
Doggett; brook tributary to Sippican River in Rochester .... New Bedford.
Dolbier; hill in Templeton; elevation, 1,280 feet .... Winchendon.
Dole Corner; cross roads in central part of Rowley .... Salem.
Dorchester; village in city of Boston .... Boston.
Dorchester; bay east of village of same name in Boston Harbor. Boston.
Dorothy; brook in Millbury .... Blackstone.
Dorothy; hill in Millbury; elevation, 460 feet .... Webster.
Dorothy; pond in Millbury .... Webster.
Double; brook in Dracut, 3 miles long; has its source in Long Pond and flows into Merrimac River .... Lowell.
Double; brook in Middleboro and Craver, 1 mile long, tributary to Weweantic River .... Middleboro.
Doublet; hill in Weston; elevation, 360 feet .... Framingham.
Dougal; mountain in town of Hardwick; altitude, 1,060 feet .. Barre.
Douglass; town in Worcester County; area, 39 square miles .. { Blackstone. Webster.
Douglass; village in town of same name .... Blackstone.
Dover; town in Norfolk County; area, 15 square miles ...... { Franklin. Framingham.
Dover; village in town of same name, on New York and New England R. R., Woonsocket division .... Franklin.
Downer Landing; village on north coast of Hingham .... Boston Bay.
Dracut; town in Middlesex County; area, 22 square miles .... Lowell.
Dracut; village in town of same name .... Lowell.
Dragon; brook in Shelburne; 6 miles long, tributary to North River .... Greenfield.
Dragon; hill in Shelburne; elevation, 780 feet .... Greenfield.
Drake; hill in northwest part of Worthington .... Chesterfield.
Dramanville; village in Millbury .... Webster.
Dread Ledge; island on southeast coast of Swampscott .... Boston Bay.
Dresser; hill in Charlton; elevation, 880 feet .... Webster.
Dresser; pond in southern part of Goshen .... Chesterfield.
Drinkwater; river in west part of Hanover .... Abington.
Dry; brook, branch of Schenob brook in western part of Sheffield .... Sheffield.
Dry; brook, branch of Hoosic River in eastern part of Cheshire. Greylock.
Dry; brook in northwestern part of South Hadley .... Northampton.
Dry; brook in Bernardsten and Gill .... Greenfield.
Dry; hill in Montague; elevation, 1,100 feet .... Warwick.
Dry; hill in southern part of Conway; elevation, 1,380 feet.... Northampton.
Dry; hill in northern part of New Marlboro; elevation, 1,746 feet .... Sandisfield.
Dry Brook; hill in northwestern part of South Hadley; elevation, about 240 feet .... Northampton.
Duck; creek in Wellfleet; tributary to Wellfleet Harbor ...... Wellfleet.
Duck; harbor on west coast of Wellfleet .... Wellfleet.

	Atlas sheets.
Duck; islands in Merrimac River, near city of Lowell	Lowell.
Duck; pond in Groton	Groton.
Duck Hill; river in northeastern part of Duxbury, emptying into Duxbury Bay	Duxbury.
Duckville; village in Palmer	Palmer.
Dudley; town in Worcester County; area, 22 square miles	Webster.
Dudley; village in town of same name	Webster.
Dudley; brook in Sudbury	Framingham.
Dudley; pond in Wayland	Framingham.
Dudleyville; village in Leverett	Belchertown.
Dug; brook in southwestern part of Sunderland, emptying into Connecticut River	Northampton.
Dug; hill in Blandford; elevation, 1,600 feet	Granville.
Dug; pond in Natick	Framingham.
Dumpling; mountain in Palmer; altitude, 741 feet	Palmer.
Dumpling Rock; a fifth order, fixed white light, off Round Hill Point, Dartmouth; lantern, 42 feet above sea level and visible 11¼ miles	New Bedford.
Dunbar; brook in Monroe and Florida, tributary to Deerfield River	Hawley.
Dunham; pond in Lakeville	Middleboro.
Dunn; brook flowing into Quaboag River in Brookfield	Brookfield.
Dunn; pond in Auburn	Webster.
Dunstable; Town in Middlesex County; area, 18 square miles	{ Groton. Lowell.
Dunstable; village in town of same name	Lowell.
Duxbury; an old seaboard town in eastern part of Plymouth County; area, 27 square miles	Duxbury.
Duxbury; village in eastern part of Duxbury, on Duxbury Bay	Duxbury.
Duxbury; bay, large arm of Cape Cod Bay, between the mainland and Duxbury Beach	Duxbury.
Duxbury; lighthouse at entrance to Duxbury Harbor, Duxbury	Plymouth.
Duxbury; marsh in eastern part of Duxbury	Duxbury.
Duxbury; railway station in eastern part of Duxbury	Duxbury.
Duxbury; beach extending southeasterly from Duxbury, between Duxbury Bay and Cape Cod Bay	Duxbury.
Dwight; village in Belchertown, on New London Northern R. R.	Belchertown.
Eagle; island about 2 miles off northeast coast of Marblehead	Salem.
Eagle; pond in Dennis	Yarmouth.
Eagle; pond in southwest part of Barnstable	Barnstable.
Eagleville; village in Holden	Worcester.
Eagleville; village in Athol	Warwick.
East; pond on coast of Tuckernuck Island	Muskeget.
East; point on southeast coast of Nahant	Boston Bay.
East; pond in southeastern part of New Marlboro	Sandisfield.
East; pond in Greenwich	Belchertown.
East; mountain in Bernardston; altitude, 1,160 feet	Greenfield.
East; mountain, long ridge forming part of Taconic range in Hancock; extreme altitude, 2,360 feet	Berlin.
East; hill in town of Monson; elevation, 860 feet	Palmer.
East; village in central part of Amherst	Northampton.
East; hill in Shelburne; elevation, 1,120 feet	Greenfield.
East; village in Webster	Webster.
East; brook tributary to Quinebaug River in Brimfield	Brookfield.

	Atlas sheets.
East Blackstone; village in Blackstone.......................	Blackstone.
East Boston; part of the city of Boston on island in Boston Harbor..	Boston.
East Braintree; village in northeast part of Braintree........	Abington.
East Branch; stream on south boundary of Chesterfield......	Chesterfield.
East Brewster; village in town of Brewster....................	Wellfleet.
East Bridgewater; town in Plymouth County; area, 18 square miles..	Abington.
East Brimfield; village in Brimfield............................	Brookfield.
East Brookfield; river tributary to Quaboag Pond in Brookfield	Brookfield.
East Brookfield; village in northwestern part of Brookfield..	Brookfield.
East Charlemont; village in town of Charlemont	Hawley.
East Chop; lighthouse on north coast of Cottage City, Marthas Vineyard..	Marthas Vineyard.
East Dedham; village in town of Dedham, on Dedham branch of Boston and Providence R. R...................................	Dedham.
East Dennis; village in town of Dennis	Yarmouth.
East Douglas; village in town of Douglas	Blackstone.
East Falmouth; village in southern part of Falmouth	Falmouth.
East Farms; village in Westfield................................	Springfield.
East Foxboro; village in town of Foxboro, on Boston and Providence R. R..	Dedham.
East Freetown; village in town of Freetown..................	Middleboro.
East Freetown; station on Old Colony R. R., New Bedford branch, in Freetown	Middleboro.
East Gloucester; village or extension of city of Gloucester on East Point at head of Gloucester harbor, Gloucester......	Gloucester.
East Granville; village in town of Granville	Granville.
East Groton; station on Nashua, Acton and Boston R. R., in town of Groton	Groton.
East Harwich; village in town of same name	Yarmouth.
East Holliston; village in town of Holliston, on Boston and Albany R. R...	Franklin.
East Lee; village in central part of Lee	Becket.
East Lexington; village in Lexington, on Boston and Lowell R. R...	Boston.
East Littleton; station on Nashua, Acton and Boston R. R., in Westford..	Lowell.
East Longmeadow; village in town of Longmeadow, on New York and New England R. R......................................	Springfield.
East Mansfield; village in town of Mansfield	Dedham.
East Marshfield; village in northeastern part of Marshfield..	Duxbury.
East Medford; village in town of Medford, on Boston and Maine R. R...	Boston.
East Middleboro; village in town of Middleboro.............	Middleboro.
East Milton; village in town of Milton.........................	Boston.
East Orleans; village in town of Orleans	Wellfleet.
East Otis; village in southeastern part of Otis................	Sandisfield.
East Pembroke; village in eastern part of Pembroke	Abington.
East Pepperell; village in town of Pepperell, on Boston and Maine R. R...	Groton.
East Phillipston; village in town of Phillipston.............	Winchendon.
East Princeton; village in Princeton...........................	Worcester.

A GEOGRAPHIC DICTIONARY OF MASSACHUSETTS. 39

Atlas sheets

East Rock; rocky point in central part of Great Barrington; elevation, 1,560 feet................................... Sheffield.
East Rocky Gutter; brook in Middleboro, tributary to Double Brook... Middleboro.
East Salisbury; village in town of Salisbury, on Boston and Maine R. R... Newburyport.
East Sandwich; village in Sandwich, on Cape Cod branch Old Colony R. R... Barnstable.
East Saugus; village in eastern part of Saugus.............. Boston Bay.
East Shelburne; village in town of Shelburne............... Greenfield.
East Stoughton; village in town of Stoughton............... Dedham.
East Sudbury Station; in Sudbury, on Massachusetts Central R. R... Framingham.
East Sutton; village in town of Sutton..................... Blackstone.
East Taunton; village in town of Taunton, on Middleboro and Taunton R. R... Taunton.
East Templeton; village in town of Templeton............... Winchendon.
East Wachusett; brook in Princeton, 4 miles long, tributary to Stillwater River................................... Worcester.
East Walpole; village in town of Walpole................... Dedham.
East Waushaccum; pond in town of Sterling................ Marlboro.
East Weymouth; village in eastern part of Weymouth........ Abington.
East Whately; village in eastern part of Whately........... Northampton.
East Woburn; village in town of Woburn.................... Boston.
Eastern; point in southern part of Gloucester, extending into Atlantic Ocean....................................... Gloucester.
Eastern; part of Boston and Maine R. R. system.
Eastham; town in Barnstable County; area, 16 square miles... Wellfleet.
Eastham Center; village in town of Eastham................ Wellfleet.
Easthampton; town in southern part of Hampshire County; area, 15 square miles................................ Northampton.
Easthampton; village and railway station in central part of town of same name................................... Northampton.
Easton, town in Bristol County; area, 32 square miles......... Dedham.
Easton Center; village in town of Easton on Old Colony R. R. Dedham.
Eastville; village in Cottage City, Marthas Vineyard......... Marthas Vineyard.
Eastville; village in east part of East Bridgewater........... Abington.
Eddyville; village in Middleboro........................... Middleboro.
Edgartown; town in Dukes County; area, 30 square miles.... Marthas Vineyard.
Edgartown; village in town of same name, Marthas Vineyard. Marthas Vineyard.
Edgartown; harbor of Edgartown............................ Marthas Vineyard.
Edgartown; light-house in Edgartown Harbor, Marthas Vineyard... Marthas Vineyard.
Edmund; hill in Northboro................................. Marlboro.
Eel; point on west coast of Nantucket...................... Muskeget.
Eel; pond (salt) in southern part of Falamouth, opening into Waquoit Bay... Falmouth.
Eel; pond in Edgartown, opens into Edgartown Island........ Marthas Vineyard.
Eel; river in northern part of Plymouth..................... Plymouth.
Egg; island in New Bedford Harbor......................... New Bedford.
Egg Rock; light-house east of Nahant at south entrance of Nahant Bay, 87 feet above sea level. Fixed red light, visible 12 miles... Boston Bay.

	Atlas sheets.
Egremont; town in southwestern part of Berkshire County; area, 19 square miles	Sheffield.
Egremont; village in town of same name	Sheffield.
Elbow; pond in southern part of Plymouth	Plymouth.
Elder; pond in Lakeville	Middleboro.
Eldridge; pond in Harwich	Yarmouth.
Elizabeth; group of islands forming town of Gosnold	Gay Head.
Ellinwood; brook in Athol	Winchendon.
Ellis; pond in northern part of Plymouth	Plymouth.
Ellis; river, right tributary of Quaboag River on the boundary between West Brookfield and Warren	Brookfield.
Ellsworth; village in Acton	Framingham.
Elm; brook in Bedford	Framingham.
Elm Grove; village in Coleraine	Greenfield.
Elmer; brook tributary to Bachelor Brook in northern part of South Hadley	Northampton.
Elmwood; village in south part of East Bridgewater	Abington.
Elmwood; railway station in south part of East Bridgewater	Abington.
Elwell; island in Connecticut River between Hadley and Northampton	Northampton.
Emerson; brook in Uxbridge, tributary to Blackstone River	Blackstone.
Emerson; hill in Douglas; elevation, 700 feet	Webster.
Emerson; point in eastern extremity of Rockport	Gloucester.
Enfield; town in Hampshire County; area, 18 square miles	Belchertown.
Enfield; village in town of same name on Boston and Albany R. R.	Belchertown.
Ephraim; mountain in Lexington	Boston.
Erving; town in Franklin County; area, 14 square miles	Warwick.
Essex; low, marshy river in eastern part of Essex County, draining Chebacco Lake and emptying into Annisquam Harbor	Salem.
Essex; village in eastern part of Essex	Salem.
Essex; town in western part of Essex County; area, 18 square miles.	{ Salem. Gloucester.
Essex Branch; stream in southern part of Essex County, emptying into Beverly Harbor	Salem.
Essex Falls; railway station in central part of Essex	Salem.
Esther; mountain in northern part of Whately; altitude, 987 feet	Northampton.
Ethel; mountain in northwestern part of Mount Washington; altitude, 1,900 feet	Sheffield.
Everett; town in Middlesex County; area, 4 square miles	Boston.
Everett; village in town of same name on Boston and Maine R. R.	Boston.
Everett; mountain in eastern part of Mount Washington; altitude, 2,624 feet	Sheffield.
Evergreen; mountain in Stockbridge; altitude, 1,060 feet	Pittsfield.
Erving; village in town of same name on Fitchburg R. R.	Warwick.
Ezekiel; pond in southern part of Plymouth	Plymouth.
Facing; hills in Granby, Belchertown, and Ludlow; elevation, 780 feet	Palmer.
Facing Rock; hill in Ludlow; elevation, 620 feet	Palmer.
Factory; village in Gill	Greenfield.
Factory; brook tributary to Westfield River, flowing southerly through Peru and Middlefield	Becket.

	Atlas sheets.
Factory Hollow; village in northern part of Amherst........	Northampton.
Fair Haven; town in southeastern part of Bristol County on New Bedford Harbor; area, 12 square miles.................	New Bedford.
Fair Haven; village on New Bedford Harbor in Fair Haven...	New Bedford.
Fair Haven; hill in Concord; elevation, 320 feet..............	Framingham.
Fair Haven; pond in Concord...................................	Framingham.
Fairmount; hill in Marlboro; elevation, 520 feet..............	Marlboro.
Fall; brook in Middleboro, 3 miles long, tributary to Namasket River...:.......................	Middleboro.
Fall; brook in Leominster.......................................	{ Worcester. { Fitchburg.
Fall; brook in Royalston	Winchendon.
Fall; brook in eastern part of Freetown, emptying into Long Pond.	{ Middleboro. { New Bedford.
Fall; hill in Orange; elevation, 1,067 feet......................	Warwick.
Fall Hill; brook in Orange, 2 miles long	Warwick.
Fall Hill; meadow in town of Orange ..;.......................	Warwick.
Fall River; manufacturing city of Bristol County, located on shore of Mount Hope Bay at mouth of Taunton River. Original name was Troy. Area, 34 square miles................	Fall River.
Falls; river in Bernardston, and between Gill and Greenfield, tributary to Connecticut River............................	Greenfield.
Fallulah; brook in Fitchburg and Ashby.......................	Fitchburg.
Falmouth; seaboard town on southwestern part of Cape Cod between Buzzards Bay and Vineyard Sound, named from Falmouth, England; area, 45 square miles................	Falmouth.
Falmouth; village in southwestern part of Falmouth.........	Falmouth.
Falmouth Harbor; village in Falmouth, on shore of Vineyard Sound	Falmouth.
Falmouth Heights; watering place in southern part of Falmouth, on shore of Vineyard Sound	Falmouth.
Faqua; pond in Edgartown, Marthas Vineyard	Marthas Vineyard.
Farley; brook in Chelmsford, tributary to River Meadow Brook	Lowell.
Farm; hill in Marlboro; elevation, 430 feet.....................	Marlboro.
Farm; hill in Stoneham; elevation, 200 feet....................	Boston.
Farm; pond in Sherborn..	Franklin.
Farm; pond in Cottage City, Marthas Vineyard...............	Marthas Vineyard.
Farm; pond in Framingham....................................	Framingham.
Farmerville; village in Sandwich	Barnstable.
Farmington; river flowing southerly through eastern part of Berkshire County into state of Connecticut	Sandisfield.
Farnumsville; village in Grafton, on Providence and Worcester R. R..	Blackstone.
Farrow; hill in Barre; elevation, 1,115 feet....................	Barre.
Fawn; lake in town of Bedford	Lowell.
Fay; mountain in Hopkinton; altitude, 700 feet..............	Blackstone.
Fayville; village in Bolton.....................................	Marlboro.
Fayville; village in town of Southboro.......................	Marlboro.
Feake, Mount; hill in Waltham................................	Boston.
Fearing; pond in southern part of Plymouth...................	Plymouth.
Feeding Hill; village in Agawam	Springfield.
Felchville; village in Natick, on Boston and Albany R. R.....	Framingham.
Fenton; brook, in southern part of Egremont	Sheffield.

	Atlas sheets.
Fenton; mountain in town of Brimfield; altitude, 960 feet	Palmer.
Fentonville; village in town of Brimfield	Palmer.
Ferry; point on east coast of Quincy, projecting into Weymouth Fore River, Quincy	Abington.
Field; brook in Chicopee, 3¼ miles long	Springfield.
Fields; hill in southeastern part of Conway; elevation, 1,200 feet	Northampton.
Fife; brook in Florida, 1¼ miles long, tributary to Deerfield River	Hawley.
Filley; mountain in central part of Otis; also called Tilley Mountain; altitude, 1,717 feet	Sandisfield.
First; branch of Jones River, in Kingston	Plymouth.
First; branch of Connecticut River, in eastern part of Whately	Northampton
First; brook in Buckland	Hawley.
First Herring; branch of North River, in southern part of Scituate	Duxbury.
First Herring; brook in south part of Scituate	Abington.
Fish; brook, branch of Ipswich River, flowing through Boxford.	Lawrence. Salem.
Fish; brook in Andover, tributary to Merrimac River	Lawrence.
Fish; island off eastern coast of Sconticut Neck, Fair Haven	New Bedford.
Fish; pond in northern part of Plymouth	Plymouth.
Fishing; river in Plaistow, N. H., and Haverhill, Mass., 4 miles long, tributary to Little River	Haverhill.
Fisk; hill in New Salem; elevation, 1,000 feet	Warwick.
Fisk; hill in eastern part of Sturbridge	Brookfield.
Fiskdale; village in Sturbridge	Brookfield.
Fitchburg; city in Worcester County; area, 29 square miles	Fitchburg.
Fitchburg; railroad connecting Fitchburg with Troy, N. Y.	
Fivemile; pond in southern part of Plymouth	Plymouth.
Fivemile; pond in Springfield	Springfield.
Fivemile; river in North Brookfield, 5 miles long; flows into Furnace Pond	Barre.
Fivepound; island in the head of Gloucester Harbor	Gloucester.
Flag; brook in Westminster and Fitchburg	Fitchburg.
Flagg Meadow; brook in Dracut and Lowell, 1 mile long; flows into Merrimac River	Lowell.
Flat; brook in towns of Hardwick and Ware	Belchertown.
Flat; hill in Spencer; elevation, 1,060 feet	Webster.
Flat; hill in Southampton; elevation, 440 feet	Granville.
Flat; hill in Lunenburg; elevation, 523 feet	Groton.
Flat; pond on southeast coast of Mashpee	Barnstable.
Flat; pond in Brewster	Wellfleet.
Flat; pond in Groton	Groton.
Flax; pond in Yarmouth	Yarmouth.
Flax; pond in southern part of Bourne	Falmouth.
Flax; pond in Dennis	Yarmouth.
Flax; pond in Wareham	Plymouth.
Flax; pond in Harwich	Yarmouth.
Flint; pond in Grafton	Blackstone.
Florence; village on Mill River in Northampton	Northampton.
Florida; mountainous town in northern part of Berkshire County; area, 24 square miles	Hawley. Greylock.
Florida; village in northern part of town of same name	Greylock.
Flower; hill in Warwick; elevation, 1,200 feet	Warwick.

	Atlas sheets.
Flushing; hill in Westford; elevation, 300 feet	Lowell.
Flushing; pond in Westford	Lowell.
Folger; hill in Nantucket	Nantucket.
Follins; pond on eastern boundary of Yarmouth	Yarmouth.
Folly; cove in northern coast of Cape Arm, between northern extremity of Gloucester and Rockport	Gloucester.
Folly; hill in eastern part of Danvers; elevation about 200 feet	Salem.
Folsom; pond in Wayland	Framingham.
Forest; river in eastern part of Salem	Boston Bay.
Forest; pond in Palmer	Palmer.
Forest; pond in Middleton	Lawrence.
Forest; hill in Dunstable; elevation, 340 feet	Lowell.
Forestdale; village in southern part of Sandwich; also called Greenwich	Falmouth.
Forest Hills; village in city of Boston	Boston.
Forge; hill in Hawley; elevation, 1,845 feet	Hawley.
Forge; pond in Freetown	Taunton.
Forge; pond in Raynham	Taunton.
Forge; pond in Granby	Belchertown.
Forge; pond in Westford	Lowell.
Forge; village in Westford, on Stoney Brook R. R.	Lowell.
Forked; pond in Nantucket	Nantucket.
Fort; hill in Ashby; elevation, 800 feet	Fitchburg.
Fort; hill in Oxford; elevation, 860 feet	Webster.
Fort; hill in Lowell; elevation, 260 feet	Lowell.
Fort; point on southwestern coast of Fair Haven	New Bedford.
Fort; pond in Lancaster	Groton.
Fort; pond in Littleton	Lowell.
Fort; river in Pelham and Amherst	{ Northampton. Belchertown.
Fort Hill; village in western part of Hingham	Abington.
Fort Meadow; reservoir in Marlboro	Marlboro.
Fort Pond; brook in Boxboro, Acton, and Concord	Framingham.
Foster; brook in town of Gardner	Fitchburg.
Foster; hill in southern part of West Brookfield; altitude, 800 feet	Brookfield.
Foster; pond in south part of Andover	Lawrence.
Fourmile; pond in Boxford	Lawrence.
Fourmile; brook in Northfield, tributary to Connecticut River.	Warwick.
Foundry; brook in Coleraine, 4 miles long, tributary to east branch of North River	Greenfield.
Foundry; village in Palmer	Palmer.
Four Corners; village in Palmer	Palmer.
Fox; brook in Blackstone; flows into Blackstone River	Blackstone.
Fox; creek in eastern part of Ipswich	Salem.
Fox; hill in eastern part of Peabody; elevation, 120 feet	Salem.
Fox; hill in Dedham; elevation, 320 feet	Dedham.
Fox; hill in Billerica; elevation, 300 feet	{ Lawrence. Lowell.
Fox Ledge; hill in Tyngsboro; elevation, 260 feet	Lowell.
Foxboro; town in Norfolk County; area, 22 square miles	{ Dedham. Franklin.

	Atlas sheets.
Foxboro; village in town of Foxboro	Franklin. Dedham.
Framingham; town in Middlesex County; area, 27 square miles.	Framingham.
Framingham and Lowell; branch of Old Colony R. R. system.	
Framingham Center; village in town of Framingham, on Old Colony R. R.	Framingham.
Francis; hill on eastern boundary line of Westford	Lowell.
Franklin; town in Norfolk County; area, 29 square miles	Franklin.
Franklin; village in town of Franklin, on New York and New England R. R.	Franklin.
Franklin Park; railroad station in Revere	Boston.
Freeland; brook in Blandford and Montgomery, 3¼ miles long.	Granville.
Freeman; brook in Webster	Webster.
Freeman; pond in Brewster	Wellfleet.
Freetown; an inland town in eastern part of Bristol County; area, 41 square miles.	Taunton. Middleboro. New Bedford.
French; brook in Boylston, tributary to Nashua River, 2 miles long	Marlboro.
French; hill in central part of Peru; elevation, 2,240 feet	Becket.
French; river in Oxford	Webster.
French; stream in west part of Rockland	Abington.
French Watering Place; village on south coast of Naushon Island, in town of Gosnold	Gay Head.
Fresh Brook; village in Wellfleet	Wellfleet.
Fresh; pond in Belmont and Cambridge	Boston.
Fresh; pond in Plymouth	Plymouth.
Fresh; pond in Dennis	Yarmouth.
Fresh; pond in southwestern part of Falmouth	Falmouth.
Fresh; river in western part of Hingham	Abington.
Freshwater Cove; village in Gloucester, on west side of head of Gloucester Harbor	Gloucester.
Frizzell; hill in Leyden; elevation, 1,343 feet	Greenfield.
Frizzell; mountain in southwestern part of Mount Washington; altitude, 2,420 feet	Sheffield.
Frost Fish; brook, principal tributary to Porter River, in eastern part of Danvers	Salem.
Frye; village in Andover	Lawrence.
Fryville; village in Orange	Winchendon.
Fuller; brook tributary to middle branch of Westfield River, in Peru and Worthington	Becket.
Fuller; brook in Hawley and Plainfield, tributary to Chickley River, 2 miles long	Hawley.
Furnace; branch of Jones River, in Kingston	Plymouth.
Furnace; pond in west part of Pembroke	Abington.
Furnace; pond in North Brookfield	Brookfield.
Furnace; pond in Middleboro	Middleboro.
Furnace ; village in Orange	Winchendon.
Furnace ; village in Easton	Dedham.
Further; creek on coast of Nantucket	Muskeget.
Gale ; brook in Warwick	Warwick.
Gale ; point on southern coast of Manchester at east entrance to Manchester Harbor	Salem.
Gallop; island east of north part of Long Island, Boston Bay.	Boston Bay.

A GEOGRAPHIC DICTIONARY OF MASSACHUSETTS. 45

	Atlas sheets.
Galloway; brook in Barre, 2 miles long	Barre.
Gallows; pond in Plymouth	Plymouth.
Gammon; point of Great Island	Barnstable.
Gannett Corners; village in west part of Scituate	Abington.
Gap Head; point on east coast of Rockport, east of Sandy Bay	Gloucester.
Gardner; lake on boundary line between Amesbury and Salisbury	Newburyport.
Gardner; village in town of Gardner, on Fitchburg R. R.	{ Fitchburg. Winchendon.
Gardner; town in Worcester County; area, 23 square miles	{ Winchendon. Fitchburg.
Gardener Neck; peninsula in southern part of Swansea between Cole and Lee rivers	Fall River.
Garfield; pond in southeastern part of Monterey	Sandisfield.
Gates; pond in town of Berlin	Marlboro.
Gates; brook in West Boylston, 3 miles long, tributary to Nashua River	Worcester.
Gates Crossing; village in Leominster	Marlboro.
Gay Head; town in Dukes County; area, 6 square miles	Gay Head.
Gay Head; point on northwest coast of Marthas Vineyard, so named from its bright-colored cliffs	Gay Head.
George; hill in town of Lancaster	Marlboro.
George; hill on boundary line between Grafton and Upton; elevation, 600 feet	Blackstone.
George; island in Boston Bay, east of Long Island	Boston Bay.
Georgetown; town in Essex County; area, 11 square miles	{ Salem. Lawrence.
Georgetown; village in town of same name	Salem.
German; hill in Yarmouth	Yarmouth.
Germantown; village in eastern part of Quincy	Boston Bay.
Gerry; island near the northeast coast of Marblehead	Salem.
Ghost; hill in Marlboro	Marlboro.
Gibbett; hill in Groton; elevation, 516 feet	Groton.
Gibbs; hill in Framingham	Framingham.
Gibbs; pond in Nantucket	Nantucket.
Gibbs Crossing; village in Ware	Palmer.
Gilbertville; village in Hardwick, on Boston and Albany R. R.	Barre.
Gill; town in Franklin County; area, 14 square miles	{ Greenfield. Warwick.
Gill; village in town of same name	Greenfield.
Gill Station; village in Northfield, on New London Northern R.R.	Warwick.
Gilson; brook in Westford, 1¼ miles long; flows into Stony Brook.	Lowell.
Gilson; hill in Billerica; elevation, 320 feet	Lowell.
Glades, The; name applied to tract of low land in north part of Scituate	Abington.
Gleason; pond in Framingham	Framingham.
Glen; pond in Wareham	Plymouth.
Glen; brook in Leyden and Greenfield, 6 miles long; flows into Green River	Greenfield.
Glen Mills; village in northern part of Rowley	Salem.
Glendale; village in Stockbridge, on Housatonic R. R.	Pittsfield.
Glenmen; pond in eastern part of Lynn	Boston Bay.
Globe; village in Southbridge	Brookfield.

	Atlas sheets.
Globe; brook tributary to Quinebang River, in Charlton, Sturbridge, and Southbridge	Brookfield.
Globe Village; village in southern part of Fall River	Fall River.
Gloucester; city in eastern part of Essex County, on Cape Ann. It took its name from Gloucester, England; area, 34 square miles	Gloucester.
Goat; hill in town of Hardwick; elevation, 986 feet	Barre.
Goat; island in Long Pond, in Lakeville	Middleboro.
Gobble Mountain; one of the Berkshire Hills, in Chester; elevation, 1,680 feet	Chesterfield.
Goddard; brook in Montague, 2 miles long; tributary to Saw Mill River	Greenfield.
Goddard; pond in Grafton	Blackstone.
Golden; hill in Haverhill; elevation, 253 feet	Haverhill.
Golden Cove; brook in Chelmsford, one-half mile long; tributary to River Meadow Brook	Lowell.
Goldthwait; brook tributary to North River, in southeastern part of Peabody, draining Cedar Pond	Salem.
Goodman; hill in Sudbury; elevation, 360 feet	Framingham.
Goodrich; pond in southeastern part of Pittsfield	Becket.
Goodrich Hollow; valley in Taconic Range in Hancock	Berlin.
Goods; hill in town of Northbridge	Blackstone.
Goose; pond on boundary line between Tyringham and Lee	Becket.
Goose; pond in Chatham	Yarmouth.
Goose; island in Slocum River, Dartmouth	New Bedford.
Goose; cove in northern coast of Gloucester at head of Annisquam Harbor	Gloucester.
Goose Branch; brook in Nashua and Attleboro tributary to Wading River; 2 miles long	Taunton.
Gooseberry; island in Poponesset Bay on southeast coast of Mashpee	Barnstable.
Gooseberry Neck; island in west entrance to Buzzards Bay off coast of Westport	Sakonnet.
Gore; pond in Charlemont and Dudley	Webster.
Goshen; town in Hampshire County; area, 15 square miles	Chesterfield.
Gosnold; town in Dukes County; area, 14 square miles	{ Gay Head. Falmouth.
Gosnold; pond in Cuttyhunk Island, Gosnold	Gay Head.
Goss; hill near western boundary line of Huntington	Chesterfield.
Governors; island in Boston Harbor	Boston.
Grace; brook in Warwick, 2¼ miles long; flows into Lake Moore.	Warwick.
Grace, Mount; hill in town of Warwick; elevation, 1,620 feet.	Warwick.
Grafton; town in Worcester County; area, 23 square miles	Blackstone.
Grafton; village in town of Grafton	Blackstone.
Granby; town in southern part of Hampshire County; area, 28 square miles.	{ Belchertown Springfield. Palmer. Northampton.
Granby; village in central part of Granby	Northampton.
Grand; cove in Dennis	Yarmouth.
Grandy; hill in western part of Wales; elevation, 1,140 feet	Brookfield.
Graniteville; village in Westford on Stony Brook R. R	Lowell.
Granny; hill in Lexington; elevation, 360 feet	Boston.
Granville; town in Hampden County: area, 41 square miles	Granville.

A GEOGRAPHIC DICTIONARY OF MASSACHUSETTS. 47

	Atlas sheets.
Granville; village in town of Granville	Granville.
Grape; hill on boundary line between Salisbury, Mass., and Seabrook, N. H.; elevation, 240 feet	Newburyport.
Grape; island north of Weymouth	Boston Bay.
Grass; hill in Millbury; elevation, 760 feet	Webster.
Grass; hill on line between Williamsburg and Whately; elevation, 440 feet	Northampton.
Grass; brook in Dunstable, tributary to Salmon Brook	Lowell.
Grass; pond in Westminster	Fitchburg.
Grass; pond in Harwich	Yarmouth.
Grassy; island in Taunton River	Taunton.
Grassy; pond in Dennis	Yarmouth.
Grassy; pond in northern part of Plymouth	Plymouth.
Grassy; pond in southern part of Plymouth	Plymouth.
Grassy; pond in Acton	Lowell.
Gravel; pond in southeastern part of Hamilton	Salem.
Graves; island off southern coast of Manchester	Gloucester.
Great; bay at head of Osterville Harbor on southwest coast of Barnstable	Barnstable.
Great; brook in Shelburne, 2 miles long, flows into Hawkes Brook	Greenfield
Great; brook in Southwick and Westfield, 7 miles long, tributary to Westfield River.	{ Granville. Springfield.
Great; brook flowing into Quaboag Pond in Brookfield	Brookfield.
Great; creek flowing from Great Marshes into Barnstable Harbor	Barnstable.
Great; harbor in Woods Holl between Long Neck Island and mainland	Falmouth.
Great; hill in Bridgewater; elevation, 160 feet	Middleboro.
Great; hill.in north part of Weymouth	Abington.
Great; hill in Acton; elevation, 340 feet	Framingham.
Great; hill in Topsfield; elevation, 240 feet	Salem.
Great; hill on Great Neck, in Marion, 127 feet above sea level.	Falmouth.
Great; island in Great Quittacas Pond, Lakeville	Middleboro.
Great; island in east branch of Westport River, Westport	Fall River.
Great; island in Wellfleet, Barnstable County	Wellfleet.
Great; lake in eastern part of Otis	Sandisfield.
Great; pond on boundary line between Randolph and Braintree	Dedham.
Great; pond in North Andover	Lawrence.
Great; pond in Montague	Greenfield.
Great; pond in Brimfield	Brookfield.
Great; pond in Plymouth	Plymouth.
Great; pond in Wellfleet	Wellfleet.
Great; pond in Eastham	Wellfleet.
Great; pond about 2 miles long in southern part of Falmouth, opening into Vineyard Sound	Falmouth.
Great; pond in Barnstable	Barnstable.
Great; pond in southwest part of Weymouth	Abington.
Great; point on northeast extremity of Nantucket	Nantucket.
Great; swamp in Tewksbury	Lawrence.
Great; swamp lying between village of Brookfield and East Brookfield in town of Brookfield	Brookfield.
Great Barrington; large town in southwestern part of Berkshire County; area, 46 square miles.	{ Pittsfield. Sheffield.

48   A GEOGRAPHIC DICTIONARY OF MASSACHUSETTS.   [BULL. 116.

	Atlas sheets.
Great Barrington; village and railway station in central part of town of same name on Housatonic River	Sheffield.
Great Beach; hill in Wellfleet	Wellfleet.
Great Blue; hill on western boundary line of Milton; elevation, 635 feet	Dedham.
Great Brewster; island in Boston Bay	Boston Bay.
Great Calf; island in Boston Bay	Boston Bay.
Great Cedar; swamp in north part of Halifax and south part of Hanson	Abington.
Great Cedar; swamp in Easton, Taunton, Bridgewater, and West Bridgewater	Taunton.
Great Cedar; swamp in New Bedford on line of Dartmouth	New Bedford.
Great Cedar; swamp in Halifax and Middleboro	Middleboro.
Great Drain; brook in southwestern part of Sunderland, emptying into Connecticut River	Northampton.
Great Duck; pond in Provincetown	Provincetown.
Great Egg Rock; islet about 1 mile south of Manchester	Gloucester.
Great Fawn; stone beacon east of Deer Island	Boston Bay.
Great Herring; pond in southern part of Plymouth	Plymouth.
Great Hill; point about one-half mile southeast of Great Hill in Plymouth, projecting into Buzzards Bay	Falmouth.
Great Indian; pond on western boundary of Kingston	Middleboro.
Great Island; peninsula on south side of Lewis Bay	Barnstable.
Great; marshes (salt) at head of Barnstable Harbor, 6 or 8 miles in extent	Barnstable.
Great Meadow; hill in Rehoboth; elevation, 263 feet	Taunton.
Great Mioxes; pond in Nantucket	Nantucket.
Great Misery; island about three-fourths mile southeast of Beverly	Salem.
Great Morse; hill in Huntington; elevation, 1,240 feet	Granville.
Great Neck; name given to land on southeast coast of Mashpee between Flat and Deans ponds	Barnstable.
Great Neck; point of land in southern part of Dartmouth in the bend of Slocum River	New Bedford.
Great Neck; peninsula in Nantucket	Nantucket.
Great Neck; peninsula in eastern part of Ipswich	Salem.
Great Rock; hill in Rehoboth; elevation, 248 feet	Providence.
Great Sandy Bottom; pond in west part of Pembroke	Abington.
Great Swamp; brook tributary to Mill Creek in northwestern part of Rowley	Salem.
Great Thatcher; island in Barnstable Harbor	Barnstable.
Great Tisbury; pond in southwestern part of town of Tisbury, Marthas Vineyard	Marthas Vineyard.
Green; river tributary to Housatonic River in western part of Great Barrington	Sheffield.
Green; river on boundary between Coleraine and Leyden and in Greenfield and Deerfield and in Vermont State, tributary to North River	Greenfield.
Green; river tributary to Hoosic River flowing northerly through western part of Berkshire County	Greylock.
Green; brook in Carver	Middleboro.
Green; creek in northeastern part of Ipswich, emptying into Plum River	Salem.

A GEOGRAPHIC DICTIONARY OF MASSACHUSETTS. 49

	Atlas sheets.
Green; harbor in eastern coast of Marshfield at mouth of Green Harbor River	Duxbury.
Green; hill in Blandford; elevation, 1,560 feet	Granville.
Green; hill in Sudbury; elevation, 320 feet	Framingham.
Green; pond in southern part of Falmouth, opening into Vineyard Sound	Falmouth.
Green; pond in Montague	Greenfield.
Green; point in Assawompsett Pond, Lakeville	Middleboro.
Green; island in Boston Bay	Boston Bay
Green, The; village in Middleboro	Middleboro
Greenbush; railway station in southern part of Scituate	Duxbury.
Greenfield; town in Franklin County; area, 20 square miles	Greenfield.
Greenfield; village in town of Greenfield on Connecticut River R. R.	Greenfield.
Greenfield; hill in Shelburne	Greenfield.
Green Harbor; marsh in eastern part of Marshfield	Duxbury.
Green Harbor; river in southern part of Marshfield	Duxbury.
Greenleaf; hill in Burlington; elevation, 260 feet	Boston.
Green Lodge; village in Dedham	Dedham.
Greenville; village in town of Leicester	Webster.
Greenville; reservoir near village of Greenville, town of Leicester	Webster.
Greenwater; pond in western part of Becket	Becket.
Greenwich; town in Hampshire County; area, 21 square miles	Belchertown.
Greenwich; village in town of same name	Belchertown.
Greenwood; village in Wakefield	Boston.
Greenwood; hill in Wakefield; elevation, 260 feet	Boston.
Greenwood; hill in town of Gardner; elevation, 1,260 feet	Fitchburg.
Grews; pond in southwestern part of Falmouth	Falmouth.
Greylock; mountain in western part of Adams; altitude, 3,505 feet, the highest point in the State	Greylock.
Griffin; brook in Richmond, 4 miles long	Pittsfield.
Griffin; island in Wellfleet	Wellfleet.
Griffith; pond in Brewster	Yarmouth.
Griswoldville; village in Coleraine	Greenfield.
Groton; town in Middlesex County; area, 39 square miles	Groton.
Groton; village in town of Groton and Maine R. R.	Groton.
Grover; cliff on northeast coast of Winthrop	Boston Bay.
Growl; hill in Auburn; elevation, 860 feet	Webster.
Groveland; town in Essex County; area, 7 square miles	{ Haverhill. Lawrence. Newburyport.
Groveland; village in town of same name	Haverhill.
Groveland; station on Georgetown branch of Boston and Maine R. R., town of Groveland	Haverhill.
Gulf; arm of Cohasset Cove on east coast of Cohasset	Abington.
Gulf; brook in Orange, flows into Millers River	Warwick.
Gulf; brook in town of Pepperell and in New Hampshire	Groton.
Gulf; island on east coast of Cohasset	Abington.
Gull; one of the Elizabeth Islands, Gosnold	Gay Head.
Gull; island in Snipatuit Pond, Rochester	Middleboro.
Gull; pond in Wellfleet	Wellfleet.
Gunners Exchange; pond in Plymouth	Plymouth.

Bull. 116——4

	Atlas sheets.
Gunning; point on southwestern coast of Falmouth	Falmouth.
Gurnet; southeastern point of peninsula east of Duxbury, Plymouth	Duxbury.
Gurnet; light-house on Gurnet Point, Plymouth	Duxbury.
Gurney Corners; village in east part of Hanson	Abington.
Gushee; pond in Raynham	Taunton.
Hacker; pond in New Salem	Warwick.
Hadley; harbor between Uncatena and Monamesset Islands	Falmouth.
Hadley; town in northern part of Hampshire County; area, 22 square miles	Northampton.
Hadley; village in southwestern part of Hadley on Connecticut River	Northampton.
Haggett; pond in Andover	Lawrence.
Haggett; station on Lawrence branch of Boston and Lowell R. R. in Andover	Lawrence.
Half Moon; island north of Quincy in Boston Bay	Boston.
Halfway; pond in eastern part of Barnstable	Barnstable.
Halfway; pond in Yarmouth	Yarmouth.
Halibut; point at northern extremity of Cape Ann, Rockport	Gloucester.
Halifax; town in Plymouth county; area, 18 square miles	Abington.
Halifax; village in town of same name	Middleboro.
Hall; brook in northern part of Kingston, emptying into Blackstone Pond	Duxbury.
Hamant; brook, right branch of Quinebaug River in Sturbridge.	Brookfield.
Hamilton; town in eastern part of Essex County; area, 15 square miles	Salem.
Hamilton; reservoir in Holland	Brookfield.
Hamilton; village in eastern part of town of same name	Salem.
Hamilton; station in eastern part of town of same name	Salem.
Hamlin; point on southwestern coast of Falmouth	Falmouth.
Hammond; brook in Wareham	Middleboro.
Hammond; hill in Charlton; elevation, 880 feet	Webster.
Hammond; pond in Newton	Boston.
Hampden; town in Hampden county; area, 18 square miles	Palmer.
Hampden; village in town of same name	Palmer.
Hampton; pond in Westfield and Southampton	Springfield.
Hancock; brook in Hancock and Williamstown, tributary to Hoosic River	Berlin.
Hancock; hill in Milton; elevation, 540 feet	Dedham.
Hancock; town in Berkshire County; area, 36 square miles	{ Pittsfield. Berlin.
Hancock; village in town of same name	Berlin.
Hanging; mountain in north part of Westhampton	Chesterfield.
Hanging; mountain in southeastern part of Sandisfield; altitude, 1,294 feet	Sandisfield.
Hangman; island in south part of group of islands in Boston Bay	Boston Bay.
Hanover; town in Plymouth County; area, 16 square miles	Abington.
Hanover Four Corners; village in southeast part of Hanover.	Abington.
Hanson; town in Plymouth County; area, 16 square miles	Abington.
Hanson; village in central part of town of same name	Abington.
Harbor; pond in town of Townsend	Groton.
Harbor Bluff; slight projection at southeast part of Barnstable County, extending into Lewis Bay	Barnstable.

A GEOGRAPHIC DICTIONARY OF MASSACHUSETTS. 51

	Atlas sheets.
Harding; sand beach in Chatham, facing Vineyard Sound	Chatham.
Harding Beach Light; a fourth-order fixed white light; lantern 45 feet above sea level; visible 12 miles	Chatham.
Hardwick; town in Worcester County; area, 41 square miles.	{ Barre. Belchertown.
Hardwick; village in town of Hardwick	Barre.
Harlow; pond in northern part of Plymouth	Plymouth.
Harmon; pond, on boundary line between Sheffield and Egremont	Sheffield.
Harmon; pond in western part of New Marlboro	Sandisfield.
Harris; hill in New Salem; elevation, 1,000 feet	Warwick.
Harris; pond in Blackstone	Blackstone.
Harris; pond in Warwick	Warwick.
Harrison Square; part of the city of Boston.	Boston.
Harrisville; village in town of Winchendon	Winchendon.
Harrisville; village in West Boylston, on Massachusetts Central R. R.	Worcester.
Harry Rocks; rocks east of Peddock Island, in Boston Bay	Boston Bay.
Hart; pond in Chelmsford and Westford	Lowell.
Hartsville; village in northern part of New Marlboro, on Mill River	Sheffield.
Hartwell; brook in Bedford, 2 miles long	Framingham.
Hartwell; brook in Charlemont, tributary to Deerfield River	Hawley.
Harvard; station on Boston and Maine R. R., in town of Harvard	Groton.
Harvard; town in Worcester County; area, 30 square miles	{ Groton. Marlboro.
Harvard Center; village in town of Harvard	Groton.
Harvard College, in Cambridge	Boston.
Harvey; mountain on western boundary of West Stockbridge; altitude, 2,065 feet	Pittsfield.
Harwich; village in town of Harwich	Yarmouth.
Harwich; town in Barnstable County; area, 23 square miles	Yarmouth.
Harwichport; village in town of Harwich	Yarmouth.
Haskell; swamp in southern part of Rochester	New Bedford.
Haskins; railway station on Old Colony R. R., Fall River branch	Middleboro.
Hastings; pond in Warwick	Warwick.
Hatch; creek on boundary between Wellfleet and Eastham	Wellfleet.
Hatchet; brook, right-hand branch of Quinebaug River, in Sturbridge	Brookfield.
Hatchville; village in northern part of Falmouth	Falmouth.
Hatfield; town in central part of Hampshire County, on Connecticut River; area, 17 square miles	Northampton.
Hatfield; village in southeastern part of Hatfield, on Connecticut River.	Northampton.
Hathaway; brook in Lakeville	Middleboro.
Havenville; village in Burlington	Lawrence.
Haverhill; city in Essex County; area, 28 square miles	Haverhill.
Haverhill; village in town of same name, on Boston and Maine R. R.	Haverhill.
Hawes; hill in town of Barre; elevation, 1,227 feet	Barre.
Hawk; mountain on northern boundary of Hawley; altitude, 1,870 feet	Hawley.
Hawkes; brook in Methuen	Haverhill.

	Atlas sheets.
Hawkes; brook in Shelburne, 2 miles long; flows into Dragon Brook	Greenfield.
Hawkes; brook in Lynnfield and Saugus, about 3 miles long, and tributary to Saugus River.	{ Lawrence. { Boston.
Hawley; town in Franklin County; area, 32 square miles	Hawley.
Hawley; village in town of same name	Hawley.
Hayden; pond in Dudley	Webster.
Hayden Row; village in town of Hopkinton	Blackstone.
Haydenville; village in southern part of Williamsburg, on Mill River	Northampton.
Hayes; pond in northwestern part of Otis	Sandisfield.
Haynes; hill in northern part of Wales; elevation, 1,080 feet	Brookfield.
Haystack; mountain in western part of Norfolk	Sandisfield.
Hayward; brook in Wayland and Weston, 1¼ miles long; flows into Sudbury River	Framingham.
Hayward; creek in southeast part of Quincy	Abington.
Hazlewood; village in Hyde Park	Boston.
Hazzard; pond in Russell	Granville.
Head of the Harbor; head of Nantucket Harbor, on coast of Nantucket	Nantucket.
Head of Hummock; pond in Nantucket	Nantucket.
Head of Westport; village in eastern part of Westport, on Westport River	Fall River.
Heald; pond in Pepperell	Groton.
Heartbreak; hill in southeastern part of Ipswich; elevation, 160 feet	Salem.
Heath; town in Franklin County; area, 25 square miles	Hawley.
Heath; brook in Tewksbury, 1 mile long	Lawrence.
Heath; village in town of same name	Hawley.
Heathen Meadow; brook in Boxford, Acton, and Stow	{ Framingham. { Marlboro.
Hebronville; village in Attleboro, on Boston and Providence R. R.	Providence.
Heird; pond in Wayland	Framingham.
Hell; pond in Harvard	Groton.
Hemlock; mountain in Northfield	Warwick.
Hemlock; point in Long Pond in Freetown	Middleboro.
Hermon; mountain on western boundary of Gill; altitude, 440 feet	Warwick.
Herring; brook in Carver, one-half mile long, tributary to South Meadow Brook	Middleboro.
Herring; brook in north part of Pembroke	Abington.
Herring; pond in Wellfleet	Wellfleet.
Herring; pond in town of Eastham	Wellfleet.
Herring; pond in Edgartown, Marthas Vineyard	Marthas Vineyard.
Herring; pond in western part of Falmouth	Falmouth.
Herring; river in Brewster; flows into Cape Cod Bay	Wellfleet.
Herring; river in town of Eastham; flows into Cape Cod Bay.	Wellfleet.
Herring; river in Wellfleet, 4 miles long; flows into Wellfleet River	Wellfleet.
Herring; river in Harwich, 5 miles long; flows into Nantucket Sound	Yarmouth.
Hibbard; brook in Leyden, 1¼ miles long, tributary to Green River	Greenfield.

GANNETT.] A GEOGRAPHIC DICTIONARY OF MASSACHUSETTS. 53

	Atlas sheets.
Hickory; mountain in northwestern part of Huntington	Chesterfield.
Hicks; pond in Charlton	Webster.
Hicksville; village in northwestern part of Dartmouth	Fall River.
Higgins; island in Barnstable Harbor	Barnstable.
Higgins; pond in Wellfleet	Wellfleet.
Higgins; pond in Truro	Wellfleet.
Higgon; cape on coast of Chilmark, Marthas Vineyard	Gay Head.
High; hill in Ludlow; elevation, 600 feet	Palmer.
High Bush; island in Snipatuit Pond, Rochester	Middleboro.
High Cliff; bluff on east coast at entrance to Plymouth Harbor, town of Plymouth	Plymouth.
High Head; life-saving station upon Atlantic coast of Truro	Provincetown.
High Knob; hill in Athol; elevation, 980 feet	Winchendon.
High Ridge; mountain in northeastern part of Williamsburg; altitude, 1,484 feet	Northampton.
High Rock; picturesque cliff in city of Lynn	Boston Bay.
High Rock; hill in Needham, elevation, 240 feet	Boston.
High Rock; hill in Brookfield; altitude, 760 feet	Brookfield.
Higher; brook in Ludlow and Chicopee	{ Palmer. Springfield.
Highland; life-saving station upon Atlantic coast of Truro	Provincetown.
Highland; village in Norfolk, on New York and New England R. R.	Franklin.
Highland Light; life-saving station upon Atlantic coast of Truro	Provincetown.
Highland Station; village in Boston, on Boston and Providence R. R.	Boston.
Highlandville; village in Needham, on Woonsocket division on New York and New England R. R.	Boston.
Highlands; village in Cottage City, Marthas Vineyard	Marthas Vineyard.
Highlands; elevated section of country in northeastern part of Marshfield	Duxbury.
Highlands; hill in Merrimac; elevation, 270 feet	Haverhill.
Hill; brook in north part of Kingston	Abington.
Hill; pond in Woburn	Boston.
Hill Crossing; railway station in Belmont, on Massachusetts Central R. R.	Boston.
Hillsville; village in town of Spencer	Barre.
Hinckley; pond in Barnstable	Barnstable.
Hinckley; pond in Harwich	Yarmouth.
Hingham; harbor on north coast of Hingham	{ Boston Bay. Abington.
Hingham; town in Plymouth County; area, 26 square miles	{ Abington. Boston Bay.
Hingham Center; village in Hingham	Abington.
Hinsdale; town in eastern part of Berkshire County; area, 20 square miles	Becket.
Hinsdale; village in western part of Hinsdale	Becket.
Hinsdale; brook in Coleraine, Shelburne, and Greenfield; flows into Allan Brook	Greenfield.
Hitchcock; mountain in Wales; altitude, 1,160 feet	Palmer.
Hitchcock; pond in Holyoke	Springfield.
Hither; creek on Nantucket	Muskeget.
Hobb; brook, left branch of Quinebaug River, in Sturbridge	Brookfield.

54 A GEOGRAPHIC DICTIONARY OF MASSACHUSETTS. [BULL. 116.

	Atlas sheets.
Hobb; brook in Lincoln, Waltham, and Weston	Framingham.
Hobomak; pond in south central part of Pembroke	Abington.
Hockanum; hill in Warwick; elevation, 1,120 feet	Warwick.
Hockanum; village in southwestern part of Hadley, on Connecticut River	Northampton.
Hockomock; river in West Bridgewater	Dedham.
Hocomonco; pond in Westboro	Marlboro.
Hodge; brook in Warwick, 2 miles long; tributary to Gales Brook	Warwick.
Hodge; brook in Mansfield and Norton; tributary to Wading River.	{ Dedham. Taunton.
Hodge; pond in northern part of Plymouth	Plymouth.
Hodge; pond in southern part of Plymouth	Plymouth.
Hodge; village in Oxford, on Boston and Albany R. R.	Webster.
Hog; brook in Hudson and Berlin, 1¼ miles long; tributary to Assabet River	Marlboro.
Hog; island off north coast of Orleans	{ Chatham. Wellfleet.
Hog; island in large marsh near mouth of Essex River, Essex.	Salem.
Hog; island in northern part of Buzzards Bay, off east coast of Wareham	Falmouth.
Hog; ponds in Sandwich	Barnstable.
Hog; mountain in Buckland; altitude, 1,540 feet	Hawley.
Hog Island; harbor on western coast of Falmouth	Falmouth.
Hog Island; point on western coast of Falmouth	Falmouth.
Hog Neck; on southeastern coast of Wareham, extending about one-half mile into the bay	Falmouth.
Holbrook; town in Norfolk County; area, 7 square miles	{ Abington. Dedham.
Holbrook; village in town of same name	Abington.
Holden; town in Worcester County; area, 36 square miles	Worcester.
Holden; pond near central part of Lynn	Boston Bay.
Holden; reservoir in town of Holden	Worcester.
Holden Center; village in Holden, on Boston, Barre, and Gardner R. R.	Worcester.
Holland; town in Hampden County; area, 14 square miles	Brookfield.
Holland; principal village in town of same name	Brookfield.
Holland; pond in northern part of Holland	Brookfield.
Holliston; town in Middlesex County; area, 20 square miles	Franklin.
Holliston; village in town of same name, on Boston and Albany R. R.	Franklin.
Hollow; brook, tributary to Quinebaug River, in Wales and Brimfield	Brookfield.
Holmes; point projecting into Plymouth Harbor	Plymouth.
Holt; hill in Andover; elevation, 400 feet	Lawrence.
Holy; island in northeastern part of Ipswich, in Rowley River.	Salem.
Holyoke; city in Hampden County; area, 18 square miles	Springfield.
Holyoke; village in town of same name, on Connecticut River R. R.	Springfield.
Holyoke; mountain in northwestern part of South Hadley; altitude, 954 feet	Northampton.
Holyoke; range of mountains in south central part of Hampshire County.	{ Belchertown. Northampton.
Hood; pond in southwestern part of Ipswich, on line of Topsfield	Salem.

A GEOGRAPHIC DICTIONARY OF MASSACHUSETTS 55

	Atlas sheets.
Hoop Pole; cove in northwestern part of Rockport	Gloucester.
Hoop Pole; hill in north part of Scituate	Abington.
Hoop Pole; swamp in central part of South Scituate..........	Abington.
Hopper; pond in Plymouth....................................	Plymouth.
Hoosac; mountain trending north and south in northeastern part of Berkshire County	Greylock.
Hoosac; tunnel on Fitchburg R. R. through Hoosac mountain from Deerfield River to valley of Hoosic River.	{ Greylock. Hawley,
Hoosic; river flowing through Berkshire County into State of Vermont...	Greylock.
Hop; brook in Shrewsbury and Northboro, 2 miles long.......	Marlboro.
Hop; brook in Framingham	Framingham.
Hop; brook in Sudbury.......................................	Framingham.
Hop; brook in New Salem, 3 miles long; flows into Hop Brook Pond..	Belchertown.
Hop; brook in Mendon and Blackstone, tributary to Mill River..	Blackstone.
Hop; brook in Tyringham, Otis and Lee, 7 miles long, tributary to Housatonic River.	{ Becket. Sandisfield.
Hop Brook; pond in New Salem	Belchertown.
Hopedale; town in Worcester County; area, 6 square miles ..	Blackstone.
Hopedale; village in town of same name.....................	Blackstone.
Hopkins; island in Town Cove...............................	Wellfleet.
Hopkins; pond in Wellfleet...................................	Wellfleet.
Hopkinton; town in Middlesex County; area, 25 square miles..	{ Marlboro. Blackstone.
Hopkinton; village in town of same name.....................	Blackstone.
Hopper, the; deep chasm in side of Mount Greylock, in southeastern part of Williamsburg...............................	Greylock.
Hopping; brook in Holliston and Medway	Franklin.
Horn; pond in eastern part of Becket	Becket.
Horn; pond in Woburn	Boston.
Horn Pond; brook between Horn Pond and Winter Pond, in Woburn and Winchester, one-half mile long...............	Boston.
Horn Pond; hill in Woburn; elevation, 240 feet	Boston.
Horner; pond in town of Tisbury, Marthas Vineyard.........	Marthas Vineyard.
Horse; pond in Westfield	Springfield.
Horse; pond in North Brookfield.............................	Barre.
Horse; hill on boundary line between Dunstable and Groton; elevation, 370 feet	Groton.
Horse; hill in southeast part of Huntington..................	Chesterfield.
Horse; island on west coast of Wellfleet	Wellfleet.
Horse; mountain on line between Williamsburg and Hatfield; altitude, 780 feet	Northampton.
Horse Neck; beach in mouth of Westport River, Westport....	Fall River.
Horse Neck; brook in Carver, one-half mile long, tributary to South Meadow Brook	Middleboro.
Horse Race; island in Connecticut River.....................	Greenfield.
Hospital; hill in Berkley.....................................	Taunton.
Hough Neck; in north part of Quincy........................	Boston.
Houghton; pond in Milton	Dedham.
Housatonic; village in Great Barrington on Housatonic R. R.	Pittsfield.
Housatonic; part of New York, New Haven and Hartford Railroad system running northward up the Housatonic Valley to Pittsfield.	

	Atlas sheets.
Housatonic; river, heading in western part of State and flowing southerly, crosses Connecticut into Long Island Sound.	Becket. Pittsfield. Greylock. Sheffield.
House; brook in Chelmsford and Carlisle, one-half mile long; tributary to River Meadow Brook	Lowell.
House; island about one-half mile south of entrance to Manchester Harbor	Salem.
House Point; island in Provincetown Harbor	Provincetown.
Howard; brook in southeast part of Pembroke	Abington.
Howard; brook in Northboro; flows into Assabet River	Marlboro.
Howe; hill in Gardner; elevation, 1,240 feet	Fitchburg.
Howe; station on Salem and Lawrence R. R. in eastern part of Middleton	Salem.
Howland; station on Old Colony R. R., in Lakeville	Middleboro.
Howlet; brook tributary to Mile Brook in Topsfield	Salem.
Hovey; pond in Boxford	Lawrence.
Hoxie; creek tributary to Hoosic River, in western part of Adams	Greylock.
Hubbard; brook in Tolland and Granville 4 miles long	Granville.
Hubbard; brook tributary to Housatonic River, flowing through Mill Pond in Sheffield	Sheffield.
Hubbard Corners; village in Agawam	Springfield.
Hubbardston; town in Worcester County; area, 53 square miles.	Worcester. Winchendon. Barre. Fitchburg.
Hubbardston; principal village in town of same name	Barre.
Hudson; town in Middlesex County; area, 13 square miles	Framingham. Marlboro.
Hudson; village in town of same name on Massachusetts Central R. R. and Fitchburg R. R., Marlboro branch	Marlboro.
Hudson; brook tributary to north branch Hoosic River, in Clarksburg	Greylock.
Hull; town in Plymouth County; area, 3 square miles	Boston Bay.
Hummock; pond in Nantucket	Nantucket.
Humphrey; island in Suntaug Lake, Peabody	Lawrence.
Hunger, Mount; in town of Ashburnham; altitude, 1,420 feet.	Fitchburg.
Hunt Hill; point on northwest coast of Weymouth	Abington.
Hunter; hill in Dighton; elevation, 160 feet	Taunton.
Hunting; brook in Royalston	Winchendon.
Hunting; hill in Lunenburg and Shirley; elevation, 542 feet	Groton.
Hunting House; brook in Carver, 1 mile long	Middleboro.
Huntington; town in Hampshire County; area, 27 square miles.	Chesterfield. Granville.
Huntington; village in town of same name on Boston and Albany R. R.	Granville.
Huy Slow; hill in central part of Rowley; elevation, 160 feet.	Salem.
Hyannis; village in Barnstable, on Cape Cod branch Old Colony R. R.	Barnstable.
Hyannis; harbor in south part of Barnstable	Barnstable.
Hyannis Light; fixed, red light at north part of Hyannis Harbor; lantern 22 feet above sea level	Barnstable.
Hyannis; point at southern extremity of Squam Island, in Barnstable	Barnstable.

A GEOGRAPHIC DICTIONARY OF MASSACHUSETTS.

	Atlas sheets.
Hyannis Port; village in Barnstable	Barnstable.
Hyde Park; town in Norfolk County; area, 5 square miles	Boston.
Hyde Park; village in town of same name on New York and New England R. R.	Boston. Dedham.
Hydeville; village in town of Winchendon	Winchendon.
Ilsley; hill in West Newbury; elevation, 200 feet	Newburyport.
Indian; brook in Hopkinton	Blackstone. Marlboro.
Indian; hill on coast of Plymouth; elevation, 80 feet	Plymouth.
Indian; hill in Billerica; elevation, 200 feet	Lawrence.
Indian; hill in north part of Lynn	Boston Bay.
Indian; hill in West Newbury	Newburyport.
Indian; hill in Tisbury, Marthas Vineyard; elevation, 264 feet	Marthas Vineyard.
Indian; hills in Groton; elevation, 460 to 480 feet; three in number	Groton.
Indian; river in West Newbury, 3 miles long, flows into Merrimac river	Newburyport.
Indian Branch; stream flowing into Cape Cod Bay from Plymouth	Plymouth.
Indian Head; brook in east part of Hanson	Abington.
Indian Head; hill in Marlboro; elevation, 420 feet	Marlboro.
Indian Head; pond in eastern part of Hanson	Abington.
Indian Head; river in northern part of Hanson	Abington.
Indian Meeting House; church in Mashpee	Barnstable.
Indian Neck; extending into Wellfleet Harbor in Wellfleet	Wellfleet.
Indian Orchard; village in Springfield, on Springfield, Athol and Northern R. R.	Springfield.
Independence; fort on Castle Island, in Boston Harbor	Boston.
Ingall; station on Salem and Lawrence R. R., in North Andover.	Lawrence.
Ingleside; station on New Haven and Northampton R. R., in Holyoke	Springfield.
Ingraham; hill in northwestern part of Leverett	Northampton.
Inman; hill in town of Mendon; elevation, 480 feet	Blackstone.
Inward; northern point of entrance of Wreck Cove, Monomoy Island	Chatham.
Ipswich; seaboard town on eastern coast of Essex County; area, 41 square miles	Salem.
Ipswich; village near central part of town of same name	Salem.
Ipswich; river in counties of Essex and Middlesex, is 30 miles long and empties into Atlantic Ocean.	Lawrence. Salem.
Ipswich; light-house on northern coast of Castle Neck, Ipswich	Salem.
Ireland; parish in Holyoke	Springfield.
Ironstone; village in Uxbridge on Providence and Worcester R. R.	Blackstone.
Ironstone; reservoir in Uxbridge and State of Rhode Island	Blackstone.
Iron Works; village in northern part of Bridgewater	Abington.
Iron Works; brook tributary to Housatonic River in eastern part of Sheffield, draining Three Mile Pond	Sheffield.
Island; creek in southern part of Duxbury, draining Island Creek Pond	Duxbury.
Island; pond in southern part of Plymouth	Plymouth.
Island; pond in Plymouth	Plymouth.

	Atlas sheets.
Island Creek; pond about one-half mile long in southern part of Duxbury, of which Island Creek forms an outlet into Kingston Bay	Duxbury.
Islington; village in town of Dedham	Dedham.
Israel; pond in eastern part of Barnstable	Barnstable.
Jabish; brook in Belchertown, tributary to Swift River	Palmer.
Jabish; river in Hampshire County	Belchertown.
Jack; brook in Erving and Northfield, 2¼ miles long; flows into Keyup Brook	Warwick.
Jackson; hill in western part of Blandford; elevation, 1,680 feet	Sandisfield.
Jacob; hill in Royalston; elevation, 1,100 feet	Winchendon.
Jacob; pond in west part of South Scituate	Abington.
Jacob Neck; peninsula on southeastern coast of Wareham, between Onset Bay and Cohasset Narrows	Falmouth.
Jamaica; pond in Berkshire	Boston.
Jamaica Plain; village in city of Boston	Boston.
James; brook in Ayer and Groton, 3¼ miles long; tributary to Nashua River	Groton.
James; pond in Yarmouth	Yarmouth.
James; pond in Tisbury, Marthas Vineyard; opens into Lambert Cove	Marthas Vineyard.
Jamesville; village in Worcester on Boston and Albany R. R.	Webster.
Jefferson; peak in Ludlow	Palmer.
Jeffersonville; village in Holden on Boston, Barre and Gardner R. R	Worcester.
Jenk; reservoir in Bellingham	Franklin.
Jenkin; pond in central part of Falmouth	Falmouth.
Jenkin Hole; pond in Plymouth	Plymouth.
Jenning; pond on eastern boundary of Natick	Framingham.
Jericho; hill in Marlboro; elevation, 560 feet	Marlboro.
Jerusalem; village in northwest part of Cohasset	Boston Bay.
Jewell; hill in Ashburnham; elevation, 1,460 feet	Fitchburg.
Jewett; hill in northern part of Ipswich; elevation, 180 feet	Salem.
Job; hill in Haverhill	Haverhill.
Job Neck; pond in Edgartown, Marthas Vineyard	Marthas Vineyard.
Joe Rock; hill in Wrentham; elevation, 486 feet	Franklin.
John; pond in eastern part of Mashpee, drained by Child River into Waquoit Bay, containing 240 acres	{ Barnstable. { Falmouth.
John; pond in southeast part of Mashpee	Barnstable.
Johnson; creek tributary to Wareham River, emptying into same from the west about 1 mile above its mouth in Plymouth County.	{ Plymouth. { Falmouth.
Johnson; hill in Buckland; elevation, 900 feet	Hawley.
Johnson; pond in southwest part of Groveland	Lawrence.
Joice; creek in Yarmouth, 1 mile long; flows into Chase Garden Creek	Yarmouth.
Joint Grass; brook in Dunstable	Groton.
Jonathan; pond in Wareham	Plymouth.
Jones; hill in Ashby; elevation, 1,220 feet	Fitchburg.
Jones; river in northern part of Gloucester, emptying into Squam River	Gloucester.
Jones; river in Plympton and Kingston	{ Plymouth. { Middleboro.

GANNETT.] A GEOGRAPHIC DICTIONARY OF MASSACHUSETTS. 59

	Atlas sheets.
Jones River; brook in Plympton, 4 miles long; tributary to Jones River	Middleboro.
Joppa Flats; shallows at mouth of Merrimac River	Newburyport.
Jordan; pond in Shrewsbury	Marlboro.
Jordansville, or East Windsor; village in southeast part of Windsor	Chesterfield.
Jayner Marsh; pond in central part of Egremont	Sheffield.
Jug End; north end of Mount Bushwell, Egremont	Sheffield.
Juniper; hill in Ashby	Fitchburg.
Juniper; pond in northwestern part of New Marlboro	Sheffield.
Justice; brook in Leominster and Sterling, 3 miles long; tributary to Stillwater River	Worcester.
Katama; village on Marthas Vineyard	Marthas Vineyard.
Katama; bay between Chappaquiddick Island and the mainland of Eagartown, Marthas Vineyard	Marthas Vineyard.
Katama; point on east coast of Edgartown, Marthas Vineyard	Marthas Vineyard.
Kearney; brook in south part of Cummington	Chesterfield.
Keen; brook in west part of Duxbury	Abington.
Keen; creek tributary to South River in western part of Duxbury	Duxbury.
Keith; mountain peak in central part of Great Barrington; altitude 1,592 feet	Sheffield.
Keith; hill in Grafton; elevation, 620 feet	Blackstone.
Kelley; bay on western boundary of Dennis, opens into Bass River	Yarmouth.
Kelley; pond in Dennis	Yarmouth.
Kendall; hill in town of Gardner; elevation, 1,120 feet	Fitchburg.
Kendall; hill in Dunstable; elevation, 320 feet	Lowell.
Kendall; hill in town of Sterling; elevation, 500 feet	Marlboro.
Kendall; pond in Gardner	Winchendon.
Kendall Green; village on Fitchburg R. R. in Weston	Framingham.
Kenoza; lake in Haverhill	Haverhill.
Kettle; brook in Auburn	Webster.
Kettle; cove in Nanshon Island in town of Gosnold	Gay Head.
Kettle; cove in northwestern coast of Manchester	Gloucester.
Kettle; island about one-half mile off southeast coast of Manchester	Gloucester.
Key; brook in Westford, 2 miles long; has its source in Key Pond and flows into Stony Brook	Lowell.
Key; pond in Westford	Lowell.
Keyes; brook in Princeton	Worcester.
Keyup; brook in Erving and Northfield, 5 miles long; flows into Connecticut River	Warwick.
Kickamuit; river in Swansea	Taunton.
Kidder; brook in Warwick, 1 mile long; unites with Mountain Brook	Warwick.
Kidd Lookout; hill in southeast part of Chesterfield	Chesterfield.
Kiln; brook in Bedford and Lincoln	Framingham.
Kimball; hill in Haverhill; elevation, 204 feet	Haverhill.
Kimball; island in Merrimac River	Haverhill.
Kimball; pond on western boundary of Amesbury	Newburyport.
King; brook in Hawley and Plainfield, 3 miles long, flows into Chickley River	Hawley.
King; brook in Palmer, 3 miles long, tributary to Chicopee River	Palmer.

	Atlas sheets.
King; pond in northern part of Plymouth	Plymouth.
King; pond in Raynham	Taunton.
King Oak; hill in north part of Weymouth	Abington.
Kingsbury; mountain in northwestern part of Otis; altitude, 1,960 feet	Sandisfield.
Kingsbury; pond in Norfolk	Franklin.
Kingston; seaboard town in Plymouth County; area, 21 square miles.	{ Plymouth. Duxbury. Abington. Middleboro.
Kingston; principal village in town of same name	Plymouth.
Kingston; bay on southeast coast of Duxbury	Duxbury.
Kneeland; brook in Gardner	{ Winchendon. Fitchburg.
Knickup; hill in Wrentham; elevation, 360 feet	Franklin.
Knightsville; village in west part of Huntington	Chesterfield.
Knop; pond in Groton	Groton.
Knubble; peninsula in southwestern part of Westport, at mouth of Westport River	Fall River.
Konkapot; brook in Great Barrington and Stockbridge; tributary to Housatonic River	{ Pittsfield. Sheffield.
Labor in Vain; creek in Dighton and Somerset, 2 miles long, tributary to Cranston River	Taunton.
Labor in Vain; creek tributary to Ipswich River, in eastern part of Ipswich	Salem.
Lagoon; pond on western boundary of Cottage City, Marthas Vineyard	Marthas Vineyard.
Lake Crossing; station on Boston and Albany R. R. in Wellesley	Framingham.
Lakeville; town in Plymouth County; area, 29 square miles	{ Middleboro. Taunton.
Lakeville; village in town of same name	Middleboro.
Lakey; bay between Nonamesset Island and Naushon Island	Falmouth.
Lambert; cove on north coast of Tisbury, Marthas Vineyard	Marthas Vineyard.
Lancaster; town in Worcester County; area, 39 square miles.	{ Groton. Marlboro.
Lancaster; village in town of same name	Marlboro.
Lancaster Commons; village in town of Lancaster	Marlboro.
Landham; brook in Sudbury	Framingham.
Lane; pond in Lunenburg	Groton.
Lane; village in town of Ashburnham	Fitchburg.
Lanesboro; town in northwestern part of Berkshire County; area, 30 square miles.	{ Berlin. Pittsfield. Greylock.
Lanesboro; village in southern part of town of same name	Greylock.
Lanesville; village in northwestern part of Gloucester	Gloucester.
Lanesville; village in Attleboro	Providence.
Larkin; pond in Otis	Springfield.
Larned; pond in Dudley	Webster.
Larned; pond in Framingham	Framingham.
Larnedville; village in Oxford	Webster.
Laundry; brook in Newbury, tributary to Charles River	Boston.
Laura Tower; hill in Stockbridge; elevation, 1,565 feet	Pittsfield.

# A GEOGRAPHIC DICTIONARY OF MASSACHUSETTS. 61

	Atlas sheets.
Laurel; hill of the Taconic range in Lanesboro	Berlin.
Laurel; lake on boundary between Lee and Lenox	Pittsfield.
Lawrence; city in Essex County; area, 8 square miles	Lawrence.
Lawrence; brook in Tyngsboro, 2 miles long	Lowell.
Lawrence; brook in Royalston and Orange	Winchendon.
Lawrence; pond in Sandwich	Barnstable.
Leach; mountain in southeastern part of Essex; altitude, 160 feet	Salem.
Leach; pond on southern boundary of Sharon	Dedham.
Lead Mine; brook below Lead Mine Pond in southern part of Sturbridge	Brookfield.
Lead Mine; mountain in southern part of Sturbridge; altitude, 860 feet	Brookfield.
Lead Mine; pond in southern part of Sturbridge	Brookfield.
Lebanon; brook tributary to Quinebaug River in Sturbridge	Brookfield.
Lebanon Mills; village in Seekonk, on Ten Mile River	Providence.
Ledge; hill near southern boundary of Dracut	Lowell.
Lee; mountainous town in central part of Berkshire County; area, 28 square miles.	Pittsfield. Becket.
Lee; village in central part of town of same name	Pittsfield. Becket.
Lee; pond in central part of Mount Washington	Sheffield.
Lee; river forming part of boundary line between Somerset and and Swansea and flowing into Mount Hope Bay	Fall River.
Lee Pond; brook in Mount Washington, flowing northwest into New York	Sheffield.
Leech; pond in northern part of Plymouth	Plymouth.
Leed; village in northwestern part of Northampton, on Mill River	Northampton.
Legate; hill in Charlemont; elevation, 1,848 feet	Hawley.
Leicester; town in Worcester County; area, 25 square miles.	Worcester. Webster.
Leicester; village in town of same name	Webster.
Leland; hill in Sutton; elevation, 660 feet	Blackstone.
Lenox; mountain in Lenox; elevation, 1,880 feet	Pittsfield.
Lenox; town in western part of Berkshire County; area, 22 square miles	Becket.
Lenox; village in town of same name	Pittsfield.
Lenox; railway station in eastern part of town of same name.	Becket.
Lenox Furnace; village in southeastern part of Lenox	Becket.
Leominster; town in Worcester County; area, 30 square miles.	Groton. Marlboro. Worcester. Fitchburg.
Leominster; principal village in town of same name, on Old Colony R. R., Fitchburg branch	Fitchburg.
Leonard; pond in Rochester	Middleboro.
Leverett; town in southern part of Franklin County; area, 23 square miles.	Belchertown. Northampton. Warwick. Greenfield.
Leverett Center; village in southwestern part of Leverett	Northampton.
Lewin; brook in Swansea	Taunton.

	Atlas sheets.
Lewis; bay at southwest part of Yarmouth, opening into Nantucket Sound.	Yarmouth. Barnstable.
Lewis; pond in Yarmouth	Yarmouth.
Lewis; pond in eastern part of Barnstable	Barnstable.
Lewis; island in Long Pond in Lakeville	Middleboro.
Lewis Neck; narrow point of land in southern part of Falmouth, between Green Pond and Great Pond	Falmouth.
Leyden; town in Franklin County; area, 19 square miles	Greenfield.
Leyden Center; village in town of same name	Greenfield.
Lexington; town in Middlesex County; area, 17 square miles.	Boston. Framingham.
Lexington; village in town of same name on Boston and Lowell R. R.	Boston.
Liberty; hill in Granville; elevation, 1,437 feet	Granville.
Liberty Plain; village in south part of Hingham	Abington.
Lily; pond in Cohasset	Abington.
Lily; pond in Northfield	Warwick.
Lilly; pond in Yarmouth	Yarmouth.
Lincoln; town in Middlesex County; area, 15 square miles	Framingham.
Lincoln; village in town of same name	Framingham.
Lincoln; mountain in Pelham; elevation, 1,240 feet	Belchertown.
Linden; village in Malden and Revere	Boston.
Linebrook; village in western part of Ipswich	Salem.
Linwood; village in town of Northbridge, on Providence and Worcester R. R.	Blackstone.
Liswell; hill in Agawam; elevation, 340 feet	Springfield.
Little; bay on southern coast of Fair Haven, east of Sconticut Neck	New Bedford.
Little; creek tributary to North River, in northeastern part of Marshfield	Duxbury.
Little; island in Osterville Harbor, on southwest coast of Barnstable	Barnstable.
Little; mountain in Southampton; elevation, 500 feet	Springfield.
Little; pond (salt) on southern coast of Falmouth	Falmouth.
Little; pond in northern part of Plymouth	Plymouth.
Little; pond in Mendon	Blackstone.
Little; pond in Bradford	Lawrence.
Little; pond in Braintree	Dedham.
Little; pond in Bolton	Marlboro.
Little; river in State of New Hampshire and in Haverhill, 10 miles long, and flows into Merrimac River	Haverhill.
Little; river in Newbury and Newburyport; flows into Parker River	Newburyport.
Little; river in northwest part of Huntington	Chesterfield.
Little; river in southwestern part of Dartmouth; flows into Buzzards Bay	New Bedford.
Little; river in southwestern part of Gloucester; flowing into Squam River	Gloucester.
Little; river in Charlton; 5 miles long	Webster.
Little Allen; pond in eastern part of Brimfield	Brookfield.
Little Bear; hill in Westford; elevation, 320 feet	Lowell.
Little Black Rock; island north of Cohasset	Boston Bay.
Little Brewster; island in Boston Bay	Boston Bay.
Little Calf; island in Boston Bay	Boston Bay.

A GEOGRAPHIC DICTIONARY OF MASSACHUSETTS. 63

	Atlas sheets.
Little Cedar; swamp in Middleboro	Middleboro.
Little Chauncey; pond in Northboro	Marlboro.
Little Clear; pond in northern part of Plymouth	Plymouth.
Little Cliff; pond in Brewster	Wellfleet.
Little Creek; pond in southern part of Duxbury	Duxbury.
Little Five Mile; pond in southern part of Plymouth	Plymouth.
Little; harbor on southwestern coast of Falmouth	Falmouth.
Little; harbor; irregular shaped arm of Buzzards Bay, extending into southern border of Wareham	Falmouth.
Little Herring; pond in southern part of Plymouth	Plymouth.
Little Hog; island west of Hull	Boston Bay.
Little Island; pond in Plymouth	Plymouth.
Little Mioxes; pond in Nantucket	Nantucket.
Little Misery; island lying immediately south of Great Misery Island	Salem.
Little Moose; hill in southwest part of Huntington	Chesterfield.
Little Mugget; hill in Charlton; elevation, 1,078 feet	Webster.
Little Nahant; village in Nahant	Boston Bay.
Little Nahant; beach on east coast of Nahant	Boston Bay.
Little Neck; peninsula on southern extremity of Great Neck, in eastern part of Ipswich	Salem.
Little Pudding; brook in central part of Pembroke	Abington.
Little Quittacas; pond in Lakeville and Rochester	Middleboro.
Little River; village in Westfield	Springfield.
Little Rest; village in Brimfield	Brookfield.
Little Sandy; pond in southern part of Plymouth	Plymouth.
Little Sandy; pond in southwest part of Yarmouth	Barnstable.
Little Sandy Bottom; pond in southwest part of Pembroke	Abington.
Little South; pond in northern part of Plymouth	Plymouth.
Little Spectacle; pond in Lancaster	Groton.
Little Thatcher; island in Barnstable Harbor	Barnstable.
Littleton; town in Middlesex County; area, 18 square miles	{ Groton. Lowell.
Littleton Station; village in town of Littleton, on Fitchburg R. R.	Groton.
Littletown; village in northeastern part of Marshfield	Duxbury.
Little Tully; mountain in Orange; elevation, 800 feet	Winchendon.
Littleville; village in Chester	Chesterfield.
Little Wachusett; hill in Princeton; elevation, 1,560 feet	Worcester.
Little Watatic; mountain in Ashburnham	Fitchburg.
Little Wigwam; pond in Dedham	Dedham.
Livermore; mountain peak in western part of Monterey; altitude, 1,863 feet	Sheffield.
Lizzie; mountain in town of Greenwich; altitude, 900 feet	Belchertown.
Loagy; bay on west coast of Wellfleet; opens into Wellfleet Harbor	Wellfleet.
Loblolly; cove in eastern coast of Rockport	Gloucester.
Lobster; cove; narrow arm of Annisquam Harbor, extending into northern part of Gloucester Harbor	Gloucester.
Lock; pond in Shutesbury	{ Warwick. Belchertown.
Lock; village in Shutesbury	Warwick.
Locke; brook in New Hampshire and towns of Ashby and Townsend, tributary to Walker Brook; 7 miles long	Fitchburg.
Locust; pond in Tyngsboro	Lowell.

	Atlas sheets.
Locust; hill in Tyngsboro; elevation, 200 feet	Lowell.
Logging; swamp in Rochester	Middleboro.
Long; beach on southeastern coast of Rockport	Gloucester.
Long; beach consisting of long narrow reef forming east side of Plymouth Harbor, town of Plymouth	Plymouth.
Long; cove in Tisbury, Marthas Vineyard, part of Great Tisbury Pond	Marthas Vineyard.
Long; creek in Sandwich, flowing into Cape Cod Bay	Barnstable.
Long; hill in northeastern part of Manchester; elevation, 160 feet	Gloucester.
Long; hill in West Newbury; elevation, 200 feet	Newburyport.
Long; hill in southeastern part of Georgetown; elevation, 200 feet	Salem.
Long; hill in Leominster; elevation, 880 feet	Fitchburg.
Long; hill in north part of Pembroke	Abington.
Long; hill on southern boundary of Ashland; elevation, 460 feet	Franklin.
Long; hill in town of Bolton	Marlboro.
Long; island in Boston Bay, one of the group of islands lying southeast of Boston	Boston Bay.
Long; island about one-half mile long between West Island and Sconticut Point	New Bedford.
Long; pond in Wellfleet	Wellfleet.
Long; pond in Truro	Wellfleet.
Long; pond in Brewster	Wellfleet.
Long; pond on southern boundary of Brewster	Yarmouth.
Long; pond in Yarmouth	Yarmouth.
Long; pond south of Yarmouthport	Barnstable.
Long; pond in west part of Barnstable	Barnstable.
Long; pond in south part of Barnstable	Barnstable.
Long; pond in Lakeville and Freetown	Middleboro.
Long; pond in Rochester	Middleboro.
Long; pond about one-half mile long in southeastern part of Bourne	Falmouth.
Long; pond about 1 mile long in southwestern part of Falmouth	Falmouth.
Long; pond in Plymouth	Plymouth.
Long; pond in Plymouth	Plymouth.
Long; pond in southern part of Plymouth	Plymouth.
Long; pond in Nantucket	Nantucket.
Long; pond in western part of Blandford	Sandisfield.
Long; pond on boundary line between Tyringham and Lee	Becket.
Long; pond in Royalston	Winchendon.
Long; pond in northwestern part of Great Barrington	Sheffield.
Long; pond on boundary between Ayer and Groton	Groton.
Long; pond in western part of Sturbridge	Brookfield.
Long; pond in Rutland	Worcester.
Long; pond in Tewksbury	{ Lowell. / Lawrence. }
Long; pond on northwest boundary of Dracut	Lowell.
Long; pond in Littleton	Lowell.
Long; point between Pocksha and Great Quittacas Pond, Lakeville and Middleboro	Middleboro.
Long; point extending into Herring Pond in Edgartown, Marthas Vineyard	Marthas Vineyard.

	Atlas sheets.
Long; point, sand reef projecting from Cape Cod and inclosing within it Provincetown Harbor	Provincetown.
Long Beach; point on southern coast of Wareham, projecting southwesterly into mouth of Wareham River and Buzzards Bay	Falmouth.
Long Drain; brook flowing into Connecticut River in northern part of Hadley	Northampton.
Long Island Headlight; light-house at northern extremity of Long Island, Boston Bay; height, 121 feet; fixed light, and is visible 16 miles	Boston Bay.
Longmeadow; town in Hampden County; area, 28 square miles	{ Springfield. Palmer.
Longmeadow; brook in town of Longmeadow, 4 miles long; tributary to Connecticut River	Springfield.
Longmeadow; brook in Rutland, 2 miles long; tributary to Ware River	Worcester.
Longmeadow; brook in Burlington, 1 mile long; tributary to Vine Brook	Boston.
Longmeadow; station on New York, New Haven and Hartford R. R., in town of Longmeadow	Springfield.
Long Neck; irregular-shaped island in Buzzards Bay at west entrance of Woods Holl	Falmouth.
Long Plain; village in Acushnet	New Bedford.
Long Point Light; light-house upon extreme end of Cape Cod.	Provincetown.
Long Pond; brook tributary to Seekonk Brook in northwestern part of Great Barrington, draining Long Pond	Sheffield.
Long Pond Brothers; three hills near Long Pond in Littleton; elevation, 340, 360, and 360 feet, respectively	Lowell.
Longwood; village in Brookline, on Boston and Albany R. R., Brookline branch	Boston.
Longwood; hills on boundary between Woburn and Reading; elevation, 200 feet	Lawrence.
Lookout; point on coast of Plymouth	Plymouth.
Loon; hill in Dracut; elevation, 200 feet	Lowell.
Loon; pond in town of Springfield	Palmer.
Loon; pond in Lakeville	Middleboro.
Loring; hill in Lexington; elevation, 360 feet	Boston.
Loudville; village in northeastern part of Southampton	Northampton.
Lout; pond in northern part of Plymouth	Plymouth.
Lovell Corners; village in eastern part of Weymouth	Abington.
Lovell; island east of north part of Long Island, in Boston Bay.	Boston Bay.
Lovell; pond in southwest part of Barnstable	Barnstable.
Low Bush; island in Snipatuit Pond	Middleboro.
Lowell; city in Middlesex County; area, 13 square miles	Lowell.
Lowell; island off east coast of Marblehead	Salem.
Lowell Junction; station on Boston and Maine R. R., in Andover	Lawrence.
Lower; village in Stow	Framingham.
Lower; pond in Belchertown	Belchertown.
Lower Barkerville; village in Pittsfield, on Boston and Albany R. R.	Pittsfield.
Lower Massapoag; pond in Dunstable	Lowell.
Lower Mills; village in city of Boston	Boston.
Lower Naukeag; pond in Ashburnham	Fitchburg.

	Atlas sheets.
Lower Plain; village in Hingham............................	Abington.
Lubber; brook in Wilmington and Billerica...................	Lawrence.
Ludlow; town in Hampden County; area, 29 square miles.....	Palmer.
Ludlow; principal village in town of same name..............	Palmer.
Ludlow Center; village in Ludlow............................	Palmer.
Lulu; brook in Pittsfield; flows into Lake Onota...............	Pittsfield.
Lunenburg; town in Worcester County; area, 29 square miles	{ Groton. Fitchburg.
Lunenburg; village in town of same name.....................	Groton.
Lunenburg; station on Fitchburg R. R., in town of Lunenburg.	Groton.
Luther Station; village in southwestern part of Swansea....	Fall River.
Lynde; hill in town of Gardner; elevation, 1,180 feet...........	Fitchburg.
Lynn; seaboard city in Essex County, on north coast of Massachusetts Bay; area, 12 square miles........................	Boston Bay.
Lynn; beach between Lynn and Nahant......................	Boston Bay.
Lynn; harbor south of Lynn and opening into Boston Bay....	Boston Bay.
Lynnfield; town in Essex County; area, 10 square miles.......	Lawrence.
Lynnfield Center; village in town of Lynnfield, on Newburyport branch of Boston and Maine R. R......................	Lawrence.
Lyon; pond in Ludlow...	Palmer.
Lyonsville; village in Coleraine...............................	Greenfield.
Mace Crossing; railway station in Tewksbury, on Boston and Maine R. R., Lowell branch...............................	Lowell.
Machine Shop; station on Salem and Lawrence R. R., in North Andover..	Lawrence.
Maddaket; harbor on west coast of Nantucket..............	{ Nantucket. Muskeget.
Madequecham; pond in Nantucket...........................	Nantucket.
Mad Mares Neck; a broad area of high ground in Middleboro.	Middleboro.
Magnolia; village in southwestern part of Gloucester........	Gloucester.
Magnolia; point at southern extremity of Gloucester.........	Gloucester.
Magnolia; railway station in eastern part of Manchester......	Gloucester.
Magog; brook in Acton, 1 mile long...........................	Lowell.
Magog; pond in Acton and Littleton	Lowell.
Magunco; hill in Ashland; elevation, 380 feet.................	Framingham.
Major; cove on boundary between Cottage City and Edgartown, Marthas Vineyard...	Marthas Vineyard.
Malden; city in Middlesex County; area, 5 square miles......	Boston.
Malden; brook in West Boylston, 3 miles long; tributary to Nashua River...	Worcester.
Malden; river, left-hand branch of Mystic River..............	Boston.
Mallard; hill in Warwick	Warwick.
Manchaug; village in town of Sutton	{ Webster. Blackstone.
Manchaug; pond in Sutton and Douglas......................	Webster.
Manchester; seaboard town in eastern part of Essex County; area, 9 square miles...	{ Salem. Gloucester.
Manchester; village in southern part of town of same name..	Salem.
Manchester; harbor, indenting southern coast of Manchester..	Salem.
Mandell; hill in town of Hardwick; elevation, 1,020 feet.....	Barre.
Mangus; hill in Wellesley....................................	Framingham.
Manhan; brook in north part of Southampton.................	Chesterfield.
Manhan; river flowing northeasterly through East Hampton into Connecticut River at Ox Bow	Northampton.

A GEOGRAPHIC DICTIONARY OF MASSACHUSETTS. 67

	Atlas sheets.
Mann; hill in northeast part of Scituate	Abington.
Manning; brook in Florida, 1 mile long, tributary to Cold River	Hawley.
Manomet; hill near coast of Plymouth; elevation, 360 feet	Plymouth.
Manomet; point on coast of Plymouth	Plymouth.
Mansfield; town in Bristol County; area, 22 square miles	{ Taunton. Dedham.
Mansfield; village in town of same name on Boston and Providence R. R. and Old Colony R. R	Dedham.
Mansfield; pond in central part of Great Barrington	Sheffield.
Manwhague; swamp in Rehoboth	Taunton.
Manwhague Plain; valley in Rehoboth	Taunton.
Maple; hill in West Stockbridge; elevation, 1,780 feet	Pittsfield.
Maple Meadow; brook in Wilmington and Burlington, 3 miles long	Lawrence.
Maplewood; village in Malden on Saugus branch of Boston and Maine R. R.	Boston.
Maquam; pond in eastern part of Hanson	Abington.
Marble; hill in Stow; elevation, 481 feet	Marlboro.
Marblehead; seaboard town in southern part of Essex county; area, 6 square miles.	{ Boston Bay. Salem.
Marblehead; village in eastern part of town of same name on Marblehead Harbor	Salem.
Marblehead; harbor on east coast of Marblehead between Marblehead Neck and the mainland	Boston Bay.
Marblehead Neck; peninsula on eastern coast of Marblehead, which, with the mainland, forms Marblehead Harbor.	{ Boston Bay. Salem.
Marbleridge; railway station on Salem and Lawrence R. R. in North Andover	Lawrence.
Mare; pond in central part of Falmouth	Falmouth.
Marion; town in Plymouth county; area, 13 square miles	Falmouth.
Mark; cove in Buzzards Bay extending westerly into Wareham between Cromeset Neck and Swift Neck	Falmouth.
Mark; mountain between villages of Warren and West Warren in Warren; altitude, 1,100 feet	Brookfield.
Marlboro; town in Middlesex county; area, 22 square miles	{ Marlboro. Framingham.
Marlboro; principal village in town of same name	Marlboro.
Marlboro; village in southern part of Georgetown	Salem.
Marsh; hill in Dracut; elevation, 260 feet	Lowell.
Marsh; brook in Stockbridge, 1¼ miles long, tributary to Housatonic River	Pittsfield.
Marshfield; town in northern part of Plymouth County. It took its name from its extensive marshes. Area, 30 square miles.	{ Abington. Duxbury.
Marshfield; village in southwestern part of town of same name	Duxbury.
Marshfield Center; railway station in central part of Marshfield	Duxbury.
Marshfield Neck; in eastern part of Marshfield between waters of Green Harbor and South River	Duxbury.
Marston Mills; village in southwest part of Barnstable	Barnstable.
Marthas Vineyard; island off southeast coast of Massachusetts, containing towns of Edgartown, Cottage City, Tisbury, Chilmark, and Gay Head; area 96 square miles.	{ Marthas Vineyard Gay Head.

	Atlas sheets.
Martin; brook in North Reading and Wilmington; tributary to Ipswich River	Lawrence.
Martin; pond in Groton	Groton.
Martin; pond in North Reading	Lawrence.
Martin Pond; brook in Groton, 3 miles long	Groton.
Mary; lake in northern part of Naushon Island	Falmouth.
Mary; pond in Rochester	Middleboro.
Mary; pond in Plymouth	Plymouth.
Mashpee; island in northern part of Buzzards Bay, off southeast coast of Wareham	Falmouth.
Mashpee; town in Barnstable County; area, 28 square miles	Barnstable.
Mashpee; pond in town of same name, containing about 395 acres, and connected with Wakeby Pond on the north	Barnstable.
Mashpee; river in town of same name flowing south from Mashpee Pond into Poponesset Bay	Barnstable.
Mashpee Neck; lying between mouth of Mashpee River and head of Poponessett Bay in southeast part of Mashpee	Barnstable.
Mason; brook in town of Mason, N. H., and town of Townsend, Mass.; flows into Walker Brook	Fitchburg.
Mason; hill in Gill; elevation, 647 feet	Greenfield.
Massachusetts Central; railroad, part of Boston and Maine system, running westward from Boston.	
Massapoag; pond on west boundary of town of Tyngsboro	Lowell.
Massapoag; pond in Sharon	Dedham.
Massapoag; pond in Lunenburg	Groton.
Matapan; village in city of Boston, on New York and New England R. R.	Boston.
Matfield; river on southern boundary of East Bridgewater	Abington.
Matfield; river in Bridgewater	Middleboro.
Mattakeset; bay on east coast of Edgartown, Marthas Vineyard.	
Mattapoisett; seaboard town in southern part of Plymouth County; area, 18 square miles	New Bedford.
Mattapoisett; village in southern part of Mattapoisett on Mattapoisett Harbor	New Bedford.
Mattapoisett; harbor on southern coast of Mattapoisett	New Bedford.
Mattapoisett; river in Rochester and Mattapoisett, flows into Mattapoisett Harbor	Middleboro.
Mattapoisett Rock; point at southern extremity of Gardner Neck, Swansea	Fall River.
Mattapoisett Neck; peninsula on southern coast of Mattapoisett, south of Mattapoisett Harbor	New Bedford.
Maxey; pond in Nantucket	Nantucket.
Maynard; town in Middlesex County; area, 6 square miles	Framingham.
Maynard; village in town of same name on Marlboro branch of Fitchburg R. R.	Framingham.
Maynard; brook in Oakham, 2 miles long	Barre.
Mayo Beach; light-house in Wellfleet Harbor	Wellfleet.
McCard; brook in Leyden and Greenfield, 3 miles long, tributary to Mill Brook	Greenfield.
McCarthy; hill in Longmeadow; elevation, 340 feet	Springfield.
Mead; pond in Waltham	Boston.
Meadow; brook in central part of East Bridgewater	Abington.
Meadow; brook in Uxbridge and Mendon, tributary to Blackstone River	Blackstone.

	Atlas sheets.
Meadow; brookd in North Brookfiel and New Braintree	Barre.
Meadow; brook in Westford, 2 miles long, flows into Key Pond	Lowell.
Meadow; brook in Hudson, 2 miles long, tributary to Assabet River	Marlboro.
Meadow; brook in Norton and Taunton, 2 miles long, tributary to Birch Brook	Taunton.
Meadow; island in Sippican Harbor, about one-fourth mile southwest of Sippican Neck	Falmouth.
Mechanicsville; village on Taunton River, Fall River	Fall River.
Mechanicsville; village in town of Bellingham	Franklin.
Medfield; town in Norfolk County; area, 15 square miles	Franklin.
Medfield; village in town of same name on Old Colony R. R., Framingham and Mansfield branch	Franklin.
Medfield Junction; railroad junction of Old Colony R. R., Framingham and Mansfield branch, and New York and New England R. R., Woonsocket division, in town of Medfield	Franklin.
Medford; town in Middlesex County; area, 9 square miles	Boston.
Medford; village in town of same name on Medford branch of Boston and Maine R. R., west division	Boston.
Medway; town in Norfolk County; area, 12 square miles	Franklin.
Medway; village in town of same name on New York and New England R. R., Woonsocket division	Franklin.
Meeting House; hill in Ashburnham; elevation, 1,320 feet	Fitchburg.
Meeting House; hill in Methuen; elevation, 220 feet	Lawrence.
Meeting House; pond in town of Westminster	Fitchburg.
Meeting House; swamp in Middleboro	Middleboro.
Melrose; town in Middlesex County; area, 6 square miles	{ Lawrence. Boston.
Melrose; principal village in town of same name on Boston and Maine R. R., west division	Boston.
Melville; lake in Pittsfield	Pittsfield.
Menauhant; village on southern coast of Falmouth	Falmouth.
Mendal; hill in eastern part of Acushnet; elevation, 146 feet	New Bedford.
Mendon; town of Worcester County; area, 17 square miles	Blackstone.
Mendon; village in town of same name	Blackstone.
Menemsha; pond in Gay Head and Chilmark, Marthas Vineyard	Gay Head.
Menemsha Bight; bay on north coast of Gay Head, Marthas Vineyard	Gay Head.
Merino; pond in Dudley	Webster.
Merino; village in Dudley on New York and New England R. R., Southbridge branch	Webster.
Merriam; hill in Lexington; elevation, 280 feet	Boston.
Merriam; hill in Framingham; elevation, 360 feet	Framingham.
Merrimac; town in Essex County; area, 9 square miles	{ Haverhill. Newburyport.
Merrimac; village in town of same name	Haverhill.
Merrimac; river heading in New Hampshire, flows southerly into Massachusetts, and then northeasterly to its mouth. The eastern part of north boundary of State is a line 3 miles north of course of this river.	{ Lowell. Lawrence. Haverhill. Newburyport.
Merrimacport; village in Merrimac	Newburyport.
Merritt; hill in northwest part of Williamsburg	Chesterfield.

	Atlas sheets.
Metcalf; village in Holliston	Franklin.
Methodist; camp ground in Eastham	Wellfleet.
Methuen; town in Essex County; area, 24 square miles	Lawrence.
Methuen; principal village in town of same name on Manchester and Lawrence R. R.	Lawrence.
Miacomet; pond in Nantucket	Nantucket.
Micajah; pond in northern part of Plymouth	Plymouth.
Mid; village in Deerfield	Greenfield.
Middle; pond in Belchertown	Belchertown.
Middle Brewster; island in group of islands in Boston Bay	Boston Bay.
Middle Point; creek in Tisbury, Marthas Vineyard, tributary to Great Tisbury Pond	Marthas Vineyard.
Middle Small; pond in Kingston	Plymouth.
Middleboro; town in Plymouth County; area, 73 square miles	Middleboro.
Middleboro; principal village in town of same name on Old Colony R. R.	Middleboro.
Middlefield; town in western part of Hampshire County; area, 23 square miles.	{ Chesterfield. Becket.
Middlefield; village in central part of town of same name	Becket.
Middlesex; village in town of Lowell on Boston, Lowell and Nashua R. R.	Lowell.
Middlesex Fells; tract of wild broken country in towns of Stoneham, Medford, Melrose, Malden, and Manchester	Boston.
Middleton; town in southwestern part of Essex County; area, 16 square miles.	{ Lawrence. Salem.
Middleton; principal village in town of same name on Salem and Lawrence R. R.	Lawrence.
Mile; brook in northern part of Kingston, flowing into Blackstone Pond	Duxbury.
Mile; brook tributary to Ipswich River in Topsfield	Salem.
Mile; river tributary to Ipswich River, draining Wenham Lake.	Salem.
Milford; town in Worcester County; area, 16 square miles	{ Blackstone. Franklin.
Milford; village in town of same name	Blackstone.
Milham; brook in Marlboro, 2 miles long, tributary to Assabet River	Marlboro.
Milk; island about 1 mile southeast of Rockport	Gloucester.
Mill; village in Ashby	Fitchburg.
Mill; river tributary to Connecticut River in Franklin and Hampshire counties	Northampton.
Mill; brook in Springfield, 1 mile long, tributary to Connecticut River	Springfield.
Mill; river in eastern part of Gloucester, flowing northerly into Annisquam Harbor	Gloucester.
Mill; river in western part of Weymouth	Abington.
Mill; river, left branch of Blackstone River	Blackstone.
Mill; river, tributary to Housatonic River flowing southerly through New Marlboro	Sheffield.
Mill; river in Taunton, tributary to Taunton River	Taunton.
Mill; pond 1 mile long through which Hubbard Brook flows, in central part of Sheffield	Sheffield.
Mill; pond about one-half mile long in northwestern part of Bourne	Falmouth.

A GEOGRAPHIC DICTIONARY OF MASSACHUSETTS.

	Atlas sheets.
Mill; pond in northern part of Plymouth	Plymouth.
Mill; pond on Acushnet River, Acushnet	New Bedford.
Mill; pond in Littleton	{ Lowell. { Groton.
Mill; pond, arm of Stage Harbor, Chatham	Chatham.
Mill; pond northwest of Yarmouthport	Barnstable.
Mill; hill in Orleans	Wellfleet.
Mill; cove on east side of Weymouth Fore River in northwest part of Weymouth	Abington.
Mill; creek in north part of Sandwich flowing into Cape Cod Bay	Barnstable.
Mill; creek in Newbury	Newburyport.
Mill; creek tributary to Parker River flowing northeasterly through Rowley	Salem.
Mill; brook in New Braintree and West Brookfield	Barre.
Mill; brook tributary to Quinebaug River in Brimfield	Brookfield.
Mill; brook in southeast part of Goshen	Chesterfield.
Mill; brook in north part of Cummington	Chesterfield.
Mill; brook in Concord and Lincoln, 3 miles long, tributary to Concord River	Framingham.
Mill; brook tributary to Deerfield River in Monroe	Greylock.
Mill; brook in Leyden, Bernardston, and Greenfield, 7 miles long, flowing into Green River	Greenfield.
Mill; brook in Monroe, flowing into Dunbar Brook	Hawley.
Mill; brook in Heath and Charlemont, 7 miles long, flowing into Deerfield River	Hawley.
Mill; brook in Webster, 1 mile long, between Lake Chaubunagungamaug and French River	Webster.
Mill; brook in Rutland	Worcester.
Mill River; village in western part of New Marlboro on Mill River	Sheffield.
Mill Valley; village in southwestern part of Amherst	Northampton.
Millbury; town in Worcester County; area, 17 square miles	{ Webster. { Blackstone.
Millbury; village in town of same name, on Providence and Worcester R. R.	Webster.
Miller; brook in Agawan, 1 mile long, tributary to Westfield River	Springfield.
Miller; hill in southern part of Williamsburg; elevation, 640 feet	Northampton.
Miller; river, left-hand branch of Connecticut River in northern part of State.	{ Winchendon. { Warwick.
Miller Falls; village in Montague on Fitchburg R. R.	Warwick.
Miller Neck; brook in Middleboro	Middleboro.
Millington; village in New Salem	Belchertown.
Millis; village in town of same name on New York and New England R. R., Woonsocket division	Franklin.
Millis; town in Norfolk County; area, 13 square miles	Franklin.
Millstone; hill in Westford; elevation, 360 feet	Lowell.
Millville; village in town of Blackstone	Blackstone.
Milton; town in Norfolk County; area, 18 square miles	{ Boston. { Dedham.
Milton; village in town of same name	Boston.
Milton Mills; village in Milton	Boston.
Milton Upper Mills; village in Milton	Boston.

	Atlas sheets.
Milward; village in Charlton.................................	Webster.
Mine; brook in Franklin and Bellingham, tributary to Charles River..	Franklin.
Mine; brook in Dover, Medfield, Walpole, and Foxboro, 8 miles long; flows into Neponsett Reservoir.......................	Franklin.
Mine; brook in town of Pepperell and in New Hampshire, 2 miles long; tributary to Nissitissit River....................	Groton.
Mine; brook in Webster, 1 mile long, tributary to Sucker Brook.	Webster.
Mine; hill in Templeton; elevation, 1,220 feet.................	Winchendon.
Minechoag; mountain in Ludlow; elevation, 700 feet.........	Palmer.
Minechoag; pond in Ludlow..................................	Palmer.
Mineral; hill in Shutesbury	Belchertown.
Minots Ledge Light; light-house built of granite on low reef of rocks; fixed light; height, 92 feet above sea level, and visible 16 miles..	Boston Bay.
Miscoe; brook in Grafton..	Blackstone.
Miscoe; hill in town of Mendon; elevation, 580 feet............	Blackstone.
Mishaum; point at southern extremity of Smith Neck, Dartmouth..	New Bedford.
Mishawum; railway station on Boston and Lowell R. R. in Woburn...	Lawrence.
Mittineaque; village in West Springfield on Boston and Albany R. R..	Springfield.
Moccasin; brook in Phillipston and Petersham..............	{ Barre. Winchendon.
Moffatt; hill in Newton; elevation, 200 feet.....................	Boston.
Mohawk; brook in southwestern part of Sunderland flowing into Connecticut River...	Northampton.
Mohawk; lake in Stockbridge...................................	Pittsfield.
Monday; hill in Salisbury; elevation, 180 feet.................	Newburyport.
Monk; hill in Kingston; elevation, 220 feet....................	Plymouth.
Monumet; river in Bourne......................................	Plymouth.
Monomonac; lake in New Hampshire and in town of Winchendon.	{ Winchendon. Fitchburg.
Monomonac; pond in Winchendon............................	Winchendon.
Monomony; island in Nantucket Sound......................	Yarmouth.
Monomoy; long, sandy island at southeast angle of Cape Cod in town of Orleans..	Chatham.
Monomoy; life-saving station on Monomoy Island 3 miles north of Monomoy Point light................................	Chatham.
Monomoy Point; light-house, fourth order, fixed white light in 30-foot tower; lantern 41 feet above sea level; visible 12 miles..	Chatham.
Monoosnoc; brook in Leominster and Fitchburg.............	Fitchburg.
Monoosnoc; hill on boundary between Leominster and Fitchburg; elevation, 1,000 feet	Fitchburg.
Monponset; pond in north part of Halifax...................	{ Middleboro. Abington.
Monroe; town in Franklin County; area, 10 square miles....	{ Greylock. Hawley.
Monroe; village in town of same name........................	Hawley.
Monroe Bridge; village and bridge in town of Monroe.........	Hawley.
Monserat; station on Gloucester branch of Boston and Maine R. R. in southern part of Beverly	Salem.

GANNETT.] A GEOGRAPHIC DICTIONARY OF MASSACHUSETTS. 73

<table>
<tr><td></td><td>Atlas sheets.</td></tr>
<tr><td>Onson; town in Hampden County; area, 44 square miles</td><td>Palmer.</td></tr>
<tr><td>Monson; village in town of same name</td><td>Palmer.</td></tr>
<tr><td>Montague; town in Franklin County; area, 41 square miles</td><td>{ Greenfield.
Warwick.</td></tr>
<tr><td>Montague; village in town of same name</td><td>Greenfield.</td></tr>
<tr><td>Montague City; village in town of Montague on New Haven and Northampton R. R</td><td>Greenfield.</td></tr>
<tr><td>Monterey; town in southern part of Berkshire County; area, 28 square miles.</td><td>{ Sheffield.
Sandisfield.</td></tr>
<tr><td>Monterey; village in town of same name</td><td>Sandisfield.</td></tr>
<tr><td>Montgomery; town in Hampden County; area, 14 square miles</td><td>Granville.</td></tr>
<tr><td>Montgomery; village in town of same name</td><td>Granville.</td></tr>
<tr><td>Montrose; station in Wakefield on Boston and Maine R. R</td><td>Lawrence.</td></tr>
<tr><td>Montville; village in central part of Sandisfield</td><td>Sandisfield.</td></tr>
<tr><td>Monument; island in Oldham Pond in west part of Pembroke</td><td>Abington.</td></tr>
<tr><td>Monument; mountain in northern part of Great Barrington</td><td>{ Pittsfield.
Sheffield.</td></tr>
<tr><td>Monument Beach; village on northwestern coast of Bourne</td><td>Falmouth.</td></tr>
<tr><td>Monumet; village in northwestern part of Bourne, on Monumet River</td><td>Falmouth.</td></tr>
<tr><td>Monumet; river in northwestern part of Bourne, flowing into Buzzards Bay at Cohasset Narrows</td><td>Falmouth.</td></tr>
<tr><td>Moody Corner; village in eastern part of South Hadley</td><td>Northampton.</td></tr>
<tr><td>Moon; island in Boston Bay, southeast of Boston</td><td>Boston Bay.</td></tr>
<tr><td>Moon; mountain in town of Monson; elevation, 1,120 feet</td><td>Palmer.</td></tr>
<tr><td>Moon Pond Meadow; salt marsh in Truro</td><td>Provincetown.</td></tr>
<tr><td>Moonshine; hill in Buckland; elevation, 1,540 feet</td><td>Hawley.</td></tr>
<tr><td>Moore; brook tributary to Quaboag River, in North Brookfield.</td><td>{ Barre.
Brookfield.</td></tr>
<tr><td>Moore; lake in town of Warwick</td><td>Warwick.</td></tr>
<tr><td>Moose; brook in Barre and Hardwick, 8 miles long</td><td>Barre.</td></tr>
<tr><td>Moose; brook in Southampton, 2 miles long, tributary to Manhan River</td><td>Springfield.</td></tr>
<tr><td>Moose; hill in Sharon; elevation, 560 feet</td><td>Dedham.</td></tr>
<tr><td>Moose; pond in Spencer</td><td>Worcester.</td></tr>
<tr><td>Moose Horn; brook in New Salem</td><td>Belchertown.</td></tr>
<tr><td>Moose Horn; pond in Hubbardston</td><td>Worcester.</td></tr>
<tr><td>Moose Meadow; brook in Montgomery and Westfield, 4 miles long, tributary to Westfield River</td><td>Granville.</td></tr>
<tr><td>More; brook in southeast part of Goshen</td><td>Chesterfield.</td></tr>
<tr><td>Morley; hill in northwestern part of Sandisfield; elevation, 1,860 feet</td><td>Sandisfield.</td></tr>
<tr><td>Moromoesoy; island in Waquoit Bay; also called Moromascoy Island</td><td>Falmouth.</td></tr>
<tr><td>Morse; brook in Marlboro, 1 mile long, flows into Broad Meadow Brook</td><td>Marlboro.</td></tr>
<tr><td>Morse; hill in southeastern part of Essex County</td><td>Salem.</td></tr>
<tr><td>Morse; pond in Wellesley</td><td>Framingham.</td></tr>
<tr><td>Morseville; village in Natick</td><td>Framingham.</td></tr>
<tr><td>Morseville; village in Charlton</td><td>Webster.</td></tr>
<tr><td>Morton; pond in Enfield</td><td>Belchertown.</td></tr>
<tr><td>Moses; hill in central part of Manchester; elevation, 180 feet</td><td>Salem.</td></tr>
<tr><td>Mosher; point on eastern coast of Dartmouth, at west entrance to Clark Cove</td><td>New Bedford.</td></tr>
</table>

	Atlas sheets.
Mosquito; brook in North Andover, nearly 4 miles long	Lawrence.
Moss; brook in Orange and Warwick	Warwick.
Mother; brook in Dedham	Dedham.
Mother; brook tributary to Copecut River, in northern part of Fall River	Fall River.
Mother; brook in Fall River and Freestone	Taunton.
Moulton; pond in Rutland	Worcester.
Mount Auburn; cemetery in Cambridge	Boston.
Mount Hope; village in city of Boston, on Boston and Providence R. R.	Boston.
Mount Hope; bay in southwestern part of Bristol County, arm of Narragansett Bay	Fall River.
Mount Tom; village in northeastern part of East Hampton	Northampton.
Mount Washington; town in southwestern corner of Berkshire County; area, 23 square miles	Sheffield.
Mount Washington; village in Everett and Chelsea	Boston.
Mound Meadow; hill in Dunstable; elevation, 341 feet	Groton.
Mountain; brook in Warwick, 2 miles long, unites with Kdider Brook	Warwick.
Mountain; brook tributary to Quinebaug River in Brimfield	Brookfield.
Mountain, The; hill in Framingham; elevation, 380 feet	Framingham
Mowry; brook in Marlboro and Southboro, 3 miles long, flows into Broad Meadow Brook	Marlboro.
Mud; creek forming part of boundary line of Chatham and Harwich, draining into Pleasant Bay	Chatham.
Mud; creek in Newbury	Newburyport.
Mud; pond in Natick	Framingham.
Mud; pond in Asburnham	Fitchburg.
Mud; pond in Pittsfield	Pittsfield.
Muddy; brook in towns of Ware and Hardwick	Barre.
Muddy; brook in Granby, Chicopee, and South Hadley	Springfield.
Muddy; brook in Mendon	Blackstone.
Muddy; cove in Great Tisbury Pond, Tisbury, Marthas Vineyard	Marthas Vineyard.
Muddy; creek on boundary between Chatham and Harwich	Yarmouth.
Muddy; pond in town of Hyde Park	Boston.
Muddy; pond in northeastern part of Washington	Becket.
Muddy; pond in Kingston	Plymouth.
Muddy; pond in Wareham	Plymouth.
Muddy; pond in southern part of Wenham Swamp, Wenham	Salem.
Muddy; pond near village of Newton, in west part of Barnstable	Barnstable.
Muddy; pond in Westminster	Fitchburg.
Muddy; pond in Rutland and Oakham	Barre.
Muddy; pond in Hardwick	Barre.
Muddy; pond in north part of Halifax	Abington.
Muddy Cove; brook in Dighton, 2 miles long, tributary to Taunton River	Taunton.
Muddy Run; marshy branch of Rowley River, in northern part of Ipswich	Salem.
Mugget; hill in Charlton; elevation, 1,012 feet	Webster.
Mulberry Mead; brook in Norton and Easton, 6 miles long, tributary to Winneconnet Pond	Taunton.
Mulpus; brook in Townsend, Shirley, and Lunenburg, 8 miles long, tributary to Nashua River	Groton.

A GEOGRAPHIC DICTIONARY OF MASSACHUSETTS. 75

Atlas sheets.

Mumford; river, right branch of Blackstone River, flowing through towns of Sutton, Northbridge, Douglas, and Uxbridge............ Blackstone.
Munn; brook in Granville, Southwick, and Westfield, 6 miles long, tributary to Westfield Little River............ Granville.
Muscle; point in western part of Gloucester Harbor............ Gloucester.
Muskeget; island northwest from western point of Nantucket. Muskeget.
Musquapog; pond in Rutland............ Worcester.
Musquashiat; pond in northeastern part of Scituate............ Abington.
Mussel; point on southeast corner of Sandy Beach and extending into Barnstable Harbor............ Barnstable.
Myrick; village in town of Berkley, on Taunton and New Bedford R. R............ Taunton.
Myrick; pond in Brewster............ Wellfleet.
Mystic; lakes which join Mystic and Arbajona rivers in Winchester on boundary between towns of Medford and Arlington............ Boston.
Mystic; pond in Methuen............ Lawrence.
Mystic; river draining northern part of Middlesex County, having upon its crooked course many lakes; enters Boston Harbor between Chelsea and Charlestown............ Boston.
Mystic Park; driving park in Medford............ Boston.
Nabnasset; pond in Westford............ Lowell.
Nahant; town in Essex County; area, 1 square mile............ Boston Bay.
Nahant; bay north of Nahant and east of Lynn............ Boston Bay.
Namasket; village in Middleboro............ Middleboro.
Namasket; river in Middleboro, 7 miles long, tributary to Taunton River............ Middleboro.
Namequoit; point on south coast of Orleans............ Wellfleet.
Namskaket; creek on boundary line between Orleans and Brewster, 1 mile long, flows into Cape Cod Bay............ Wellfleet.
Namskaket; village in Orleans............ Wellfleet.
Nantasket; village on northwest coast of Cohasset............ Boston Bay.
Nantasket; beach on east coast of Hull............ Boston Bay.
Nantucket; town in Nantucket County; area, 52 square miles. { Muskeget. Nantucket. }
Nantucket; harbor on northern coast of Nantucket............ Nantucket.
Nantucket; island off southeast coast, constituting town of Nantucket; area, 52 square miles. { Muskeget. Nantucket. }
Nantucket; sound on south side of Cape Cod............ { Nantucket. Yarmouth. Barnstable. }
Nantucket; principal village in town of same name............ Nantucket.
Nantucket; lighthouse on northeast coast of Nantucket............ Nantucket.
Nantucket; cliffs on north coast of Nantucket............ Nantucket.
Nantucket Cliff; beacons on north shore of Nantucket............ Nantucket.
Narrow; creek on coast of Nantucket............ Muskeget.
Narrows; section of Connecticut River............ Greenfield.
Narrows; light-house near Fort Warren, 46 feet above sea level, with fixed red light and visible 12 miles............ Boston Bay.
Nashaquitsa; settlement in Chilmark, Marthas Vineyard............ Gay Head.
Nashaquitsa; cliffs on south coast of Chilmark, Marthas Vineyard............ Gay Head.
Nashaquitsa; pond in Chilmark, Marthas Vineyard............ Gay Head.
Nashawena; one of the Elizabeth islands, Gosnold............ Gay Head.

	Atlas sheets.
Nashoba; brook in Acton and Westford, 3 miles long.........	Lowell
Nashoba; hill on southern boundary of Westford; elevation, 380 feet...	Lowell.
Nashua; river heading in northern part of the State, and flowing with circuitous course into the Merrimac River in southern New Hampshire.	{ Fitchburg. Groton. Worcester. Marlboro.
Nashua; reservoir in Gardner and Ashburnham................	Fitchburg.
Nashua; village on Marblehead Neck..........................	Boston Bay.
Nashua, Acton, and Boston; branch of the Concord and Montreal Railroad system...	
Nasketucket; village in eastern part of Fair Haven on Nasketucket River..	New Bedford.
Nasketucket; bay on coast of Fair Haven and Mattapoisett..	New Bedford.
Nasketucket; river in eastern part of Fair Haven, flowing into Little Bay..	New Bedford.
Nason; hill in Sherborn; elevation, 260 feet...................	Franklin.
Natick; town in Middlesex County; area, 16 square miles....	Framingham.
Natick; village in town of same name.........................	Framingham.
Natty; pond in Hubbardston..................................	Barre.
Natty Pond; brook in Hubbardston...........................	Barre.
Naugus Head; point on northwestern coast of Marblehead....	Salem.
Nauset; beach, low sand-bar extending along southeast end of Cape Cod..	Chatham.
Nauset; harbor on east boundary of Orleans....................	Wellfleet.
Nauset Beach; beacons on eastern coast of Wellfleet	Wellfleet.
Nauset Beach; life saving-station on eastern coast of Eastham.	Wellfleet.
Naushon; one of the Elizabeth islands, part of town of Gosnold.	{ Falmouth. Gay Head.
Neal; pond on boundary between Merrimac and Haverhill....	Haverhill.
Nebo, Mount; hill in town of Medfield; elevation, 240 feet...	Franklin.
Neck; hill in Hopedale...	Blackstone.
Neck; pond near coast in south of Barnstable..................	Barnstable.
Ned Point Light; light on coast of Mattapoisett, east of Mattapoisett Harbor; lantern 43 feet above sea level and visible 11 miles	New Bedford.
Needham; town in Norfolk County; area 12 square miles.	{ Framingham. Boston.
Needham; village in town of same name on Woonsocket division, New York and New England R. R.....................	Boston.
Needham Corner; village in southeastern part of Peabody...	Salem.
Neeseponset; pond in Dana......................................	Belchertown.
Negus; mountain in Rowe; altitude, 1,830 feet.................	Hawley.
Nelson; island in Long Pond, Lakeville	Middleboro.
Nelson Island; creek in eastern part of Rowley, flowing into Plum Island River	Salem.
Neponset; village in city of Boston	Boston.
Neponset; reservoir in Foxboro..............................	{ Franklin. Dedham.
Neponset; river in Norfolk and Suffolk counties, about 18 miles long; flows into Dorchester Bay.	{ Dedham. Boston.
New; harbor on south side of Barnstable, opening into Nantucket Sound	Barnstable.
New Ashford; mountainous town in northwestern part of Berkshire County, area, 14 square miles.	{ Berlin. Greylock.

	Atlas sheets.
New Ashford; village in central part of town of same name..	Greylock.
New Bedford; seaboard city in Bristol County; area, 19 square miles	New Bedford.
New Bedford; harbor in southern part of Bristol County between New Bedford and Fair Haven	New Bedford.
New Bedford; reservoir in Freetown and Acushnet	Middleboro.
New Boston; village in eastern part of Sandisfield on Farmington River	Sandisfield.
New Boston; village in town of Winchendon	Winchendon.
New Boston; village in town of Framingham	Framingham.
New Boston; river in Dennis, flows into Chase Garden Creek.	Yarmouth.
New Braintree; town in Worcester County; area, 21 square miles	Barre.
New Braintree; principal village in town of same name	Barre.
New England; village in town of Grafton	Blackstone.
New Haven and Northampton; part of New York, New Haven and Hartford Railroad system running from New Haven, Conn., to Northampton and Holyoke.	
New Lenox; village in northeastern part of town of same name	Becket.
New London Northern; part of Central Vermont Railroad system running from New London northward across the State into Vermont.	
New Marlboro; town in southern part of Berkshire County; area, 50 square miles.	{ Sheffield. { Sandisfield.
New Marlboro; village in central part of town of same name.	Sandisfield.
New Salem; town in Franklin County; area, 28 square miles.	{ Belchertown. { Warwick.
New Salem; village in town of Salem	{ Belchertown. { Warwick.
Newtown; hill in Littleton; elevation, 400 feet	Lowell.
New York and New England; railroad extending from Boston southwestward through Connecticut to New York.	
New York, New Haven and Hartford; railroad system connecting New York City with New Haven and Hartford, Conn., and Springfield, Holyoke, Northampton and other places in Massachusetts.	
Newbury; town in Essex County; area, 27 square miles	Newburyport.
Newbury Old Town; village in town of Newbury	Newburyport.
Newburyport; city in Essex County; area, 18 square miles	Newburyport.
Newburyport; village in town of same name	Newburyport.
Newburyport; light-house on Plum Island	Newburyport.
Newcomb; pond in Truro	Wellfleet.
Newfield; pond in Chelmsford	Lowell.
Newton; city in Middlesex County; area 18 square miles	Boston.
Newton; village in town of same name	Boston.
Newton; village in west part of Barnstable	Barnstable.
Newton Center; village in Newton on Boston and Albany R. R.	Boston.
Newton Highlands; village in Newton, on Boston and Albany R. R.	Boston.
Newton Lower Falls; village in town of Newton	Framingham.
Newton Upper Falls; village in town of Newton, on Woonsocket division, New York and New England R. R.	Boston.
Newtonville; village in town of Newton, on Boston and Albany R. R.	Boston.

	Atlas sheets.
Nichewaug; village in town of Petersham	Barre.
Nichol; brook tributary to Ipswich River, rising in Danvers and forming boundary line between Topsfield and Middleton	Salem.
Nichol; brook in Amesbury, 1 mile long, flows into Merrimac River	Newburyport.
Nichol; hill in Lunenburg; elevation, 542 feet	Groton.
Nickerson Neck; peninsula on north of Crow Pond and Bassing Harbor, Chatham	Chatham.
Niles; pond in southern part of Gloucester	Gloucester.
Nine Acre Corner; village in Concord	Framingham.
Nine Mile; pond in Wilbraham	Palmer.
Nineteenth; hill in Winchendon; elevation, 1,180 feet	Winchendon.
Nipmuck; pond in Mendon	Blackstone.
Nipmuck; pond in Webster	Webster.
Nippenicket; pond in Bridgewater	Taunton.
Nissitissit; hills in Pepperell; elevation, 380 to 470 feet	Groton.
Nissitissit; river in town of Pepperell and in New Hampshire, tributary to Nashua River	Groton.
No Bottom; pond in Brewster	Wellfleet.
No Bottom; pond in west part of Pembroke	Abington.
No Mans Land; island lying south of Gay Head, Marthas Vineyard	Gay Head.
Nobadee; pond in Nantucket	Nantucket.
Nobscot; hill in Framingham; elevation, 600 feet	Framingham.
Nobscusset; harbor on north coast of Dennis	Yarmouth.
Nobscusset; point on north coast of Dennis	Yarmouth.
Nobska; point on eastern coast of Cromeset Neck, south of Mark Cove	Falmouth.
Nobska Point; light on southwestern corner of Falmouth at eastern entrance of Woods Holl	Falmouth.
Nod; brook in Groton, 1 mile long, tributary to Nashua River	Groton.
Nonacoicus; brook in Ayer, 1 mile long, tributary to Nashua River	Groton.
Nonamesset; island southwest of Woods Holl, in Vineyard Sound	Falmouth.
Nonantum; village in Newton	Boston.
None Such; pond in Webster	Framingham.
Nonotuck; mount, summit of Holyoke range, in Northampton; altitude, 852 feet	Northampton.
Nonquitt; village in southeastern part of Dartmouth	New Bedford.
Nonset; brook in Westford, 2 miles long	Lowell.
Nookagee; river in Fitchburg, Westminster, and Ashburnham	Fitchburg.
Norcross; hill in Templeton; elevation, 1,100 feet	Winchendon.
Norfolk; town in Norfolk County; area, 16 square miles	Franklin.
Norfolk; village in town of same name, on New York and New England R. R.	Franklin.
Norman Woe; point on southern coast of Gloucester, at west entrance of Gloucester Harbor	Gloucester.
Norman Woe; rock in western entrance to Gloucester Harbor	Gloucester.
North; brook in Northboro and Berlin, 4¼ miles long, tributary to Assabet River	Marlboro.
North; brook in Westhampton	Chesterfield.
North; cove in northern coast of West Island	New Bedford.
North; point at northern extremity of West Island	New Bedford.

	Atlas sheets.
North; pond on coast of Tuckernuck Island	Muskeget.
North; pond in Orange...	Warwick.
North; pond in Worcester......................................	Worcester.
North; pond in Hopkinton and Milford........................	Blackstone.
North; river in Coleraine and Shelburne, 3 miles long, flows into Deerfield River	Greenfield.
North; river flowing into Beverly Harbor in northern part of Salem	Salem.
North; river in northern part of Plymouth County, flowing into Massachusetts Bay.	{ Abington. { Duxbury.
North; village in Webster, on New York and New England R. R.	Webster.
North; village in Pepperell....................................	Groton.
North; village in Lancaster	Marlboro.
North Abington; village in northeast part of Abington.......	Abington.
North Acton; railway station in Acton, on Nashua, Acton and Boston R. R..	Lowell.
North Adams; town in northern part of Berkshire County; area, 19 square miles.......................................	Greylock.
North Adams; village in northern part of North Adams, on Hoosic River	Greylock.
North Amherst; village in northern part of Amherst.........	Northampton.
North Andover; town in Essex County; area, 28 square miles.	Lawrence.
North Andover; principal village in town of same name......	Lawrence.
North Andover Center; village in North Andover, near Marbleridge Station, on Salem and Lawrence R. R.............	Lawrence.
North Ashburnham; village in town of Ashburnham.........	Fitchburg.
North Ashburnham; station in town of Ashburnham, on Cheshire R. R.....	Fitchburg.
North Attleboro; town in Bristol County; area, 20 square miles.	Providence.
North Becket; village in northern part of Becket............	Becket.
North Bellingham; village in town of Bellingham, on New York and New England R. R., Woonsocket division	Franklin.
North Bernardston; village in town of Bernardston..........	Greenfield.
North Beverly; village in western part of Beverly............	Salem.
North Beverly Station; village in northern part of Beverly..	Salem.
North Billerica; village in town of Billerica, on Boston and Lowell R. R..	Lowell.
North Blandford; village in town of Blandford...............	Granville.
North Brookfield; town in Worcester County; area, 22 square miles.	{ Barre. { Brookfield.
North Brookfield; village in town of same name..............	Barre.
North Cambridge; village in city of Cambridge.............	Boston.
North Carver; village in town of Carver.....................	Middleboro.
North Charlton; village in town of Charlton.................	Webster.
North Chatham; village in Chatham..........................	Chatham.
North Chelmsford; village in town of Chelmsford, on Stony Brook R. R...	Lowell.
North Chester; village in north part of Chester..............	Chesterfield.
North Dana; village in town of Dana, on Boston and Albany R. R., Athol branch	Belchertown.
North Dartmouth; village in central part of Dartmouth......	New Bedford.
North Dighton; village in town of Dighton...................	Taunton.
North Duxbury; village in northern part of Duxbury.........	Duxbury.
North Eastham; village in town of Eastham..................	Wellfleet.

	Atlas sheets.
North Easton; village in town of Easton, on Old Colony R. R.	Dedham.
North Egremont; village in northern part of Egremont, on Green River	Sheffield.
North Falmouth; village in northeastern part of Falmouth	Falmouth.
North Farms; village in northern part of Northampton	Northampton.
Northampton; city in central part of Hampshire County; area, 37 square miles	Northampton.
Northboro; town in Worcester County; area, 19 square miles	Marlboro.
Northboro; village in town of same name	Marlboro.
Northbridge; town in Worcester County; area, 19 square miles	Blackstone.
Northbridge; village in town of same name	Blackstone.
Northfield; town in Franklin County; area, 37 square miles	Greenfield. Warwick.
Northfield; principal village in town of same name, on New London Northern R. R	Warwick.
Northfield Farms; village in town of Northfield, on New London Northern R. R.	Warwick.
North Framingham; station on Old Colony R. R., in Framingham	Framingham.
North Hadley; village in western part of Hadley, on Connecticut River	Northampton.
North Hanover; village in north part of Hanover	Abington.
North Hanson; village in northwest part of Hanson	Abington.
North Hanson; station (railway) in western part of Hanson	Abington.
North Harwich; village in town of Harwich	Yarmouth.
North Hatfield; village in northern part of Hatfield	Northampton.
North Leominster; village in town of same name, on Fitchburg R. R	Groton.
North Leverett; village in town of Leverett	Warwick.
North Lexington; village in Lexington	Boston.
North Littleton; station on Boston and Lowell R. R., in town of Littleton	Groton.
North Marshfield; village in northwest part of Marshfield	Abington.
North Meadow; pond in Blandford	Granville.
North Middleboro; village in town of Middleboro	Middleboro.
North Milford; village in town of Milford	Blackstone.
North Monson; village in town of Monson, on New London Northern R. R	Palmer.
North; mountain in Northfield; altitude, 1,340 feet	Warwick.
North Nashua; river in Lancaster and Leominster, tributary to Nashua River	Marlboro.
North New Salem; village in town of New Salem	Warwick.
North Orange; village in town of Orange	Warwick.
North Otis; village in northern part of Otis	Sandisfield.
North Oxford; village in town of Oxford, on Webster Branch Boston and Albany R. R.	Webster.
North Pembroke; village in north part of Pembroke	Abington.
North Plympton; village in town of Plympton	Middleboro.
North Pocasset; village situated upon small arm of Buzzards Bay, in western portion of Bourne	Falmouth.
North Prescott; village in town of Prescott	Belchertown.
North Quincy; village in Quincy, on Old Colony R R.	Boston.
North Raynham; village in town of Raynham	Taunton.

A GEOGRAPHIC DICTIONARY OF MASSACHUSETTS.

Atlas sheets.

Place	Description	Atlas sheet
North Reading	town in Middlesex County; area, 13 square miles	Lawrence.
North Reading	village in town of same name, on Salem and Lowell R. R.	Lawrence.
North Rehoboth	village in Rehoboth	Taunton.
North Ridge	hill in northern part of Great Neck, Ipswich; elevation, 120 feet	Salem.
North Rochester	village in town of Rochester	Middleboro.
North Rutland	village in town of Rutland	Worcester.
North Salem	village in northern part of Salem, on North River	Salem.
North Saugus	village in town of Saugus	Boston.
North Scituate	village in northwest part of Scituate	Abington.
North Shirley	village in town of Shirley	Groton.
North Spencer	village in Spencer	Worcester.
North Sudbury	village in town of Sudbury	Framingham.
North Sugarloaf	point about 760 feet high, in southeastern part of Deerfield	Northampton.
North Tewksbury	village in Tewksbury	Lawrence.
North Tisbury	village in town of Tisbury, Marthas Vineyard	Marthas Vineyard.
North Truro	village in Truro	Provincetown.
North Uxbridge	village in Uxbridge	Blackstone.
Northville	village in northeast part of East Bridgewater	Abington.
Northwest Duxbury	village in western part of Duxbury	Duxbury.
North Weymouth	village in north part of Weymouth	Abington.
North Wilbraham	village in town of Wilbraham, on Boston and Albany R. R.	Palmer.
North Wilmington	railway station on Salem and Lowell R. R., in Wilmington	Lawrence.
North Woburn	village in Woburn, on Woburn branch of Boston and Lowell R. R.	Lawrence.
North Yarmouth	village in central part of Manchester	Salem.
Norton	town in Bristol County; area, 30 square miles	Taunton.
Norton	village in town of same name	Taunton.
Norton	hill in southeastern part of Conway; elevation, 920 feet	Northampton.
Norton	reservoir in Mansfield and Norton	Taunton.
Norwell	town in Plymouth County; appears on map as South Scituate; area, 22 square miles	Abington.
Norwich	hill in south central part of Huntington	Chesterfield.
Norwich	pond in northeast part of Huntington	Chesterfield.
Norwich	village in Huntington	Chesterfield.
Norwich Bridge	village in Huntington	Granville.
Norwood	town in Norfolk County; area, 10 square miles	Dedham.
Norwood	village in town of same name, on New York and New England R. R	Dedham.
Norwottock, Mount	mountain in Holyoke range, on line between Amherst and Granby; also called Hilliard Knob; altitude, 1,115 feet	Northampton.
Notch, The	gap in Holyoke range, in Granby	Northampton.
Noyes	hill in northeastern part of Tolland; elevation, 1,700 feet	Sandisfield.
Noyes	pond in central part of Tolland	Sandisfield.
Nunket	pond on western boundary line of Bridgewater	Taunton.

Bull. 116——6

82　A GEOGRAPHIC DICTIONARY OF MASSACHUSETTS.　[BULL. 116.

	Atlas sheets.
Nut; island off northeast coast of Quincy	Boston Bay.
Nutting; hill in town of Ashburnham; elevation, 1,600 feet	Fitchburg.
Nutting; pond in Billerica	Lowell.
Nye Neck; peninsula on northwestern corner of Falmouth between Cataumet Harbor and Wild Harbor	Falmouth.
Oak; hill in Westford; elevation, 340 feet	Lowell.
Oak; hill in Harvard; elevation, 630 feet	Groton.
Oak; hill in Littleton; elevation, 420 feet	Groton.
Oak; hill in Pepperell; elevation, 380 feet	Groton.
Oak; hill in Newton	Boston.
Oak; hill in Fitchburg; elevation, 900 feet	Fitchburg.
Oak; hill in Southboro; elevation, 440 feet	Marlboro.
Oak Bluffs; village in Cottage City, Marthas Vineyard	Marthas Vineyard.
Oak Hill; pond in Lancaster	Groton.
Oak Island; railway station, northeast part of Revere	Boston Bay.
Oakdale; village in Dedham, on New York and New England R. R.	Dedham.
Oakdale; village in West Boylston, on Fitchburg and Worcester R. R.	Worcester.
Oakham; town in Worcester County; area, 21 square miles	Barre.
Oakham; principal village in town of same name	Barre.
Oakland; village in town of Taunton	Taunton.
Ocean View; village in northern part of Rockport	Gloucester.
Ockcooanganset; hill in Marlboro; elevation, 500 feet	Marlboro.
Ockway; bay; part of Poponesset Bay, on southeast coast of Mashpee	Barnstable.
Old Boat; point on west side of Weymouth Fore River, Quincy	Abington.
Old Cambridge; part of city of Cambridge in which is located Harvard University	Boston.
Old Colony; part of Boston and Providence Railroad system, extending southward and southeastward from Boston to Taunton, Fall River, New Bedford, Cape Cod, and other points	
Old Colony House; railway station in north part of Hingham.	Abington.
Old Common; village in Millbury	Webster.
Old Furnace; village in town of Hardwick, on Ware River Branch, Boston and Albany R. R.	Barre.
Old Harbor; creek in north part of Sandwich, flowing into Cape Cod Bay	Barnstable.
Old; harbor on northeast coast of Cohasset	Boston Bay.
Old Pond Meadow; hill in south part of South Scituate	Abington.
Old Spain; village in north part of Weymouth	Abington.
Old Swamp; river in southeast part of Weymouth	Abington.
Old Tower; light on Cedar Point at north entrance of Scituate Harbor, northeast coast of Scituate	Duxbury.
Oldham; pond in western part of Pembroke	Abington.
Onota; brook in Pittsfield, 3 miles long; tributary to Housatonic River	Pittsfield.
Onset; village in Wareham, on coast of Buzzards Bay	Falmouth.
Onset; bay; arm of Buzzards Bay projecting into southeastern part of Wareham	Falmouth.
Onset; island situated in mouth of Onset Bay, about one-fourth mile southwest of Jacob Neck	Falmouth.

A GEOGRAPHIC DICTIONARY OF MASSACHUSETTS. 83

	Atlas sheets.
Outer Brewster; island in Boston Bay	Boston Bay.
Open Pasture; pond in Provincetown	Provincetown.
Orange; town in Franklin County; area, 36 square miles	{ Warwick. Winchendon.
Orange; village in town of same name, on Fitchburg R. R.	Warwick.
Orchard; hill on southern boundary of Stow; elevation, 300 feet	Marlboro.
Orcutt; brook in Orange, 2 miles long; tributary to Miller River	Warwick.
Ore; hill in Granville; elevation 1,300 feet	Granville.
Orient; mountain in Pelham	Belchertown.
Orleans; town in Barnstable County; area, 15 square miles	{ Wellfleet. Chatham.
Orleans; village in town of same name, on Old Colony R. R., Cape Cod division	Wellfleet.
Orleans Beach; life-saving station on eastern coast of Orleans.	Wellfleet.
Orleans Mills; village in Rehoboth	Providence.
Orme; island near northeast coast of Marblehead	Salem.
Osceola; mountain in Richmond; altitude 1,420 feet	Pittsfield.
Osceola; island in Robbin Pond, in southeast part of East Bridgewater	Abington.
Osgood; brook on western boundary of Wendell, 2 miles long; tributary to Miller River	Warwick.
Oshar; rocks near east shore of the Glades, on northeast coast of Scituate	Abington.
Osterville; village in Barnstable	Barnstable.
Osterville Grand; island in Osterville Harbor, on southwest coast of Barnstable	Barnstable.
Osterville Landing; village at west entrance to New Harbor, on south coast of Barnstable	Barnstable.
Otis; town in southeastern part of Berkshire County; area, 36 square miles	Sandisfield.
Otis; village in southern part of Otis	Sandisfield.
Otis: hill in north part of Hingham	Boston Bay.
Otis; hill north of central part of South Scituate	Abington.
Otis; reservoir in eastern part of Otis	Sandisfield.
Otter Pond; brook in Gill	Greenfield.
Otter River; village in Templeton	Winchendon.
Otter Run; brook in Gill, flows into Connecticut River	Warwick.
Overlook; reservoir in Fitchburg	Fitchburg.
Owen; mountain in Conway; altitude 1,460 feet	Greenfield.
Owl; hill in Waltham; elevation, 240 feet	Boston.
Ox Bow; bend of Connecticut River in northeastern part of Easthampton	Northampton.
Ox Pasture; hill in northern part of Rowley; elevation, 180 feet.	Salem.
Oxford; village in western part of Fair Haven	New Bedford.
Oxford; town in Worcester County; area, 27 square miles	Webster.
Oxford; village in town of same name, on Norwich and Worcester R. R.	Webster.
Oyster; creek connecting northwest corner of Stage Harbor with Oyster Pond, Chatham	Chatham.
Oyster; pond about one-half mile long in southwestern part of Falmouth	Falmouth.
Oyster; pond in Edgartown, Marthas Vineyard	Marthas Vineyard

	Atlas sheets.
Oyster; pond at head of narrow body of water extending back from northwest corner of Stage Harbor	Chatham.
Packard; mountain in New Salem	Belchertown.
Packard; pond in Orange	Winchendon.
Packardsville; village in Pelham	Belchertown.
Page; brook in Carlisle, 2 miles long, tributary to Concord River	Lowell.
Paine; creek tributary to Green Creek, in northeastern part of Ipswich	Salem.
Pakachoag; hill in Worcester; elevation, 700 feet	Webster.
Palmer; town in Hampden County; area, 25 square miles	{ Palmer. { Brookfield.
Palmer; village in town of same name, on Boston and Albany R. R.	Palmer.
Palmer; cove in Salem Harbor indenting eastern coast of Salem	Salem.
Palmer; island in New Bedford Harbor	New Bedford.
Palmer; river in Rehoboth	{ Providence. { Taunton.
Palmer Center; village in town of Palmer	Palmer.
Pamanset; river flowing southerly through Dartmouth into Buzzards Bay	{ New Bedford. { Fall River.
Pamet River; life saving-station on Atlantic coast of Truro	Provincetown.
Pampet; river in Truro	Wellfleet.
Pampet River; life saving-station on east coast of Truro	Wellfleet.
Panker; pond near coast in south part of Barnstable	Barnstable.
Pantry; brook in Sudbury, 2 miles long	Framingham.
Parish; pond in Otis	Sandisfield.
Park; hill in Millbury; elevation, 620 feet	Webster.
Park; pond in Tyngsboro	Lowell.
Parker; hill in Hawley; elevation, 2,060 feet	Hawley.
Parker; point on southwestern coast of Falmouth projecting southward into Woods Holl	Falmouth.
Parker; river in northern part of Essex County, flowing easterly into Plum Island River	{ Lawrence. { Newburyport. { Salem.
Parker; river in Yarmouth, flowing into Nantucket Sound	Yarmouth.
Parksville; village in Brimfield	Palmer.
Parsonage; hill in Haverhill; elevation, 233 feet	Haverhill.
Partridgeville; village in Templeton	Winchendon.
Pasque; one of the Elizabeth Islands in Gosnold	Gay Head.
Pasture; brook, tributary to Mill Creek, running northwesterly through Rowley	Salem.
Patch Meadow; brook in Billerica and Chelmsford; tributary to River Meadow Brook	Lowell.
Pattaquattic; hill in Palmer; elevation, 1,080 feet	Palmer.
Pattaquattic; pond in Palmer	Palmer.
Pattenville; village in Billerica	Lawrence.
Paul; hill in Sherborn; elevation, 320 feet	Franklin.
Paul; point on north coast of Tisbury, Marthas Vineyard	Marthas Vineyard.
Pawtucketville; village in Lowell	Lowell.
Paxton; town in Worcester County; area, 19 square miles	Worcester.
Paxton Center; village in town of Paxton	Worcester.
Pea; brook in Conway, 2 miles long; tributary to Bear River	Greenfield.

A GEOGRAPHIC DICTIONARY OF MASSACHUSETTS.

	Atlas sheets.
Pea; island in Nasketucket Bay	New Bedford.
Peabody; town in southern part of Essex County; area, 17 square miles.	Lawrence. Salem.
Peabody; village in eastern part of town of same name, on North River	Salem.
Peach; point on northeast coast of Marblehead	Salem.
Peaked; cliff on coast of Plymouth	Plymouth.
Peaked; hill in Chilmark, Marthas Vineyard; elevation, 311 feet	Gay Head.
Peaked; rock near coast in Westport	Sakonnet.
Peaked; mountain in town of Monson; altitude, 1,240 feet	Palmer.
Peaked Hill Bar; life-saving station in Provincetown	Provincetown.
Pearce; island in Gloucester	Gloucester.
Pearl; hill in Fitchburg; elevation, 1,000 feet	Fitchburg.
Pearl Hill; brook in Townsend and Lunenburg, 8 miles long	Fitchburg.
Pease; point on eastern coast of Mattapoiset	New Bedford.
Pebble; brook in Blandford, 7 miles long	Granville.
Pecowsic; brook in Longmeadow, 5 miles long; tributary to Connecticut River	Springfield.
Pecuanticiot; river in Sharon, Foxboro, and Mansfield; flows into Canoe River	Dedham.
Peddock; island west of Hull, in Boston Bay	Boston Bay.
Pegan; hill in Natick; elevation, 320 feet	Framingham.
Pegan; hill in Dover; elevation, 360 feet	Franklin.
Pelham; town in Hampshire County; area, 27 square miles	Belchertown.
Pelham; village in town of same name	Belchertown.
Pelham; brook in Rowe and Charlemont, 7 miles long; flows into Deerfield River	Hawley.
Pembroke; town in Plymouth County; area, 24 square miles	Abington.
Pendleton; hill in Sudbury; elevation, 260 feet	Framingham.
Penikese; one of the Elizabeth Islands, in town of Gosnold	Gay Head.
Penn; brook, tributary to Parker River, in Georgetown	Salem.
Penny; brook in Ware	Palmer.
Penny; brook in Saugus, 1 mile long	Boston.
Pentucket; pond in northwestern part of Georgetown	Salem.
Peppercorn; hill in town of Upton	Blackstone.
Pepperell; town in Middlesex County; area, 27 square miles	Groton.
Pepperell; village in town of same name	Groton.
Pequoig; railway station in Winchendon	Winchendon.
Perkins; hill in western part of Essex; elevation, 180 feet	Salem.
Perry; pond in North Brookfield	Brookfield.
Perry; mountain peak in Richmond; altitude, 2,060 feet	Pittsfield.
Perryville; village in Rehoboth	Providence.
Peru; town in eastern part of Berkshire County; area, 27 square miles.	Chesterfield. Becket.
Peru; village in central part of town of same name	Becket.
Peru; hill in western part of Peru; elevation, 2,180 feet	Becket.
Peter; hill in Sherborn; elevation, 240 feet	Framingham.
Peter; pond in Dracut	Lowell.
Peter; pond in Dudley	Webster.
Peter; pond in Sandwich, covering about 176 acres	Barnstable.
Peter; river in Wrentham and Bellingham, and in State of Rhode Island	Franklin.

	Atlas sheets.
Petersham; town in Worcester County; area, 40 square miles	Winchendon. Barre. Belchertown. Warwick.
Petersham; village in town of same name	Barre
Petticoat; hill in west part of Williamsburg	Chesterfield.
Pew; brook in Gardner	Fitchburg.
Phelps; brook in Hancock and Pittsfield, 4 miles long; flows into Housatonic branch of Housatonic River	Pittsfield.
Phillip; beach on east coast of Swampscott	Boston Bay.
Phillip; brook tributary to South River, in Duxbury	Duxbury.
Phillip; brook in Ashburnham	Fitchburg.
Phillip; brook tributary to Hoosic River, in eastern part of North Adams	Greylock.
Phillip; pond on east coast of Swampscott	Boston Bay.
Phillip Beach; railway station in east part of Swampscott	Boston Bay.
Phillipston; town in Worcester County; area, 40 square miles	Winchendon. Barre.
Phillipston; pond in town of same name	Winchendon.
Phillipston Center; village in town of Phillipston	Winchendon.
Phillis; island in Barnstable Harbor	Barnstable.
Philo; brook in Agawam	Springfield.
Phinney; harbor in Buzzards Bay between north end of Bennett Neck and the mainland	Falmouth.
Picard; point on southern coast of Manchester	Salem.
Pickerel; pond in Ludlow	Palmer.
Pickerel; pond in Natick	Framingham.
Pickle; pond in Wareham	Plymouth.
Pierce; brook in West Brookfield	Barre.
Pier Head; northern extremity of reef known as Long Beach, which forms eastern boundary of Plymouth Harbor	Plymouth.
Pierpoint Meadow; pond in Charlton and Dudley	Webster.
Pigeon; hill in northern part of Rockport; elevation, 180 feet	Gloucester.
Pigeon Cove; village in northern part of Rockport	Gloucester.
Pilling; pond in Lynnfield	Lawrence.
Pine; brook in north part of Kingston	Abington.
Pine; creek in southern part of Plum Island, flowing into Plum Island River	Salem.
Pine; mountain in Hampden; altitude, 1,040 feet	Palmer.
Pine; point extending into Weymouth Fore River, in northwest part of Weymouth	Abington.
Pine; hill in eastern part of Bourne; elevation, 260 feet	Falmouth.
Pine; hill in Southboro; elevation, 500 feet	Marlboro.
Pine; hill in Fitchburg; elevation, 720 feet	Fitchburg.
Pine; hill in Lynnfield; elevation, 200 feet	Lawrence.
Pine; hill in Andover; elevation, 300 feet	Lawrence.
Pine; hill in Tyngsboro; elevation, 280 feet	Lowell.
Pine; hill in Chelmsford; elevation, 320 feet	Lowell.
Pine; hill in Lynn	Boston Bay.
Pine; hill in Conway; elevation, 1,060 feet	Greenfield.
Pine; hill on western boundary of Kingston	Middleboro.
Pine; hill in Princeton; elevation, 1,400 feet	Worcester.
Pine; hill in Bolton	Marlboro.
Pine; hill in Sherborn; elevation, 360 feet	Franklin.

	Atlas sheets.
Pine Hill; brook in Barre and Hardwick, 3 miles long	Barre.
Pine Neck; cove in southeastern part of Mattapoiset	New Bedford.
Pine Point; river in Duxbury Marsh, Duxbury	Duxbury.
Pine Swamp; brook in Taunton and Raynham	Taunton.
Pine Dale; village in Athol	Winchendon.
Pingree; hill in southern part of Topsfield; elevation, 200 feet.	Salem.
Pinney; brook in northeast part of Chester	Chesterfield.
Pipestave; hill in West Newbury; elevation, 180 feet	Newburyport.
Pisgah; hill in Gill; elevation, 700 feet	Greenfield.
Pisgah; mountain in Northboro	Marlboro.
Pisgah; mountain in northwest part of Westhampton	Chesterfield.
Pisgah; mountain in northern part of Wales; altitude, 1,220 feet.	Brookfield.
Pismire; island in Great Quittacas pond, Lakeville	Middleboro.
Pitman; hill in New Salem; elevation, 760 feet	Belchertown.
Pitt; hill on western boundary of Orange; elevation, 1,240 feet.	Warwick.
Pittsfield; town in western part of Berkshire County; area, 43 square miles.	{ Pittsfield. { Becket.
Pittsfield; village in central part of town of same name	{ Pittsfield. { Becket.
Plain; meadow in southwest part of Northfield	Warwick.
Plainfield; town in Hampshire County; area, 39 square miles	{ Chesterfield. { Hawley.
Plainfield; pond in town of same name	Hawley.
Plainville; village in eastern part of Hadley	Northampton.
Plainville; village in Wrentham	Franklin.
Plantain; mountain in southeastern part of Mount Washington; altitude, 1,980 feet	Sheffield.
Plantain; pond in southeastern part of Mount Washington	Sheffield.
Planter; hill south of World's End, on north coast of Hingham.	Boston Bay.
Planting; island about one-half mile long, situated in Sippican Harbor	Falmouth.
Plashes; pond in Yarmouth	Yarmouth.
Pleasant; bay about 1¼ miles in extent, on Cape Cod between Orleans and Chatham	Chatham.
Pleasant; brook in Barre, 3 miles long	Barre.
Pleasant; mountain in northern part of Peabody; altitude, 200 feet	Salem.
Pleasant; mountain in town of Barre; altitude, 1,080 feet	Barre.
Pleasant; mountain in Winchendon; altitude, 1,280 feet	Winchendon.
Pleasant; mountain in Woburn; altitude, 300 feet	Boston.
Pleasant; pond about one-half mile long in southern part of Wenham Swamp, Wenham	Salem.
Pleasantdale; pond in Sutton	Blackstone.
Plover; hill in southern part of Great Neck, Ipswich; elevation, 120 feet	Salem.
Plow Shop; pond in Ayer	Groton.
Plug; pond in Haverhill	Haverhill.
Plum; island in northeastern part of Essex County, belonging to towns of Ipswich, Rowley, Newbury, and Newburyport, and separated from the mainland by Plum Island River.	{ Newburyport. { Salem.
Plum Island; river in northeastern part of Essex County, connecting mouths of Ipswich and Merrimac rivers and separating Plum Island from the mainland.	{ Newburyport. { Salem.
Plunkett; reservoir in southeastern part of Hinsdale	Becket.

	Atlas sheets.
Plymouth; town in Plymouth County; area, 116 square miles.	Plymouth. Duxbury.
Plymouth; principal village in town of same name	Plymouth.
Plymouth; harbor in village of Plymouth, inclosed between the mainland and a long reef	Plymouth.
Plympton; town in Plymouth County; area, 16 square miles	Middleboro.
Plympton; village in town of same name	Middleboro.
Pocasset; harbor, arm of Buzzards Bay on western coast of Bourne	Falmouth.
Pochassic; mountain in Westfield; altitude, 300 feet	Granville.
Pochet; island off east coast of Orleans	Wellfleet.
Pochet Neck; peninsula in Orleans	Wellfleet.
Pocksha; pond in Lakeville and Middleboro	Middleboro.
Pocomo Head; point extending into Nantucket Harbor, Nantucket	Nantucket.
Pocumtuck: mountain in Charlemont; altitude, 1,887 feet	Hawley.
Pocumtuck; rock in Deerfield; elevation, 822 feet	Greenfield.
Podonk; pond in Brookfield and Sturbridge	Brookfield.
Poge; cape on northern extremity of Great Neck, Chappaquiddick Island, in Edgartown, Marthas Vineyard	Marthas Vineyard.
Point of Pines; at south entrance to Saugus River	Boston Bay.
Point Shirley; village on southeast coast of Winthrop	Boston Bay.
Pole; hill in Andover; elevation, 140 feet	Lawrence.
Pollock Rip; lightship anchored off Pollock Rip Shoals, 2¼ miles east of south end of Monomoy Island	Chatham.
Polpis; harbor on coast of Nantucket opening into Nantucket Harbor	Nantucket.
Pomeroy; mountain in town of Greenwich; altitude, 900 feet.	Belchertown.
Pomeroy; mountain in northern part of Southampton; altitude, 1,233 feet.	Chesterfield. Northampton.
Pomp; pond in Andover	Lawrence.
Pond; brook in Montague, 2 miles long, tributary to Saw Mill River	Greenfield.
Pond; brook in Huntington	Chesterfield.
Pond; brook in Granville, 4 miles long	Granville.
Pond; brook in Blandford, 2 miles long, tributary to Pebble Brook	Granville.
Pond; brook in Leverett and Amherst	Belchertown.
Pond; brook in Gardner	Fitchburg.
Pond; brook in Westfield, 3 miles long	Springfield.
Pond; hill in town of Mendon; elevation, 460 feet	Blackstone.
Pond; hill in Amesbury; elevation, 200 feet	Newburyport.
Pond; mountain in Northfield; elevation, 1,190 feet	Greenfield.
Pondville; village in Auburn	Webster.
Pondville; village in Barnstable	Barnstable.
Ponkapoag; pond on western boundary of Randolph	Dedham.
Pontoosic; lake on boundary line between Pittsfield and Lanesboro.	Pittsfield. Becket.
Pool; mountain peak in southeastern part of Great Barrington; altitude, 1,680 feet	Sheffield.
Poole; hill in central part of Rockport; elevation, 180 feet	Gloucester.
Poor Meadow; brook in western part of Hanson	Abingdon.
Poponesset; bay on southeast coast of Mashpee	Barnstable.
Poponesset; beach between Poponesset Bay and Nantucket Sound, southeast coast of Mashpee	Barnstable.

	Atlas sheets.
Poponesset; island in Poponesset Bay on southeast coast of Mashpee..	Barnstable.
Popple; hill in southern part of Conway; elevation, 940 feet..	Northampton.
Popple Hill; brook tributary to Roaring Brook in southwestern part of Conway..	Northampton.
Populatic; pond on northwestern boundary of Norfolk.......	Franklin.
Poquoy Trout; brook in Middleboro and Lakeville, 3¼ miles long, tributary to Taunton River............................	Middletown.
Porter; island in Merrimac River.................................	Haverhill.
Porter; river in eastern part of Danvers, flowing into Beverly Harbor..	Salem.
Porter; swamp in western part of Granby......................	Northampton.
Potash; brook in Barre..	Barre.
Potash; brook tributary to Wright River in eastern part of Williamsburg...	Northampton.
Potash; brook in Blandford and Russell, 5 miles long, tributary to Westfield River..	Granville.
Potash; brook in Dracut, one-half mile long, tributary to Richardson Brook...	Lowell.
Potomska; point on southern coast of Dartmouth.............	New Bedford.
Pottapaug; hill in Dana; elevation, 880 feet...................	Barre.
Pottapaug; pond in Dana..	Barre.
Potter; hill in Sutton; elevation, 794 feet......................	Webster.
Potter; mountain in Taconic Range in Lanesboro; altitude 2,400 feet...	Berlin.
Pottersville; village in Somerset................................	Taunton.
Pottersville; village in eastern part of Somerset, on Taunton River..	Fall River.
Poucha; pond in Chappaquiddick Island in Edgartown, Marthas Vineyard...	Martha's Vineyard.
Ponnakin; hill in Charlton; elevation, 800 feet................	Webster.
Pound; hill in Rutland; elevation, 1,160 feet..................	Worcester.
Poverty; hill in Hardwick; elevation, 1,080 feet...............	Barre.
Poverty; point projecting into Plymouth Harbor..............	Plymouth.
Powder; hill in southern part of Beverly; elevation, 100 feet..	Salem.
Powder; point in head of Duxbury Bay, extending from eastern part of Duxbury...	Duxbury.
Powder Hole; on western coast of Monomoy Island...........	Yarmouth.
Powder House; hill in Methuen; elevation, 200 feet..........	Lawrence.
Powder Mill; brook in Montgomery and Westfield, 7 miles long...	Granville.
Powder Mill; brook in Westfield, 3 miles long.................	Springfield.
Power Mills; village in Phillipston..............................	Winchendon.
Power Neck; in Yarmouth..	Yarmouth.
Powow; hill in Salisbury; elevation, 330 feet..................	Newburyport.
Powow; river on boundary between Salisbury and Amesbury and in Amesbury, tributary to Merrimac River............	Newburyport.
Pranker; pond in Saugus..	Boston.
Pratt; brook in Barre...	Barre.
Pratt; hill in town of Upton; elevation, 608 feet..............	Blackstone.
Pratt Junction; village and railroad junction in Sterling on Old Colony R. R..	Marlboro.
Pratt; pond in town of Upton....................................	Blackstone.
Prattville; village in Raynham on main line Old Colony R. R.	Taunton.
Prescott; town in Hampshire County; area, 17 square miles..	Belchertown.

	Atlas sheets.
Prescott; village in town of same name.....................	Belchertown.
Prescott; hill in town of Prescott; elevation, 1,100 feet	Belchertown.
Pride Crossing; village in southeastern part of Beverly......	Salem.
Priest; brook in Royalston	Winchendon.
Prince Head; point on southeast coast of Peddock Island in Boston Bay..	Boston Bay.
Prince; river in Barre, 7 miles long.............................	Barre.
Princeton; town in Worcester County; area, 36 square miles.	Worcester.
Princeton Center; village in Princeton........................	Worcester.
Proctor; brook tributary to North River in northern part of Peabody...	Salem.
Prospect; hill in town of Barre; elevation, 1,000 feet.........	Barre.
Prospect; hill in Waltham; elevation, 400 feet................	Framingham.
Prospect; hill in Westminster; elevation, 1,220 feet	Fitchburg.
Prospect; hill in town of Gardner; elevation, 1,200 feet	Fitchburg.
Prospect; hill in eastern part of South Hadley; elevation, 300 feet	Northampton.
Prospect; hill in Chilmark, Marthas Vineyard; elevation, 308 feet...	Gay Head.
Prospect; hill in Auburn; elevation, 860 feet	Webster.
Prospect; hill in Charlton; elevation, 925 feet................	Webster.
Prospect; hill in Taunton; elevation, 200 feet	Taunton.
Prospect; hill in West Springfield; elevation, 380 feet........	Springfield.
Prospect; hill in northwestern part of Mount Washington; elevation, 1,900 feet	Sheffield.
Prospect; hill in southeast part of Hingham..................	Abington.
Prospect; hill in Phillipston; elevation, 1,380 feet............	Winchendon.
Prospect; hill in southeastern part of Rowley; elevation, 264 feet...	Salem.
Prospect; hill in Plympton; elevation, 100 feet................	Middleboro.
Prospect; hill in Groton; elevation, 503 feet	Groton.
Prospect; hill in Harvard; elevation, 557 feet..................	Groton.
Prospect; hill in Westford; elevation, 440 feet	Lowell.
Prospect; hill in Tewksbury; elevation, 340 feet..............	Lawrence.
Prospect; lake containing 140 acres in northwestern part of Egremont	Sheffield.
Prospect Hill; pond on eastern boundary of Taunton..........	Taunton.
Prospectville; village in Waltham.............................	Framingham.
Provens; mountain in Agawam; altitude, 640 feet	Springfield.
Providence; hill in Westford; elevation, 360 feet..............	Lowell.
Providence and Worcester; railroad connecting Worcester with Providence, R. I.	
Provincetown; town in Barnstable County; area, 11 square miles	Provincetown.
Provincetown; principal settlement within town of same name.	Provincetown.
Pudding; brook in eastern part of Pembroke..................	Abington.
Puffer; pond in Maynard......................................	Framingham.
Pulpit; hill in northern part of Amherst; elevation, 340 feet ...	Northampton.
Pulpit Rock; hill in Rowe......................................	Hawley.
Pumpkin; brook in Townsend and Shirley, 1 mile long, tributary to Squannacook River	Groton.
Punch; brook in Greenfield and Shelburne, 2 miles long, tributary to Green River..	Greenfield.
Punch; brook in Fitchburg	Fitchburg.

A GEOGRAPHIC DICTIONARY OF MASSACHUSETTS. 91

Atlas sheets.

Punkatasset; hill in Concord; elevation, 300 feet	Framingham.
Purgatory; brook in Sutton; flows into Whitin Pond	Blackstone.
Purgatory; brook in Norwood and Dedham, 3 miles long, tributary to Neponset River	Dedham.
Purgatory Chasm; gorge in town of Sutton	Blackstone.
Purge; brook in Pelham, 2 miles long, flows into Swift River	Belchertown.
Putnam; brook in Chelmsford, 1 mile long, tributary to river Meadowbrook	Lowell.
Putnam; hill in Buckland; elevation, 1,220 feet	Hawley.
Putnam; hill in northern part of Danvers; elevation, 200 feet	Salem.
Putnam; hill in Sutton; elevation, 783 feet	Webster.
Putnamsville; village in northeastern part of Danvers	Salem.
Pye; brook in Boxford and Topsfield	Salem.
Quabin; hill in Enfield; elevation, 1,020 feet	Belchertown.
Quaboag; river tributary to Chicopee River, in southern part of the State.	Worcester. Brookfield. Palmer.
Quaboag; pond in Brookfield	Brookfield.
Quacker Run; creek which flows into Poponesset Bay, in southeast part of Mashpee	Barnstable.
Quaker; brook in Berkley, 1¼ miles long	Taunton.
Quamquisset; harbor in southwestern coast of Falmouth	Falmouth.
Quaquechan; river, arm of Watuppa Pond, extending into city of Fall River	Fall River.
Quarantine Rocks; islands south of Rainsford Island, in Boston Bay	Boston Bay.
Queen; brook in west part of Pembroke	Abington.
Queen Anns Corners; village in western part of South Scituate	Abington.
Quicks Hole; harbor between islands of Pasque and Nashawena, in town of Gosnold	Gay Head.
Quicksand; point on southwest coast of Westport	Sakonnet.
Quinapoxet; pond in Princeton and Holden	Worcester.
Quincy; city in Norfolk County; area, 18 square miles	Boston. Boston Bay. Dedham. Abington.
Quincy; village in town of same name	Abington. Dedham.
Quincy; bay east of town of Quincy; opens into Boston Harbor.	Boston.
Quincy Center; village in town of Quincy, on Old Colony R. R.	Boston.
Quincy Neck; peninsula in eastern part of Quincy	Abington.
Quinepoxet; river in Holden and West Boylston, 6 miles long; tributary to Nashua River	Worcester.
Quinepoxet; village in Holden	Worcester.
Quinsigamond; village in Worcester, on Providence and Worcester R. R.	Webster.
Quinsigamond; lake on southwestern boundary of Shrewsbury.	Worcester. Marlboro.
Quinsigamond; river, outlet of Quinsigamond Lake, in Grafton; flows into Blackstone River	Blackstone.
Quivett; creek on boundary between Brewster and Dennis; flows into Cape Cod Bay.	Yarmouth. Wellfleet.

	Atlas sheets.
Quivett Neck; peninsula on north coast of Dennis	Wellfleet.
Quohog; point extending into Katama Bay, in Edgartown, Marthas Vineyard	Marthas Vineyard.
Quostinet; river rising in Mashpee and flowing into Waquoit Bay	Falmouth.
Raccoon; hill in town of Barre; elevation, 1,040 feet	Barre.
Raccoon; island off east coast of Quincy	Boston Bay.
Race; mountain in southeastern part of Mount Washington; altitude, 2,395 feet	Sheffield.
Race; point, most western extremity of Cape Cod, in Provincetown	Provincetown.
Race Point; life-saving station upon Race Point, Provincetown	Provincetown.
Race Point; light-house upon Race Point, Provincetown	Provincetown.
Race Run; head of inlet or lagoon back of Race Point, in Provincetown	Provincetown.
Rag Rock; hill in Woburn	Boston.
Ragged; hill in West Brookfield; elevation, 1,227 feet	Barre.
Ragged; island in Hingham Harbor	Boston Bay.
Railtree; hill in Carlisle; elevation, 400 feet	Lowell.
Railcut; hill in eastern part of Gloucester; elevation, 160 feet.	Gloucester.
Rainsford; island east of south part of Long Island, in Boston Bay	Boston Bay.
Ram; island in Sippican Harbor, off south coast of Marion	Falmouth.
Ram; island east of south coast of Marblehead	Boston Bay.
Ram; island in Merrimac River	Newburyport.
Ram; island in Buzzards Bay, south of Mattapoiset Neck	New Bedford.
Ram; islands south of entrance to Manchester Harbor	Salem.
Ram Head Bar; reef of rocks in Boston Bay	Boston Bay.
Ramshorn; brook in Millbury, 2 miles long	Webster.
Ramshorn; pond in Millbury and Sutton	Webster.
Randolph; town in Norfolk County; area, 10 square miles	Dedham.
Randolph; village in town of same name, on Old Colony R. R.	Dedham.
Range; light-house on Plum Island	Newburyport.
Rattlesnake; hill on boundary between Lunenburg and Townsend	Fitchburg.
Rattlesnake; hill in Stockbridge; elevation, 1,540 feet	Pittsfield.
Rattlesnake; hill in Dana; elevation, 840 feet	Belchertown.
Rattlesnake; hill in Sharon; elevation, 420 feet	Dedham.
Rattlesnake; hill in New Salem; elevation, 860 feet	Warwick.
Raven; brook in Middleboro and Halifax; 3 miles long	Middleboro.
Ray; hill in town of Gardner; elevation, 1,200 feet	Fitchburg.
Rayberry; hill in Leominster; elevation, 1,020 feet	Fitchburg.
Raynham; town in Bristol County; area, 21 square miles	Taunton.
Raynham; village in town of same name	Taunton.
Reading; town in Middlesex County; area 10 square miles	Lawrence.
Reading; principal village in town of same name, on main line of Boston and Maine R. R.	Lawrence.
Reading Highlands; high ground at and around village of Reading, in town of Reading; from 100 to 200 feet high	Lawrence.
Reading Highlands; railway station on main line Boston and Maine R. R., in Reading	Lawrence.
Readville; village in Hyde Park	Dedham.

GANNETT.] A GEOGRAPHIC DICTIONARY OF MASSACHUSETTS. 93

Atlas sheets.

Red; brook in Southampton, 2 miles long; tributary to Manhan River... Springfield.
Red; brook in Falmouth and Mashpee, flowing into Waquoit Bay .... Falmouth.
Red; river on boundary between Chatham and Harwich...... Yarmouth.
Red Bridge; station in Ludlow, on Springfield, Athol and Northeastern Branch of Boston and Albany R. R................. Palmer.
Red Brook; harbor of Buzzards Bay, indenting southwest coast of Bourne.. Falmouth.
Red Brush; hill in Wrentham; elevation, 440 feet............. Franklin.
Red Oak; hill in south part of Westhampton.................. Chesterfield.
Red Oak; hill in Merrimac; elevation, 308 feet................ Haverhill.
Reed; pond in Nantucket....................................... Nantucket.
Reed; island in Great Quittacas Pond, Lakeville and Middleboro .... Middleboro.
Reedy Meadow; brook in Pepperell and Groton, 2 miles long; tributary to Nashua River.................................. Groton.
Reeves; hill in Wayland; elevation, 400 feet................... Framingham.
Rehoboth; town in Bristol County; area, 47 square miles.... { Taunton. Providence.
Rehoboth; village in town of same name....................... Providence.
Remington; mountain in western part of Cummington......... Chesterfield.
Reservoir Marsh; pond on northern boundary of Wrentham.. Franklin.
Revere; town in Suffolk County; area, 7 square miles......... { Boston. Boston Bay.
Revere; beach along coast of Revere............................ Boston Bay.
Revere; brook in southern part of Lynn........................ Boston Bay.
Revere Beach; railway station on Revere Beach............... Boston Bay.
Rice; hill in Rutland; elevation, 1,260 feet..................... Worcester.
Rice Crossing; railway crossing on Boston and Albany R. R., in Wellesley... Framingham.
Richardson; brook in Dracut, 2 miles long.................... Lowell.
Richardson; pond in Woburn.................................... Lawrence.
Richmond; town in Berkshire County; area, 17 square miles.. Pittsfield.
Richmond; village in town of same name, on Boston and Albany R. R... Pittsfield.
Richmond; hill in Dighton; elevation, 180 feet................. Taunton.
Richmond; pond on boundary between Pittsfield and Richmond.. Pittsfield.
Richmond Furnace; village in town of Richmond, on Boston and Albany R. R... Pittsfield.
Ricketson; point in eastern part of Dartmouth, extending southward between Clark Cove and Apponagansett Harbor. New Bedford.
Rider; cove, connecting on southwest with Bassing Harbor.. Chatham.
Ridge; hill in Plympton... Middleboro.
Ridge; hill in Barre; elevation, 1,140 feet...................... Barre.
Ring; hill on north boundary of Amesbury; elevation, 280 feet Newburyport.
Ringville; village in Worthington.............................. Chesterfield.
Ripley; creek in Edgartown, Marthas Vineyard............... Marthas Vineyard.
River Meadow; brook in Chelmsford and Lowell, 6 miles long; tributary to Concord River.................................. Lowell.
Riverdale; village in West Springfield......................... Springfield.
Riverdale; village on Mill River, in Gloucester................ Gloucester.

	Atlas sheets.
Riverdale; village in town of Northbridge, on Providence and Worcester R. R.	Blackstone.
Riverside; village in Haverhill	Haverhill.
Riverside Station; village in Newton, on Boston and Albany R. R.	Framingham.
Roaring; brook in Freetown	Middleboro.
Roaring; brook, outlet of Clapp Pond in Washington, flowing into Housatonic River	Becket.
Roaring; brook in Chester, tributary to Westfield River	Chesterfield.
Roaring; brook in Huntington and Montgomery, tributary to Westfield River.	{ Chesterfield. Granville.
Roaring; brook in Shutesbury and Leverett	Belchertown.
Roaring; brook, branch of Mill River, in southern part of Conway	Northampton.
Roaring; brook, branch of Hoosic River, in northern part of Williamstown	Greylock.
Robb; hill in Lunenburg; elevation, 446 feet	Groton.
Robbin; hill in Chelmsford; elevation, 440 feet	Lowell.
Robbin; pond in southeast part of East Bridgewater	Abington.
Robbin; pond in Harwich	Yarmouth.
Robbin; pond in Harvard	Groton.
Robert; brook in northwestern part of Northampton	Northampton.
Robert; hill in northwestern part of Northampton; elevation, 500 feet	Northampton.
Robert; station in Weston on Massachusetts Central R. R.	Framingham.
Robert Meadow; brook in north part of Westhampton	Chesterfield.
Robinson; brook in Pepperell, 3 miles long; tributary to Nashua River	Groton.
Robinson; creek in north part of Pembroke	Abington.
Robinson Hole; between islands of Naushon and Pasque	Gay Head.
Robinsonville; village in North Attleboro	Providence.
Rochdale; village in town of Northbridge, on Providence and Worcester R. R	Blackstone.
Rochdale; village in Leicester, on Boston and Albany R. R.	Webster.
Rochdale; pond in Leicester	Webster.
Roche Run; in northwest part of Pembroke	Abington.
Rochester; town in southwestern part of Plymouth County; Indian name, Menchoisett; area, 37 square miles.	{ Middleboro. New Bedford.
Rochester; village in southern part of town of same name	New Bedford.
Rock; creek on boundary line between Eastham and Orleans, one-half mile long	Wellfleet.
Rock; creek in Orleans, one-half mile long; flows into Cape Cod Bay	Wellfleet.
Rock; island south of Marion, in Ancoot Cove	New Bedford.
Rock; hill in Northboro; elevation, 440 feet	Marlboro.
Rock; pond in Georgetown	Lawrence.
Rock Bottom; village in Stow	Marlboro.
Rock Harbor; village in town of Orleans	Wellfleet.
Rock Island; cove on east coast of Quincy	Boston Bay.
Rock Meadow; brook in Mendon and Uxbridge, tributary to Blackstone River	Blackstone.
Rock Rimmon; hill in Belchertown; elevation, 840 feet	Palmer.

A GEOGRAPHIC DICTIONARY OF MASSACHUSETTS.

Atlas sheets.

Rock Station; village in town of Middleboro, on Old Colony R. R., Cape Cód Branch	Middleboro.
Rock Valley; in Holyoke	Springfield.
Rockdale; village in western part of New Bedford	New Bedford.
Rockland; town in Plymouth County; area, 11 square miles	Abington.
Rockport; town on eastern extremity of Cape Ann; area, 7 square miles	Gloucester.
Rockport; village in town of same name on Sandy Bay	Gloucester.
Rockville; village in Millis on New York and New England R. R., Woonsocket division	Franklin.
Rockville; village in Haverhill	Haverhill.
Rocky; brook in Sterling and Douglas, 2 miles long; tributary to Stillwater River	Webster. Worcester.
Rocky; hill in Chelmsford; elevation, 220 feet	Lowell.
Rocky; hill in Groton; elevation, 460 feet	Groton.
Rocky; hill in Oxford; elevation, 840 feet	Webster.
Rocky; hill on boundary line between Winchendon and Ashburnham; elevation, 1,400 feet	Fitchburg.
Rocky; point, southern extremity of West Island, in Fairhaven	New Bedford.
Rocky; point on coast of Plymouth	Plymouth.
Rocky; pond in Boylston	Marlboro.
Rocky; pond in Leominster	Fitchburg.
Rocky; pond in southern part of Plymouth	Plymouth.
Rocky Meadow; brook in Middleboro	Middleboro.
Rocky Neck; island in head of Gloucester Harbor, between Gloucester City and East Gloucester	Gloucester.
Rocky Run; brook in Rehoboth and Swansea	Taunton.
Rocky Woods; hills on northeast boundary of Medfield, respectively 300 and 400 feet high	Franklin.
Roger; island in northeastern part of Ipswich surrounded by waters of Rowley River	Salem.
Rollston; hill in Fitchburg; elevation, 820 feet	Fitchburg.
Romp Hole; shallow boat anchorage in north end of Monomoy Island	Chatham.
Rooly Plain; village in western part of Rowley	Salem.
Root; pond in southwestern part of Great Barrington	Sheffield.
Rope; island in New Bedford Harbor opposite city of New Bedford	New Bedford.
Roslindale; village in city of Boston on Boston and Providence R. R.	Boston.
Round; cove in northeastern coast of West Island in Fairhaven	New Bedford.
Round; hill in Northfield; elevation, 1,240 feet	Warwick.
Round; hill in Sudbury	Framingham.
Round; hill in Southwick; elevation, 320 feet	Granville.
Round; island between West Island and Sconticut Neck, in Fairhaven	New Bedford.
Round; pond in northwestern part of Great Barrington	Sheffield.
Round; pond in west central part of Barnstable County	Barnstable.
Round; pond in Truro	Wellfleet.
Round; pond in Plymouth	Plymouth.
Round; pond in Haverhill	Haverhill.
Round; cove at head of Pleasant Bay, between Orleans and Chatham	Chatham.

	Atlas sheets.
Round; pond in Tewksbury.	Lawrence.
Round Hill; point on southeastern coast of Dartmouth.	New Bedford.
Round Meadow; brook in Mendon, tributary to Mill River.	Blackstone.
Round Rocks; mountain peak in western part of Cheshire; elevation, 2,480 feet.	Greylock.
Round Top; hill in Athol; elevation, 1,260 feet.	Winchendon.
Round Top; hill in Chester; elevation, 1,785 feet.	Chesterfield.
Rowe; town in Franklin County; area, 25 square miles.	Hawley.
Rowe Center; village in town of Rowe.	Hawley.
Rowe Lot; hill in Shelburn; elevation, 819 feet.	Greenfield.
Rowley; seaboard town on eastern coast of Essex County; area, 19 square miles.	Salem.
Rowley; village in southeastern part of town of same name.	Salem.
Rowley; river in northeastern part of Essex County, forming portion of boundary line between Ipswich and Rowley, and flowing into Plum Island River.	Salem.
Rowley; station in southeastern part of Rowley on Boston and Maine R. R.	Salem.
Roxbury; part of city of Boston.	Boston.
Royalston; town in Worcester County; area, 44 square miles.	{ Winchendon. Warwick. }
Royalston Center; village in town of Royalston.	Winchendon.
Rudd; pond near central part of Becket.	Becket.
Ruggles; creek in eastern part of Quincy.	Abington.
Ruggles; hill in Hardwick; elevation, 1,040 feet.	Barre.
Rumford; river in Mansfield and Norton; flows into Three-Mile River.	Taunton.
Run; brook in Sudbury.	Framingham.
Run; pond in Dennis.	Yarmouth.
Running Gutter; brook in northeastern part of Northampton.	Northampton.
Ruralville; village in Holden.	Worcester.
Russ; pond in Prescott.	Belchertown.
Russell; town in Hampden County; area, 18 square miles.	Granville.
Russell; village in town of same name.	Granville.
Russellville; village in Southampton.	Granville.
Rutland; town in Worcester County; area, 38 square miles.	{ Worcester. Barre. }
Rutland; brook in town of Petersham, 2 miles long.	Barre.
Rutland Center; village in town of Rutland.	Worcester.
Sachacha; pond in Nantucket.	Nantucket.
Sachem; spring in Tisbury, Marthas Vineyard.	Marthas Vineyard.
Sacker; brook in Pepperell, 2¼ miles long; tributary to Nissitissit River.	Groton.
Sacket; brook tributary to Housatonic River in Hinsdale and Pittsfield.	Becket.
Saco; pond in northwestern part of Brimfield.	Brookfield.
Saddle; mountain in southwestern part of North Adams; altitude, 3,040 feet.	Greylock.
Saddle Rock; mountain in western part of New Ashford; altitude, 3,240 feet.	Greylock.
Sagamore; hill in Bourne.	Plymouth.
Sagamore Head; point of land 80 feet high on southeast coast of Hull.	Boston Bay.

	Atlas sheets.
Saguish Head; point of land at entrance to Duxbury Harbor, Duxbury	Plymouth.
Sailor; island in Hingham Harbor	Boston Bay.
Salem; city in southern part of Essex County; area, 9 square miles.	{ Boston Bay. Salem.
Salem; harbor in southern part of Essex County between Marblehead and Salem	Salem.
Salem; reservoir on hill about one-half mile north of Salem in Beverly	Salem.
Salem and Lawrence; part of Boston and Maine Railroad system.	
Salem and Lowell; part of Boston and Maine Railroad system.	
Salem Neck; peninsula on northeastern coast of Salem	Salem.
Salisbury; town in Essex County; area, 18 square miles	Newburyport.
Salisbury; village in town of same name on Boston and Maine R. R.	Newburyport.
Salisbury Beach; village in town of Salisbury	Newburyport.
Salisbury Plain; river in Norfolk and Bristol counties	{ Dedham. Abington.
Salisbury Point; village in town of Salisbury	Newburyport.
Salmon; brook in Dunstable	Lowell.
Salmon Falls; village in town of Russell on Boston and Albany R. R.	Granville.
Salt; island off eastern coast of Gloucester	Gloucester.
Salt; pond in southwestern part of Falmouth	Falmouth.
Salt; pond on southern coast of Harwich	Yarmouth.
Salt; pond in Plymouth	Plymouth.
Salt Island Ledge; islet off eastern coast of Gloucester	Gloucester.
Salt Meadow; marsh in Truro	Provincetown.
Salten; point on north of Barnstable, extending into Barnstable Harbor	Barnstable.
Salter; point on southeastern coast of Dartmouth	New Bedford.
Sampson; brook in northern part of Kingston flowing into Blackwater Pond	Duxbury.
Sampson; brook in Carver	Middleboro.
Sampson; cove in Assawompsett pond in Lakeville	Middleboro.
Sampson; hill on Chappaquiddick Island in Edgartown, Marthas Vineyard	Marthas Vineyard
Sampson; island at entrance of Osterville Harbor, southwest of Barnstable	Barnstable.
Sampson; island off south coast of Orleans	Wellfleet.
Sampson; pond in Carver	{ Middleboro. Plymouth.
Sand; brook in Fitchburg	Fitchburg.
Sand; pond in Harwich	Yarmouth.
Sandersdale; village in Southbridge	Brookfield.
Sanderson; brook in Chester and Blandford, 2 miles long; tributary to Westfield River	Granville.
Sandisfield; town in southeastern part of Berkshire County; area, 54 square miles	Sandisfield.
Sandisfield; village in central part of town of same name	Sandisfield.
Sandwich; town in western part of Barnstable County, bordering on Cape Cod Bay; area, 44 square miles.	{ Barnstable. Falmouth.

	Atlas sheets.
Sandwich; principal village in town of same name	Barnstable. Plymouth.
Sandy; bay in northeastern coast of Rockport	Gloucester.
Sandy; brook in Burlington, tributary to Vine Brook	Boston.
Sandy; brook tributary to Farmington River, rising in Sandisfield, flowing southeasterly into Connecticut	Sandisfield.
Sandy; pond in Lincoln	Framingham.
Sandy; pond in southern part of Plymouth	Plymouth.
Sandy; pond in Ayer	Groton.
Sandy Neck; low sand beach on north of Barnstable	Barnstable.
Sandy Neck; light at entrance to Barnstable Harbor	Barnstable.
Sandy Pond; station on Boston and Lowell R.R., Stony Brook branch, in Groton	Groton.
Sankaty Head; light-house on east coast of Nantucket	Nantucket.
Sason; island in Sengekontacket Pond, Marthas Vineyard, opens into Vineyard Sound	Marthas Vineyard.
Sassaquin; pond in northern part of New Bedford	New Bedford.
Satucket; river in southern part of East Bridgewater	Abington.
Saugus; town in Essex County; area 12 square miles	Boston. Boston Bay.
Saugus; principal village in town of same name on Saugus branch of Boston and Maine R. R.	Boston.
Saugus; river in Essex and Middlesex counties, flowing into Lynn Harbor; is about 15 miles long	Lawrence. Boston. Boston Bay.
Savin; hill in city of Boston	Boston.
Savory; pond in Plymouth	Plymouth.
Savoy; town in northeastern part of Berkshire County; area 36 square miles.	Hawley. Greylock.
Savoy Hollow; village in southern part of Savoy	Greylock.
Sawdy; pond in western part of Westfield	Fall River.
Saw Mill; brook in Leverett	Warwick.
Saw Mill; brook in Concord, 1 mile long; flows into Concord River	Framingham.
Saw Mill; brook in Bridgewater, tributary to Taunton River, 2 miles long	Middleboro.
Saw Mill; hills in western part of Northampton, highest point being 740 feet	Northampton.
Saw Mill; river in Montague, 7 miles long, tributary to Connecticut River	Greenfield.
Saw Mill; river in Leverett	Belchertown.
Sawyer; hill in Berlin	Marlboro.
Saxonville; village in town of Framingham on Saxonville branch Boston and Albany R. R.	Framingham.
Scantic; village in Hampden	Palmer.
Scantic; brook in Hampden and Monson	Palmer.
Scargo; hill in Dennis	Yarmouth.
Scargo; lake in Dennis	Yarmouth.
Scarlet; brook in Tyngsboro and Lowell, 1 mile long, tributary to Merrimac River	Lowell.
Schenob; brook, branch of Housatonic River in Sheffield	Sheffield.
Schoolhouse; pond in Brewster	Wellfleet.
Scituate; seaboard town in northeastern part of Plymouth County; area 27 square miles.	Abington. Duxbury.

A GEOGRAPHIC DICTIONARY OF MASSACHUSETTS. 99

	Atlas sheets.
Scituate; village in town of same name	Abington.
Scituate; harbor on east coast of Scituate between Crow Point and Cedar Point	Duxbury
Scituate; hill in Cohasset	Abington.
Scituate Harbor; village in eastern part of Scituate	Duxbury.
Scituate Neck; peninsula in northeast part of Scituate	Abington.
Sconticut; point, southern extremity of Sconticut Neck, Fair Haven	New Bedford.
Sconticut Neck; peninsula on southern coast of Fair Haven, extending southeasterly into Buzzards Bay	New Bedford.
Scorton Harbor; creek north of Sandwich flowing into Cape Cod Bay	Barnstable.
Scorton Neck; reef covered with sand hills on south shore of Cape Cod Bay, in town of Sandwich	Barnstable.
Scotland; village in town of Bridgewater	Taunton.
Scotland; hill in Reading; elevation, 160 feet	Lawrence.
Scotland; hill on boundary between Haverhill and Methuen	Haverhill.
Scott; brook in Fitchburg	Fitchburg.
Scott; hill in central part of Ipswich; elevation, 180 feet	Salem.
Scott; reservoir in Fitchburg	Fitchburg.
Scraggy Neck; island in eastern part of Buzzards Bay	Falmouth.
Scribner; hill in Tyngsboro; elevation, 400 feet	Lowell.
Scudding; pond in Taunton	Taunton.
Seal; island in Buzzards Bay south of Mattapoisett Neck	New Bedford.
Seal; island in Merrimac River	Newburyport.
Sear; pond in Yarmouth	Yarmouth.
Searsville; village in west part of Williamsburg	{ Northampton. Chesterfield.
Second; brook in Buckland, 1 mile long, flows into Deerfield River	Hawley.
Second; pond in Ludlow	Palmer.
Second; branch of Connecticut River in eastern part of Franklin County	Northampton.
Second; branch of Jones River in Kingston	Plymouth.
Second Herring; brook in eastern part of South Scituate	Abington.
Seekonk; town in Bristol County; area 19 square miles	Providence.
Seekonk; village in town of same name	Providence.
Seekonk; brook tributary to Green River in western part of Great Barrington	Sheffield.
Seekonk; river in Alford	Pittsfield.
Sengekontacket; pond in Cottage City and Edgartown, Marthas Vineyard	Marthas Vineyard.
Serganset; river in Taunton and Dighton, 6 miles long, tributary to Taunton River	Taunton.
Seven Mile; river in Attleboro and North Attleboro, flows into Ten Mile River	Providence.
Seven Mile; river tributary to Quaboag River in Spencer	{ Brookfield. Barre.
Sewammock Neck; peninsula in southern part of Somerset, between Lees and Taunton rivers	Fall River.
Seymour; brook in Granville, 1 mile long	Granville.
Seymour; mountain in southeastern part of Sandisfield; altitude, 1,693 feet	Sandisfield.

	Atlas sheets.
Seymour; pond on southern boundary of Brewster	Yarmouth.
Shag Rocks; rocky islets near Boston Light in Boston Bay	Boston Bay.
Shaker; brook in Hancock and Pittsfield, 2 miles long	Pittsfield.
Shaker; village in Shirley	Groton.
Shaker; village in town of Harvard	Groton.
Shaker; village in Pittsfield	Pittsfield.
Shaker Mill; pond in West Stockbridge	Pittsfield.
Shakum; pond on southern boundary of Framingham	Framingham.
Shallow; pond in Falmouth	Falmouth.
Shallow; pond east of Great Pond, Barnstable	Barnstable.
Shallow; pond in Plymouth	Plymouth.
Shank Pooder; pond in Provincetown	Provincetown.
Sharon; town in Norfolk County; area 25 square miles	Dedham.
Sharon; village in town of same name on Boston and Providence R. R	Dedham.
Sharon Heights; village in town of Sharon on Boston and Providence R. R	Dedham.
Shatterack; brook in Montgomery and Russell, 2 miles long, tributary to Westfield River	Granville.
Shatterack; mountain in town of Montgomery; altitude, 1,200 feet	Granville.
Shatterack, pond in Montgomery	Granville.
Shattuck; brook in Phillipston, 2 miles long; unites with Bigelow Brook to form Swift River	Winchendon.
Shattuck; brook in Leyden and Bernardston and in State of Vermont	Greenfield.
Shattuckville; village in Coleraine	Greenfield.
Shaving; brook in Middleboro	Middleboro.
Shaw; pond in Leicester	Worcester.
Shaw; pond in Ludlow	Palmer.
Shaw; pond in southwestern part of Becket	Becket.
Shawkemo; hill in Nantucket	Nantucket.
Shawshine; river in Essex and Middlesex counties, tributary to Merrimac River	Framingham. / Lawrence.
Sheep; island west of Hull in Boston Bay	Boston Bay.
Sheep; pond in Brewster	Yarmouth.
Sheep Pasture; hill in northeastern part of Manchester; elevation, 140 feet	Salem.
Sheffield; town in southern part of Berkshire County; area, 52 square miles	Sheffield.
Sheffield; village in central part of town of same name	Sheffield.
Sheffield Plain; village in central part of Sheffield	Sheffield.
Shelburne; town in Franklin County; area, 23 square miles	Greenfield.
Shelburne; village in town of same name	Greenfield.
Shelburne Falls; village in town of Shelburne	Greenfield.
Sheldon; hill in Leominster; elevation, 840 feet	Fitchburg.
Sheldonville; village in Wrentham	Franklin.
Shemo; point on coast of Nantucket, extending into Nantucket Harbor	Nantucket.
Shepard: brook in Franklin, tributary to Charles River, 2 miles long	Franklin.
Shepard; pond on western boundary of Foxboro	Franklin.
Shepardville; village in Wrentham	Franklin.
Shepardville; reservoir in Wentham	Franklin.

A GEOGRAPHIC DICTIONARY OF MASSACHUSETTS. 101

Atlas sheets.

Shepherd; brook in Buckland, 1¼ miles long; tributary to Cleason Brook .... Hawley.
Shepherd; cove in Assonet Bay, Freetown .... Taunton.
Shepherd; island in Connecticut River, between southern parts of Hadley and Northampton .... Northampton.
Sherborn; town in Middlesex County; area, 17 square miles. { Framingham. Franklin.
Sherborn; village in town of same name on Old Colony R. R., Framingham and Mansfield branch .... Franklin.
Shingle; brook in Shelburne and Deerfield, 3 miles long; flows into Deerfield River .... Greenfield.
Shingle; hill in southeasterly part of Williamsburg; altitude, 900 feet .... Northampton.
Shingle; hill in Shelburne; elevation, 890 feet .... Greenfield.
Shingle Island; river tributary to Westport River in northern part of Dartmouth .... Fall River.
Shingle Swamp; brook in Orange, 2 miles long .... Warwick.
Ship; pond in Plymouth .... Plymouth.
Shirley; town in Middlesex County; area, 16 square miles .... Groton.
Shirley; village in town of same name, on Fitchburg R. R. .... Groton.
Shirley; reservoir in towns of Shirley and Lunenburg .... Groton.
Shivenick; pond in southern part of Falmouth .... Falmouth.
Shoe String; hill in Marlboro; elevation, 540 feet .... Marlboro.
Shooters; island near north end of Monomoy Island .... Chatham.
Short; brook in Middleboro, 3¼ miles long; tributary to Tispaquin Pond .... Middleboro.
Short; creek in Tisbury, Marthas Vineyard; flows into Great Tisbury Pond .... Marthas Vineyard.
Shovelfull Shoal; about 1¼ miles southeast from Monomoy Point Light, Monomoy Island .... Chatham.
Shoves Neck; peninsula in Berkley .... Taunton.
Shrewsbury; town in Worcester County; area, 21 square miles. { Marlboro. Worcester.
Shrewsbury; village in town of same name .... Marlboro.
Shubart; pond in west central part of Barnstable .... Barnstable.
Shumatuscacant; river in eastern part of Abington .... Abington.
Shutesbury; town in Franklin County; area, 27 square miles. { Belchertown. Shutesbury.
Shutesbury; village in town of same name .... Belchertown.
Siasconset; village in Nantucket, on Nantucket R. R. .... Nantucket.
Sibley; reservoir in Sutton .... Webster.
Silver; brook in east part of Hanover .... Abington.
Silver; brook in towns of Barre and Petersham, 2 miles long .. Barre.
Silver; hill in Milford; elevation, 520 feet .... Blackstone.
Silver; hill in Haverhill; elevation, 278 feet .... Haverhill.
Silver; hill in Weston; elevation, 100 feet .... Framingham.
Silver; lake in south part of Pembroke .... Abington.
Silver; lake in northwest part of Kingston .... Abington.
Silver; lake in Grafton .... Blackstone.
Silver; lake in central part of Pittsfield .... Becket.
Silver; lake in Wilmington .... Lawrence.
Silver Branch; branch of Clam River, in Sandisfield .... Sandisfield.
Silver Lake; railway station on Boston and Lowell R. R., in Wilmington .... Lawrence.

	Atlas sheets.
Simmons; two ponds in Dennis	Yarmouth.
Simon; hill in central part of South Scituate	Abington.
Simon; pond in southern part of Sandisfield	Sandisfield.
Singletary; brook in Millbury, 1 mile long; tributary to Blackstone River	Webster.
Singletary; pond in Sutton and Millbury	Webster.
Sinking; pond in Acton	Framingham.
Sippican; village in Marion on Sippican Harbor	New Bedford.
Sippican; harbor, arm of Buzzards Bay, projecting into Marion	{ Falmouth. New Bedford.
Sippican Neck; peninsula about 2 miles long on southeast coast of Marion	Falmouth.
Sipson; island in Orleans	Chatham.
Sixteen Acres; village in town of Springfield	Palmer.
Skinequit; pond in Harwich	Yarmouth.
Skug; river in Andover and North Reading, flows into Martin Pond	Lawrence.
Sky; hill in Tyringham; elevation, 1,947 feet	Sandisfield.
Slab; brook in Southwick, 3 miles long; tributary to Great Brook	Granville.
Slate; island east of Grape Island in Boston Bay	Boston Bay.
Slater; reservoir in Charlton	Webster.
Sleep; hill on northwestern coast of Castle Neck; elevation, 120 feet	Salem.
Sligo; hill in Marlboro; elevation, 580 feet	Marlboro.
Slocum; brook tributary to Farmington River in southern part of Tolland	Sandisfield.
Slocum; river in southern part of Dartmouth, flowing into Buzzards Bay	New Bedford.
Slocum Neck; peninsula on southern coast of Dartmouth	New Bedford.
Sluice; brook in Shelburne, 2¼ miles long; tributary to North River	Greenfield.
Small; hill in Truro; elevation, 140 feet	Provincetown.
Small; pond in Kingston	Plymouth.
Small; pond in eastern part of Barnstable	Barnstable.
Smead; brook in Greenfield, 2 miles long; tributary to Green River	Greenfield.
Smelt Branch; stream in Kingston	Plymouth.
Smith; brook in Florida, tributary to Deerfield River; 1¼ miles long	Hawley.
Smith; brook in Hancock and Pittsfield, 4 miles long; flows into Housatonic branch of Housatonic River	Pittsfield.
Smith; brook in Barre, 1½ miles long	Barre.
Smith; village in town of Enfield, on Boston and Albany R. R., Athol branch	Barre.
Smith Ferry; ferry and village on Connecticut River about 3 miles below Ox Bow, between South Hadley and part of Northampton	Northampton.
Smith Neck; peninsula on southern coast of Dartmouth	New Bedford.
Smith Rocks; rocks lying on northeast coast of Scituate	Abington.
Smithville; village in Barre, on Ware River branch of Boston and Albany R. R.	Barre.
Snake; brook in Wayland and on its southern boundary, 2 miles long; flows into Lake Cochituate	Framingham.

A GEOGRAPHIC DICTIONARY OF MASSACHUSETTS. 103

Atlas sheets.

Snake; hill in Tewksbury; elevation, 140 feet .... Lawrence.
Snake; hill on boundary line between Ayer and Groton .... Groton.
Snake; hill in southern part of Beverly .... Salem.
Snake; hill in eastern part of Marshfield; elevation, 100 feet.. Duxbury.
Snake; island west of south coast of Winthrop .... Boston Bay.
Snake; pond in southwestern part of Sandwich .... Falmouth.
Snake Meadow; hill in Westford; elevation, 340 feet .... Lowell.
Snipatuit; pond in Rochester .... Middleboro.
Snow; pond in Rochester .... Middleboro.
Soapstone; hill in Petersham; elevation, 860 feet............. Belchertown.
Sodden; brook in eastern part of Westhampton .... Chesterfield.
Sodom; mountain in Southwick and Granville; altitude, 1,100 feet .... Granville.
Solomon; pond in Northboro .... Marlboro.
Somerset; town in west central part of Bristol County; area, 9 square miles. { Taunton. Fall River.
Somerset; village in town of same name .... Taunton.
Somerville; city in Middlesex County; area, 4 square miles... Boston.
Soughtfor; pond in Westford .... Lowell.
South; brook, tributary to Hoosic River, in southeastern part of Cheshire .... Greylock.
South; brook in Bridgewater, tributary to Town River; 3 miles long .... Middleboro.
South; mountain in Lenox; altitude, 1,870 feet .... Pittsfield.
South; mountain in Granville; altitude, 1,200 feet .... Granville.
South; pond in Plymouth .... Plymouth.
South; river in Conway, tributary to Deerfield River .... Greenfield.
South; river rising in Duxbury and flowing through Marshfield to the sea .... Duxbury.
South Acton; village in town of Acton, on Fitchburg R. R ... Framingham.
South Amherst; village in southeastern part of Amherst..... Northampton.
South Ashburnham; village in town of Ashburnham .... Fitchburg.
South Athol; village in town of Athol, on Boston and Albany R. R., Athol branch .... Warwick.
South Attleboro; village in town of Attleboro .... Providence.
South Bellingham; village in town of Bellingham .... Franklin.
South Berlin; village in town of Berlin .... Marlboro.
South Billerica; village in town of Billerica, on Boston and Lowell R. R., Billerica branch .... Lowell.
South Boston; part of city of Boston .... Boston.
South Brewster; village in town of Brewster .... Yarmouth.
South Charlton; village in town of Charlton .... Webster.
South Charlton; reservoir in town of Charlton .... Webster.
South Chatham; village in town of Chatham .... Yarmouth.
South Chelmsford; village in Chelmsford, on Framingham and Lowell R. R .... Lowell.
South Dartmouth; village in eastern part of Dartmouth ..... New Bedford.
South Deerfield; village in southern part of Deerfield .... Northampton
South Dennis; village in town of Dennis .... Yarmouth.
South Duxbury; village in southeastern part of Duxbury.... Duxbury.
South Duxbury; station on Old Colony R. R., in southeastern part of Duxbury .... Duxbury.
South Easton; village in town of Easton .... Dedham.
South Egremont; village in eastern part of Egremont .... Sheffield.

	Atlas sheets.
South Fitchburg; village in town of Fitchburg	Fitchburg.
South Framingham; village in town of Framingham, on Boston and Albany R. R	Framingham.
South Gardner; village in town of Gardner, on Fitchburg R. R., Worcester division	Fitchburg.
South Gardner; reservoir in town of Gardner	Fitchburg.
South Georgetown; village in southern part of Georgetown	Salem.
South Groveland; village in Groveland, on Boston and Maine R. R., Georgetown branch	Lawrence.
South Hadley, town in southern part of Hampshire County; area, 22 square miles.	{ Springfield. Northampton.
South Hadley; village in central part of town of same name	Northampton.
South Hadley Falls; village in town of South Hadley	Springfield.
South Hanover; village in south part of Hanover	Abington.
South Hanson; village in south central part of Hanson	Abington.
South Hanson; station in south part of Hanson	Abington.
South Harwich; village in town of Harwich	Yarmouth.
South Hawley; village in town of Hawley	Hawley.
South Hingham; village in south part of Hingham	Abington.
South Lancaster; village in town of Lancaster	Marlboro.
South Lawrence; part of city of Lawrence lying on south side of Merrimac River	Lawrence.
South Lee; village in town of Lee, on Housatonic R. R	Pittsfield.
South Leverett; village in town of Leverett	Belchertown.
South Lincoln; village in town of Lincoln	Framingham.
South Lynnfield; village in Lynnfield, on Wakefield branch of eastern division Boston and Maine R.R.	{ Salem. Lawrence.
South Marlboro; village in town of Marlboro, on Fitchburg R. R., Marlboro branch	Marlboro.
South Meadow; brook in Shrewsbury; flows into Lake Quinsigamond; 2 miles long	Marlboro.
South Meadow; brook in Carver, 6 miles long, tributary to Weweantic River	Middleboro.
South Middleboro; village in town of Middleboro, on Old Colony R. R., Cape Cod branch	Middleboro.
South Milford; village in town of Milford	Blackstone.
South Monson; village in town of Monson, on New London Northern R. R	Palmer.
South Natick; village in town of Natick	Framingham.
South Orleans; village in town of Orleans	Wellfleet.
South Pocasset; village in southwestern part of Bourne	Falmouth.
South Purchase; swamp in Middleboro	Middleboro.
South Quincy; village in east part of Quincy	Abington.
South Royalston; village in town of Royalston, on Fitchburg R. R	Winchendon.
South Salem; village in eastern part of Salem, on Salem Harbor	Salem.
South Sandisfield; village in southwestern part of Sandisfield	Sandisfield.
South Scituate; village in eastern part of town of same name.	Abington.
South Seekonk; village in town of Seekonk	Providence.
South Sherborn; village in town of Sherborn, on Old Colony R. R., Framingham and Mansfield branch	Franklin.
South Shrewsbury; village in town of Sherborn	Marlboro.
South Spencer; village in town of Spencer	Brookfield.

A GEOGRAPHIC DICTIONARY OF MASSACHUSETTS.

Atlas sheets.

South Sudbury; village in town of Sudbury, on Massachusetts Central R. R. .... Framingham.
South Sugar Loaf; point 709 feet high in southeastern part of Deerfield .... Northampton.
South Sutton; village in town of Sutton .... Blackstone.
South Truro; village in town of Truro .... Wellfleet.
South Wachusett; brook in Princeton, 5 miles long, flows into Quinapoxet Pond .... Worcester.
South Walpole; village in town of Walpole, on Old Colony R. R., Framingham and Mansfield branch .... Franklin.
South Wareham; village in town of Wareham, on Old Colony R. R., Cape Cod branch .... Middleboro.
South Wellfleet; village in town of Wellfleet, on Old Colony R. R., Cape Cod division .... Wellfleet.
South Westport; village in the eastern part of Westport ...... Fall River.
South Weymouth; village in southern part of Weymouth .. Abington.
South Williamstown; village in southern part of Williamstown .... Greylock.
South Wilmington Station; village in Woburn, on Boston and Lowell R. R .... Lawrence.
South Worthington; village in southeast part of Worthington .... Chesterfield.
South Yarmouth; village in town of Yarmouth .... Yarmouth.
Southampton; town in Hampshire County; area, 29 square miles { Chesterfield. Granville. Springfield.
Southampton; village in town of same name .... Springfield.
Southboro; town in Worcester County; area, 16 square miles. { Marlboro. Framingham.
Southboro; village in town of same name .... Marlboro.
Southbridge; town in Worcester County; area, 21 square miles Brookfield.
Southbridge; principal village in town of same name .... Brookfield.
Southfield; village in central part of New Marlboro .... Sandisfield.
Southville; village in town of Southboro, on Boston and Albany R. R .... Marlboro.
Southwick; town in Hampden County; area, 30 square miles. { Springfield. Granville.
Southwick; village in town of same name on New Haven and Northampton R. R. .... Granville.
Southwick; creek tributary to Hoosic River, in eastern part of Adams .... Greylock.
Southwick; hill in Southwick; elevation, 380 feet .... Granville.
Southwick Jog; a departure from a right line in south boundary of Massachusetts, by which a small rectangular area which, under the definition of the boundary would have formed part of Connecticut, was included in Massachusetts. This was done by the surveyors in running the line in accordance with the wish of Oliver Wolcott, who preferred to be under the jurisdiction of Massachusetts .... Granville.
Spark; hill in Westford; elevation, 400 feet .... Lowell.
Spaulding; brook in Westford, connects Key Pond with Sought-for Pond .... Powell.
Spectacle; island in Boston Bay, lying southeast of Boston ... Boston Bay.
Spectacle; pond in central part of Falmouth .... Falmouth.

	Atlas sheets.
Spectable; pond in Sandwich; area, about 150 acres	Barnstable.
Spectacle; pond, containing 113 acres, in northern part of Sandisfield	Sandisfield.
Spectacle; pond in Lancaster	Groton.
Spectacle; pond in Wareham	Plymouth.
Spectacle; pond in Wilbraham	Palmer.
Spectacle; two ponds in eastern part of New Salem	Warwick.
Spencer; town in Worcester County; area, 34 square miles	Worcester. Barre. Webster. Brookfield.
Spencer; village in town of same name, on Boston and Albany R. R.	Brookfield. Webster.
Spencer; brook in Concord and Carlisle, 3 miles long	Lowell. Framingham.
Spencer Center; village in town of Spencer	Worcester.
Spickett; mountain in northern part of Lynn	Boston Bay.
Spickett; river in Methuen and Lawrence	Lawrence.
Spindle; hill in Stow; elevation, 400 feet	Marlboro.
Spofford; pond in Boxford	Lawrence.
Spoon; hill in Marlboro; elevation, 480 feet	Marlboro.
Spooner; pond in northern part of Plymouth	Plymouth.
Spot; pond in Stoneham	Boston.
Sprague; hill in north part of Bridgewater	Abington.
Spring; brook in Bedford	Framingham.
Spring; brook in Mendon	Blackstone.
Spring; brook in Bridgewater, tributary to Taunton River, 1 mile long	Middleboro.
Spring; brook in Bedford	Lowell.
Spring; creek flowing from Great Marshes into Barnstable Harbor	Barnstable.
Spring; lake in Needham	Framingham.
Spring; pond in Groton	Groton.
Spring; pond in southwest part of Salem	Boston Bay.
Spring Hill; stream in north part of Sandwich, flowing into Cape Cod Bay	Barnstable.
Spring Hill; beach in north part of Sandwich	Barnstable.
Springfield; city in Hampden County; area, 36 square miles	Springfield. Palmer.
Springfield; reservoir in Ludlow	Palmer.
Springfield, Athol, and Northern; part of Boston and Albany Railroad system, running northeastward from Springfield and Athol.	
Springville; village in Winchendon	Winchendon.
Spruce; hill in west part of Westhampton	Chesterfield.
Spruce; hill in southwestern part of Florida; elevation, 2,588 feet	Greylock.
Spurr; lake in Sheffield	Sheffield.
Sky; pond in Abington	Boston.
Squam; pond in Nantucket	Nantucket.
Squam; river in central part of Gloucester, connecting Annisquam Harbor with Gloucester Harbor	Gloucester.
Squam Head; point on east coast of Nantucket	Nantucket.

A GEOGRAPHIC DICTIONARY OF MASSACHUSETTS.

Atlas sheets.

Squam Light; fifth order, fixed white light at east entrance of Annisquam Harbor on Wigwam Point, Gloucester; lantern 50 feet high, visible 12¼ miles .... Gloucester.
Squannacook; river in Townsend and Shirley .... Groton.
Squannakonk; swamp in Rehoboth .... Taunton.
Squantum; village in Quincy .... Boston.
Squash Meadow; pond in Cottage City, Marthas Vineyard ... Marthas Vineyard.
Squaw; island at east entrance of New Harbor .... Barnstable.
Squibnocket; village in town of Chilmark, Marthas Vineyard. Gay Head.
Squibnocket; beach on coast of Gay Head and Chilmark, Marthas Vineyard .... Gay Head.
Squibnocket; hill in Chilmark, Marthas Vineyard .... Gay Head.
Squibnocket; pond in Gay Head and Chilmark, Marthas Vineyard .... Gay Head.
Squirrel; hill in north part of Hingham .... Abington.
Stacey; brook in southeast part of Lynn .... Boston Bay.
Stage; harbor in southern shore of Chatham, entered from Vineyard Sound .... Chatham.
Stanley; island in Merrimac River .... Haverhill.
State Line; village on boundary line between Canaan, N. Y., and West Stockbridge, Mass., on Boston and Albany R. R . Pittsfield.
State Line; station on New London Northern R. R., in Monson. Palmer.
State Muster Grounds; in Framingham .... Framingham.
Steele; brook in Rowe, 1½ miles long, flows into Pelham Brook. Hawley.
Steep; brook in northwestern part of Fall River, flowing into Taunton River .... Fall River.
Steep Brook; village in northwestern part of Fall River, on Taunton River .... Fall River.
Steep Gutter; brook in Barre, 2 miles long .... Barre.
Steep Rock; village in Natick .... Framingham.
Steerage Rock; hill in Brimfield; elevation, 1,240 feet .... Brookfield.
Sterling; town in Worcester County; area, 33 square miles ... { Marlboro. Worcester.
Sterling; mountain in northern part of Mount Washington; altitude, 1,960 feet .... Sheffield.
Sterling Camp Grounds; near Sterling Junction, in Sterling . Worcester.
Sterling Center; village in Sterling on Fitchburg R. R .... Worcester.
Sterling Junction; village and railway junction in Sterling .. Worcester.
Stetson; pond in southwest part of Pembroke .... Abington.
Steven; brook in Barre and Rutland, 1¼ miles long .... Barre.
Steven; brook in Holland .... Brookfield.
Steven; brook in north part of Worthington .... Chesterfield.
Steven; pond in Lawrence .... Lawrence.
Steward; island east of Marion, in Sippican Harbor .... New Bedford.
Steward; pond in Barnstable .... Barnstable.
Stile; pond in Boxford .... Lawrence.
Stile; reservoir in Spencer and Leicester .... Webster.
Still; brook in Agawam .... Springfield.
Still; river in Bolton and Harvard, 2 miles long, tributary to Nashua River .... Marlboro.
Still River; village in town of Harvard .... Marlboro.
Still River; station in Harvard, on Boston and Maine R. R.... Marlboro.
Stillwater; river in Princeton, Sterling, and West Boylston, 5 miles long, tributary to Nashua River .... Worcester.

	Atlas sheets.
Stirrup, brook in Northboro	Marlboro.
Stirrup; hill in Marlboro; elevation, 454 feet	Marlboro.
Stockbridge; town in Berkshire County; area, 24 square miles.	Pittsfield.
Stockbridge; village in town of same name	Pittsfield.
Stockbridge Bowl; pond in town of Stockbridge	Pittsfield.
Stoddard; pond in Winchendon	Winchendon.
Stodge Meadow; pond in town of Ashburnham	Fitchburg.
Stone; brook in northwest part of Goshen	Chesterfield.
Stone; brook in Auburn, 2 miles long	Webster.
Stone; hill in western part of Brookfield; elevation, 900 feet	Brookfield.
Stone House; hill in town of Holden; elevation, 1,100 feet	Worcester.
Stone Wall; beach on south coast of Chilmark, Marthas Vineyard	Gay Head.
Stoneham; town in Middlesex County; area, 7 square miles	Boston.
Stoneham; principal village in town of same name on Boston and Lowell R. R	Boston.
Stoneville; village in Auburn	Webster.
Stoneville; reservoir in Auburn	Webster.
Stony; brook in South Hadley	Springfield.
Stony; brook in southeast part of South Scituate	Abington.
Stony; brook in Lincoln and Weston	Framingham.
Stony; brook in Westford and Chelmsford, 7 miles long, tributary to Merrimac River	Lowell.
Stony; brook in southern part of Lynn	Boston Bay.
Stony; brook in Middleboro	Middleboro.
Stony; brook in Carver, 2¼ miles long	Middleboro.
Stony; brook in Hyde Park and Boston, 4 miles long	Boston.
Stony; brook in Granby	Palmer.
Stony Brook; village in Weston	Framingham.
Stop; river in Medfield	Franklin.
Stoughton; town in Norfolk County; area, 17 square miles	Dedham.
Stoughton; village in town of same name, on Stoughton branch Boston and Providence R. R	Dedham.
Stow; town in Middlesex County; area, 18 square miles	{ Marlboro. { Framingham.
Stow; village in town of same name	Marlboro.
Stow; brook in Framingham and Southboro	Framingham.
Straitsmouth; island near eastern coast of Rockport, near Gap Head	Gloucester.
Straw Hollow; village in Boylston	Marlboro.
Strawberry; hill in Acton; elevation, 340 feet	Framingham.
Strawberry; hill in western part of Hull	Boston Bay.
Strawberry; point on southeastern border of Mattapoiset, south of Pine Neck Cove	New Bedford.
Stream; river in eastern part of Abington	Abington.
Strobridge; hill in Northfield; elevation, 940 feet	Warwick.
Strong; island near Chatham	Chatham.
Strong; pond in Newton	Boston.
Strongwater; brook in Tewksbury, 4 miles long, tributary to Shawshine River	Lawrence.
Stump; pond in north part of Halifax	{ Abington. { Middleboro
Sturbridge; town in Worcester County; area, 38 square miles.	Brookfield.
Sturbridge; village in town of same name	Brookfield.

A GEOGRAPHIC DICTIONARY OF MASSACHUSETTS.

	Atlas sheets.
Succonesset; point on southeast coast of Mashpee	Barnstable.
Sucker; brook in Webster, 2 miles long, flows into Lake Chaubunagungamaug	Webster.
Sucker; brook in West Brookfield, 2 miles long, tributary to Wickaboag pond	Barre.
Sucker; pond in Framingham	Framingham.
Sudbury; town in Middlesex County; area, 26 square miles	Framingham.
Sudbury; pond in Framingham	Framingham.
Sudbury; river in Middlesex County	{ Marlboro. Framingham.
Sudbury Center; village in town of Sudbury, on Old Colony R. R.	Framingham.
Sugar Loaf; mountain in southern part of New Ashford; altitude, 2,040 feet	Greylock.
Sugarloaf; brook flowing through northeastern part of Whately.	Northampton.
Sugarloaf; hill in Webster; elevation, 760 feet	Webster.
Sulphur; hill in Northboro	Marlboro.
Summer; hill in Maynard; elevation, 380 feet	Framingham.
Sunderland; town in southern part of Franklin County; area, 13 square miles	Northampton.
Sunderland; village in western part of town of same name, on Connecticut River	Northampton.
Sunk; brook in Greenwich, 3 miles long, flows into Swift River.	Belchertown.
Sunk; pond in Dana	Belchertown.
Sunken; brook in Dighton, 2 miles long, tributary to Sarganset River	Taunton.
Suntaug; lake on line between Peabody and Lynnfield	{ Lawrence. Salem.
Surfside; village on south coast of Nantucket	Nantucket.
Sursuit; creek in Dennis, flows into Cape Cod Bay	{ Wellfleet. Yarmouth.
Sutton; town in Worcester County; area, 36 square miles	{ Blackstone. Webster.
Sutton; village in town of same name	Webster.
Swamp; brook in north part of Pembroke	Abington.
Swampscott; town in Essex County; area, 3 square miles	Boston Bay.
Swampscott; station in southwest part of Swampscott	Boston Bay.
Swan; pond in Yarmouth	Yarmouth.
Swan; pond in Dennis	Yarmouth.
Swan; pond in North Reading	Lawrence.
Swan Pond; river in Dennis, 2 miles long, flows into Nantucket Sound	Yarmouth.
Swansea; town in southwestern part of Bristol County; area, 23 square miles.	{ Taunton. Providence. Fall River.
Swansea; village in southern part of town of same name	Fall River.
Swansea Factory; village in Swansea	Taunton.
Sweetman; mountain in Granville; altitude, 1,503 feet	Granville.
Swift; hill in southwestern part of Falmouth	Falmouth.
Swift; pond in Wareham	Plymouth.
Swift; river in Hampshire, tributary to Chicopee River	{ Chesterfield. Palmer. Winchendon. Belchertown.

Atlas sheets

Swift Neck; peninsula projecting northeasterly from western portion of Wareham, into Wareham River.................. Falmouth.
Swift River; village in east part of Cummington.............
Taconic Range; range of broken hills trending southward { Pittsfield. through western part of Berkshire County. { Berlin.
Tallow; hill in Winchendon; elevation, 1,100 feet............. Winchendon.
Tamett; brook in Lakeville, flows into Assawompsett Pond... Middleboro.
Tapley; brook tributary to Goldthwait Brook, in eastern part of Peabody.. Salem.
Tapleyville; station in southern part of Danvers.............. Salem.
Tarkill; brook in Agawam, 1 mile long........................ Springfield.
Tarpaulin; cove on coast of Naushon, in town of Gosnold..... Gay Head.
Tarpaulin Cove; light-house on coast of Naushon Island, in town of Gosnold .... Gay Head.
Tarrot; hill in Blandford; elevation, 1,303 feet................ Granville.
Tasseltop; village in Douglas .... Blackstone.
Tatnuck; village in Worcester .... Worcester.
Tatum Station; village in West Springfield.................... Springfield.
Taunton; city in Bristol County; area 49 square miles .... Taunton.
Taunton; river in southeastern Massachusetts, flowing into { Taunton. Narragansett Bay. { Fall River. { Middleboro.
Taylor; brook tributary to Quaboag River in Warren and Brimfield .... Brookfield.
Taylor; pond in Chatham .... Yarmouth.
Tekoa; mountain in Montgomery; altitude 1,211 feet .... Granville.
Telegraph; hill in Plymouth; elevation 220 feet............... Plymouth.
Telegraph; hill in central part of Marshfield; elevation 200 feet Duxbury.
Tempe Knob; point of about 120 feet elevation on most southerly peninsula of Wareham................................ Falmouth.
Templeton; town in Worcester County; area 32 square miles.. Winchendon.
Templeton Center; village in town of Templeton............. Winchendon.
Ten Mile; river in North Attleboro and Attleboro and in Rhode Island .... Providence.
Ten Pound; island in Gloucester Harbor....................... Gloucester.
Teneriffe; hill in western part of Brookfield; elevation 880 feet Brookfield.
Tenneyville; village in Palmer on Boston and Albany R. R.... Palmer.
Terrydiddle; hill in Rehoboth; altitude 140 feet.............. Taunton.
Tespaquin; pond in Middleboro .... Middleboro.
Tewksbury; town in Middlesex County; area 24 square miles. { Lowell. { Lawrence.
Tewksbury Center; village on Salem and Lowell R. R. in Tewksbury .... Lawrence.
Tewksbury; railroad junction in town of Tewksbury on Salem and Lowell R. R .... Lawrence
Thatch; island at entrance of Poponesset Bay on southeast coast of Mashpee... Barnstable.
Thatch Bank; islet about one-half mile off northwestern coast of Gloucester .... Gloucester.
Thatcher; brook in Attleboro, tributary to Ten Mile River.... Providence.
Thatcher; island off Cape Ann, Rockport..................... Gloucester.
The Cove; bay opening into Barnstable Harbor, Barnstable.. Barnstable.
The Graves; island in Boston Bay .... Boston Bay.
The Nook; arm of Kingston Bay indenting coast of Duxbury, west of Captains Hill.. Duxbury.

GANNETT.] A GEOGRAPHIC DICTIONARY OF MASSACHUSETTS. 111

Atlas sheets.

The Throne; hill on boundary between Pepperell and Groton; elevation, 484 feet .... Groton.
Thermopylæ; gap at west end of Holyoke range .... Northampton.
Third; brook in Buckland, 1 mile long; flows into Deerfield River .... Hawley.
Third Herring; brook on southwest boundary of South Scituate. Abington.
Thompson; brook in Berkley and Lakeville, 1 mile long ...... Middleboro.
Thompson; brook tributary to Green River, in western part of New Ashford .... Greylock.
Thompson; hill in western part of Gloucester; elevation, 220 feet .... Gloucester.
Thompson; island in Boston Harbor .... Boston.
Thompson; pond in New Salem .... Belchertown.
Thompson; village in central part of Essex .... Salem.
Thompsonville; village in Newton .... Boston.
Thorndike; village in town of Palmer .... Palmer.
Three Cornered; pond in Plymouth .... Plymouth.
Three-Mile; brook in Agawam, 3 miles long .... Springfield.
Three-Mile; hill in northern part of Great Barrington; elevation, 1,240 feet .... Sheffield.
Three-Mile; pond in northeastern part of Sheffield, containing 104 acres and drained by Iron Works Brook .... Sheffield.
Three-Mile; river, 8 miles long, in Norton, Taunton, and Dighton, tributary to Taunton River .... Taunton.
Three Rivers; village in Palmer, on New London Northern R. R. Palmer.
Tibbs Meadow; brook in south part of Pembroke .... Abington.
Tilden; island in North River, in northwestern part of Marshfield .... Duxbury.
Tillison; brook in Granville .... Granville.
Tilton; hill in eastern part of Ipswich; elevation, 160 feet .... Salem.
Tinker; island east of Marblehead .... Boston Bay.
Tisbury; town in Dukes County; area, 32 square miles .... Marthas Vineyard.
Tisbury; river in Chilmark and Tisbury, Marthas Vineyard... Gay Head.
Tispaquin; pond in Middleboro .... Middleboro.
Titicut; village in Middleboro .... Middleboro.
Titicut; swamp in Raynham .... Taunton.
Tob; hill in Westhampton; elevation, 1,245 feet .... Chesterfield.
Toby; mountain in central part of Sunderland; altitude, 1,275 feet .... Northampton.
Todd; mountain in Charlemont; altitude, 1,711 feet .... Hawley.
Tolland; town in Hampden county; area 31 square miles .... { Granville. Sandisfield. }
Tolland; village in central part of town of same name .... Sandisfield.
Tom; hill on western boundary of Natick; elevation 280 feet.. Framingham.
Tom; mountain in Holyoke; elevation, 1160 feet .... Springfield.
Tom Ball; hill in West Stockbridge; elevation 1,930 feet ...... Pittsfield.
Tom Nevers Head; point of land on south coast of Nantucket Nantucket.
Tomblin; hill on eastern boundary of Shrewsbury; elevation 500 feet .... Marlboro.
Tomlin; swamp in western part of Lynn .... Boston Bay.
Tonset; village in town of Orleans .... Wellfleet.
Toovhka; pond in Nantucket .... Nantucket.
Tophet; brook tributary to Hoosic River in eastern part of Adams .... Greylock.
Tophet; swamp in north part of Carlisle .... Lowell.

	Atlas sheets.
Topsfield; town near central part of Essex county; area, 13 square miles	Salem.
Topsfield; village in town of same name	Salem.
Torrey; pond in east part of South Scituate	Abington.
Tour; mountain in Easthampton and South Hadley; altitude, 1,200 feet	Springfield.
Tower; mountain in Hancock; altitude 2,185 feet	Pittsfield.
Tower Hill; station in Weston on Massachusetts Central R. R.	Framingham.
Town; brook draining Billington Sea into Plymouth Harbor	Plymouth.
Town; cove on northern boundary line of Orleans; opens into Nauset Harbor	Wellfleet.
Town; hill in Topsfield; elevation 240 feet	Salem.
Town; hill rising back of village of Provincetown	Provincetown.
Town; hill in central part of Ipswich; elevation 160 feet	Salem.
Town; island in Barnstable Harbor, Barnstable	Barnstable.
Town; river in north part of Bridgewater	{ Middleboro. Abington.
Town; swamp in west part of Scituate	Abington.
Town Hill; village in northwestern part of Sandisfield	Sandisfield.
Town Meadow; brook in Leicester, two miles long, flows into Greenville reservoir	Webster.
Town River; bay on east coast of Quincy	Boston Bay.
Townsend; town in Middlesex County; area, 31 square miles	{ Fitchburg. Groton.
Townsend; village in town of same name, on Fitchburg R. R., Petersburg and Shirley Branch	Groton.
Townsend; hill in town of same name; elevation, 586 feet	Groton.
Townsend; hill in southwestern part of Fall River; elevation, 280 feet	Fall River.
Townsend Harbor; village in town of Townsend, on Fitchburg R. R., Petersburg and Shirley Branch	Groton.
Towser Neck; point of land extending into Haskell Swamp, Rochester	New Bedford.
Train; hill on eastern boundary of Natick	Framingham.
Trap Rock Ledge; hill in Deerfield; elevation, 440 feet	Greenfield.
Trapfall; brook in Ashby, 4 miles long, flows into Willard Brook	Fitchburg.
Traphole; brook in Norwood, Walpole, and Sharon	Dedham.
Trapp; pond in Edgartown, Marthas Vineyard; opens into Sengekontucket Pond	Marthas Vineyard.
Treadwell Island; creek in eastern part of Ipswich	Salem.
Tremont; village in Wareham	Middleboro.
Triangle; pond in northern part of Plymouth	Plymouth.
Triangle; pond in Sandwich	Barnstable.
Triphammer; pond in eastern part of Hingham	Abington.
Tripple; brook in Southampton, 2 miles long, tributary to Manhan River	Springfield.
Trouant; island in North River, Scituate	Duxbury.
Trout; brook in Templeton	Winchendon.
Trout; brook in Princeton and Holden, 3 miles long, tributary to Quinepoxet River	Worcester.
Trout; brook in Dover	Franklin.
Trout; brook in Dracut, 1¼ miles long, tributary to Richardson Brook	Lowell.

A GEOGRAPHIC DICTIONARY OF MASSACHUSETTS.

	Atlas sheets.
Trout; brook in Townsend, 1¼ miles long, tributary to Squannacook River	Groton.
Trout; brook tributary to middle branch of Westfield River, in Peru and Worthington	Becket.
Trull; brook in Tewksbury, 2 miles long, tributary to Merrimac River	Lowell.
Truro; town in Barnstable County; area, 22 square miles	{ Wellfleet. Provincetown.
Truro; village in town of same name	Wellfleet.
Tuck; point on southern coast of Beverly	Salem.
Tuckernuck; island in Nantucket County, north of western extremity of Nantucket	Muskeget.
Tuft; brook tributary to Quinebaug River, in Warren, Worcester, and Hampden counties	Brookfield.
Tuft; hill in town of New Braintree; elevation, 1,179 feet	Barre.
Tuft; village in Dudley	Webster.
Tuft Branch; stream in Dudley, 4 miles long, tributary to Quinebaug River	Webster.
Tuft College; buildings on Walnut Hill, which is partly in Medford and partly in Somerville	Boston.
Tully; brook in Warwick and Orange, flows into west branch of Tully River, 5 miles long	Warwick.
Tully; mountain in Orange; altitude, 1,160 feet	Winchendon.
Tully; river in Orange and Athol	Winchendon.
Tully; meadow in Orange	Warwick.
Tullyville; village in Orange	Warwick.
Tupper; island in Barnstable Harbor, Barnstable	Barnstable.
Turkey; hill in central part of Ipswich; elevation, 240 feet	Salem.
Turkey; hill in Lunenburg; elevation, 647 feet	Groton.
Turkey; hill in east part of Westhampton	Chesterfield.
Turkey; hill in western part of Cohasset	Abington.
Turkey; hill in Newburyport; elevation, 140 feet	Newburyport.
Turkey Hill; brook in Paxton and Spencer, 2 miles long	Worcester.
Turkey Hill; pond in Paxton and Rutland	Worcester.
Turner; hill in southwestern part of Ipswich; elevation, 260 feet	Salem.
Turner; pond in Lancaster	Groton.
Turner Falls; village in Montague, on Fitchburg R. R.	Greenfield.
Turner Mills; village in Bristol County on line between Dartmouth and New Bedford	New Bedford.
Turnpike; station on Old Colony R. R., Taunton Branch, in Lakeville	Middleboro.
Turtle; pond in Greenwich	Belchertown.
Turtle; pond in Yarmouth	Yarmouth.
Tussock; brook tributary to Jones River, in northeastern part of Kingston	Duxbury.
Tuttle; brook tributary to middle branch of Westfield River in northern part of Middlefield	Becket.
Twelve Mile; brook in Monson and Wilbraham, 6 miles long, tributary to Chicopee River	Palmer.
Twopenny Loaf; low, sandy point on northern coast of Gloucester, west of Coffin Beach	Gloucester.
Tyer; cove, part of Great Tisbury Pond, Marthas Vineyard	Marthas Vineyard.
Tyng; island in Merrimac River, in Tyngsboro	Lowell.

Bull. 116——8

	Atlas sheets.
Tyng; pond in Tyngsboro...	Lowell.
Tyngsboro; town in Middlesex County; area, 19 square miles..	Lowell.
Tyngsboro; village in town of same name, on Boston, Lowell and Nashua R. R..	Lowell.
Tyringham; mountain town in Berkshire County; area, 20 square miles.	{ Becket. { Sandisfield.
Tyringham; village in town of same name................:...	Sandisfield.
Uncas; pond in Franklin...	Franklin.
Uncatena; island in Buzzards Bay, west of Woods Holl......	Falmouth.
Unchechehaton, pond in Lunenburg............................	Groton.
Undine; brook in Mount Washington, draining Undine Lake. Also called Guilford Brook..................................	Sheffield.
Undine; lake in northeastern part of Mount Washington. Also called Guilford Pond......*...................................	Sheffield.
Undine; mountain in northeastern part of Mount Washington; altitude, 2,195 feet..:..	Sheffield.
Union Square; part of town of Somerville	Boston.
Unionville; village in Franklin, on New York and New England R. R., Franklin Branch.......................................	Franklin.
Unionville; village in Holden ....:........	Worcester.
Unkamet; brook tributary to Housatonic River, in Pittsfield..	Becket.
Unquetenassett; brook in Dunstable and Groton, 4 miles long, tributary to Nashua River	Groton.
Unquomonk; brook tributary to Mill River, in southwestern part of Williamsburg......:................................	Northampton.
Unquomonk; hill in southwestern part of Williamsburg; elevation, 1,180 feet...	Northampton.
Upper;_pond in Belchertown ...., ...	Belchertown.
Upper Gate; pond in eastern part of Barnstable...............	Barnstable.
Upper Naukeag; pond in Ashburnham........................	Fitchburg.
Upper Plain; village in Hingham ....:.....	Abington.
Upton; town in Worcester County; area, 21 square miles......	Blackstone.
Upton; village in town of same name..........................	Blackstone.
Upton; hill in Peabody; elevation, 200 feet....................	Lawrence.
Uxbridge; town in Worcester County; area, 30 square miles...	Blackstone.
Uxbridge; village in town of same name, on Providence and Worcester R. R	Blackstone.
Valley; brook in Warwick.......................................	Warwick.
Valley; brook in Granville, tributary to east branch of Farmington River...	Granville.
Valley; swamp in western part of South Scituate..............	Abington.
Van Deusenville; village and railway station in northwestern part of Great Barrington on William River................	Sheffield.
Varnum; brook in Pepperell tributary to Nashua River........	Groton.
Vaughan; hill in town of Bolton; elevation, 640 feet.........	Marlboro.
Venturer; pond in Springfield...................................	Springfield.
Very; pond near summit of Taconic range in Hancock.........	Berlin.
Vine; brook in Billerica, Burlington, and Lexington, 6 miles long, tributary to Shawshine River.	{ Lawrence. { Lowell. { Boston.
Vineyard; hill in western part of Hamilton; elevation, 120 feet.	Salem.
Vineyard; sound between Cape Cod and Elizabeth Islands on the northwest and Marthas Vineyard on the southeast.....	Falmouth.
Vineyard Haven; village in Tisbury, Marthas Vineyard.....	{ Marthas Vineyard. { Wellfleet.

A GEOGRAPHIC DICTIONARY OF MASSACHUSETTS. 115

Atlas sheets.

Vineyard Haven; harbor on coast of Tisbury and Cottage City, Marthas Vineyard	Marthas Vineyard.
Vision; mountain in Wilbraham; altitude, 860 feet	Palmer.
Vosburg; hill in southern part of Great Barrington	Sheffield.
Vose; hill in Maynard; elevation, 260 feet	Framingham.
Waban; lake in Wellesley	Framingham.
Wachusett; mountain in Princeton; altitude, 2,000 feet	Worcester.
Wachusett; pond on boundary line between Princeton and Westminster	Fitchburg.
Wachusett; village in Westminster	Fitchburg.
Wachusett; station on Fitchburg R. R., in Fitchburg	Fitchburg.
Wading; river in Mansfield and Norton, tributary to Three-Mile River	Taunton.
Wadkin; hill in Douglas; elevation, 820 feet	Webster.
Wadsworth; village in Franklin on New York and New England R. R., main line	Franklin.
Wadsworth; hill in central part of Becket; elevation, 1,880 feet	Becket.
Wakeby; village in Sandwich	Barnstable.
Wakeby; pond in Mashpee, containing about 375 acres, connected with Mashpee pond on the south	Barnstable.
Wakefield; town in Middlesex County; area, 10 square miles	{ Boston. Lawrence.
Wakefield, principal village in town of same name on Wakefield branch of eastern division of Boston and Maine R. R.	Lawrence.
Walcott; hill in west part of Williamsburg	Chesterfield.
Walden; hill in Peabody; elevation, 220 feet	Lawrence.
Walden; lake in Concord	Framingham.
Wales; town in Hampden County; area, 16 square miles	{ Palmer. Brookfield.
Wales; principal village in town of same name	Brookfield.
Wales; brook tributary to Quinebaug River in Wales and Brimfield	Brookfield.
Wales; pond in center of town of same name	Brookfield.
Walker; brook in town of Mason, N. H., and town of Townsend, Mass., 6 miles long	Fitchburg.
Walker; brook in Chester, flowing into west branch of Westfield River	Chesterfield.
Walker; brook tributary to Westfield River in Becket	Becket.
Walker; mountain in Sturbridge	Brookfield.
Walker; pond in eastern part of Sturbridge	Brookfield.
Walker; pond in Harwich	Yarmouth.
Walkerville; village in Natick	Framingham.
Wall; pond in southern part of Plymouth	Plymouth.
Wallum; pond in State of Rhode Island and in town of Douglas	Webster.
Wallum Pond; hill in Douglas; elevation, 778 feet	Webster.
Walnut; hill in Orange; elevation, 840 feet	Warwick.
Walnut; hill in north part of Hanover	Abington.
Walnut; hill in northern part of Williamsburg; altitude, 1,440 feet	Northampton.
Walnut; hill in Blandford; elevation, 1,760 feet	Granville.
Walnut; hill in southwest part of Chesterfield	Chesterfield.
Walnut; hill in Buckland; elevation, 1,240 feet	Hawley.
Walnut; hill in Brookline; elevation, 300 feet	Boston.
Walnut; hill on eastern boundary of Goshen	Chesterfield.

		Atlas sheets.
Walnut Tree; hill in south part of Scituate		Abington.
Walpole; town in Norfolk County; area, 22 square miles		Dedham. *Franklin.*
Walpole; village in town of same name on New York and New England R. R., main line		Franklin.
Waltham; city in Middlesex County; area, 15 square miles		Boston. *Framingham.*
Waltham; principal village in town of same name on Fitchburg R. R		Boston.
Wankinco Neck; point of land east of Wareham River, in Wareham		Plymouth
Wankinco; river flowing into Wareham River and forming part of boundary between Carver and Plymouth		Plymouth.
Waupenum; brook in Pittsfield		Pittsfield.
Waquoit; bay, arm of Vineyard Sound, indenting southern coast of Barnstable County		Falmouth.
Waquoit; village in southeastern part of Falmouth		Falmouth.
Ward; hill in Bradford; elevation, 272 feet		Haverhill.
Ward; hill in Phillipston; elevation, 1,340 feet		Winchendon.
Ward; mount in Marlboro; elevation, 400 feet		Framingham.
Ward; pond in Ashburnham		Fitchburg.
Ward; pond in southern part of Becket		Sandisfield.
Ward; stream in Worthington, about 4 miles long, unites with Watt stream at Ringville to form Little River		Chesterfield.
Ward Hill; station in Bradford on Boston and Maine R. R.		Lawrence.
Ware; town in Hampshire County; area, 28 square miles		Belchertown. *Barre.* *Palmer.* *Brookfield.*
Ware; principal village in town of same name, on Ware River branch, Boston and Albany R. R		Barre.
Ware; river tributary to Chicopee River, in central part of the State.		Worcester. *Barre.* *Fitchburg.* *Palmer.*
Ware Center; village in town of Ware		Belchertown.
Wareham; town in southerly part of Plymouth County, on northern border of Buzzards Bay; area, 41 square miles.		Middleboro. *Plymouth.* *New Bedford.* *Falmouth.*
Wareham; principal village in town of same name		Plymouth.
Wareham; river draining southeastern part of Plymouth County and flowing into northern part of Buzzards Bay		Falmouth.
Wareham Center; village in town of Ware		Plymouth.
Warner; mountain near eastern bank of Connecticut River, in town of Hadley; elevation, 500 feet		Northampton.
Warner; mountain in southeastern part of Great Barrington; altitude, 1,835 feet		Sheffield.
Warner; pond in Greenwich		Belchertown.
Warren; town in Worcester County; area, 29 square miles		Brookfield. *Palmer.*
Warren; principal village in town of same name		Brookfield.
Warren; brook in Upton		Blackstone.
Warren; cove on coast of Plymouth		Plymouth.

A GEOGRAPHIC DICTIONARY OF MASSACHUSETTS. 117

	Atlas sheets.
Warren; fort on George Island, Boston Bay	Boston Bay.
Warren; hill in Stow; elevation, 440 feet	Marlboro.
Warren; point on southern coast of Wareham, projecting southwesterly into Buzzards Bay at mouth of Wareham River	Falmouth.
Warren; reservoir in Swansea	Taunton.
Warren; river in Swansea and Rehoboth and in State of Rhode Island	Providence.
Warwick; town in Franklin County; area, 38 square miles	Warwick.
Warwick; village in town of same name	Warwick.
Wash; brook in Sudbury, flows into Sudbury River	Framingham.
Washing; pond in Nantucket	Nantucket.
Washington; town in central part of Berkshire County; area, 37 square miles	Becket.
Washington; village in town of same name	Becket.
Washington; village, part of Boston	Boston.
Washington Station; village and railway station in Washington	Becket.
Watatic; mountain in Ashburnham; altitude, 1,840 feet	Fitchburg.
Watatic; pond in town of Ashburnham	Fitchburg.
Watcha; pond in Tisbury, Marthas Vineyard	Marthas Vineyard.
Water; river in southern part of Essex County, on line of Danvers and Peabody	Salem.
Waterbug; hill in Blackstone; elevation, 440 feet	Blackstone.
Watertown; town in Middlesex County; area, 4 square miles	Boston.
Watertown; village in town of same name, on Watertown branch, Fitchburg R. R.	Boston.
Waterville; village in Winchendon	Winchendon.
Waterville; village in Middleboro	Middleboro.
Watson; pond in Taunton	Taunton.
Watt; stream in Worthington, 4 miles long; unites with Ward Stream at Ringville to form Little River	Chesterfield.
Wattle; pond in Groton	Groton.
Watuppa; pond of fresh water in Fall River, extending southward to Westport and covering nearly 5,000 acres	Fall River.
Wauwinet; village in Nantucket	Nantucket.
Waverly; village in Belmont, on Fitchburg R. R.	Boston.
Wayland; town in Middlesex County; area, 17 square miles	Framingham.
Wayland; village in town of same name, on Massachusetts Central R. R.	Framingham.
Webb; brook in Billerica, 2 miles long, tributary to Shawshine River	Lawrence.
Webster; town in Worcester County; area, 16 square miles	Webster.
Webster; principal village in town of same name, on New York and New England R. R., Southbridge branch	Webster.
Webster Place; station in southern part of Marshfield	Duxbury.
Wedge; pond in Winchester	Boston.
Weedweeder; two ponds in Nantucket	Nantucket.
Week; pond in southwestern part of Sandwich	Falmouth.
Weir; village in town of Taunton, on main line Old Colony R. R.	Taunton.
Weir; river in northeast part of Hingham	Boston Bay.
Wekepeke; brook in Lancaster, Leominster, and Sterling	{ Worcester. Marlboro. }
Well; creek flowing into north side of Barnstable Harbor	Barnstable.

	Atlas sheets.
Wellesley; town in Norfolk County; area, 11 square miles....	Framingham.
Wellesley; village in town of same name, on Boston and Albany R. R.	Framingham.
Wellesley Hills; village in town of Wellesley, on Boston and Albany R. R.	Framingham.
Wellfleet; town in Barnstable County; area, 23 square miles..	Wellfleet.
Wellfleet; village in town of same name, on Wellfleet Harbor and on Old Colony R. R., Cape Cod division	Wellfleet.
Wellfleet; harbor on west coast of town of same name	Wellfleet.
Wellingsly; village in northern part of Plymouth	Plymouth.
Wenatuxet; village in Plympton	Middleboro.
Wenatuxet; river in Halifax, Plymouth, and Carver, 6 miles long	Middleboro.
Wenaumet Neck; peninsula on western coast of Bourne, extending about 2 miles southwesterly into Buzzards Bay....	Falmouth.
Wendell; town in Franklin County; area, 29 square miles....	Warwick.
Wendell; village in town of same name	Warwick.
Wenham; town in southeastern part of Essex County; area, 9 square miles	Salem.
Wenham; village in eastern part of town of same name	Salem.
Wenham; lake on boundary line between Wenham and Beverly.	Salem.
Wenham; pond in Carver	Middleboro.
Wenham; swamp in western part of Wenham and Hamilton..	Salem.
Wenham; village in Carver	Middleboro.
Wenuchus; lake in central part of Lynn	Boston Bay.
Wessonville; village in Westboro	Marlboro.
West; beach on southeastern coast of Beverly	Salem.
West; brook, tributary to Mill River in Whately	Northampton.
West; brook, tributary to Hoosic River, in Cheshire and Williamstown	Greylock.
West; brook, left tributary to Quinebaug River, in Bromfield.	Brookfield.
West; brook in Hampden and Wilbraham	Palmer.
West; brook in Orange and Athol	Warwick.
West; creek in eastern part of Rowley, flowing into Rowley River	Salem.
West; hill in Marlboro; elevation, 580 feet	Marlboro.
West; hill in town of Monson; elevation, 940 feet	Palmer.
West; hill in west part of Worthington; elevation, 1,800 feet..	Chesterfield.
West; island in Buzzards Bay, south of Nasketucket Bay....	New Bedford.
West; mountain in Brimfield	Brookfield.
West; mountain in Bernardston; altitude, 1,145 feet	Greenfield.
West; pond in Bolton	Marlboro.
West; river in towns of Upton, Northbridge, and Uxbridge; flows into Blackstone River	Blackstone.
West; village in North Reading	Lawrence.
West Abington; village in north part of Abington	Abington.
West Acton; village in town of Acton, on Fitchburg R. R....	Framingham.
West Andover; village in Andover	Lawrence.
West Andover; station on Boston and Lowell R. R., in town of Andover	Lawrence.
West Barnstable; village in Barnstable, on Cape Cod branch, Old Colony R. R	Barnstable.
West Becket; village in southwestern part of Becket	Becket.
West Bedford; village in Bedford	Framingham.

	Atlas sheets.
West Berkley; village in town of Berkley	Taunton.
West Berlin; village in town of Berlin, on Massachusetts Central R. R.	Marlboro.
West Boxford; village in Boxford	Lawrence.
West Boylston; town in Worcester County; area, 25 square miles	Worcester.
West Boylston; village in town of same name, on Massachusetts Central R. R.	Worcester.
West Branch; brook in Heath tributary to west branch Green River	Hawley.
West Brewster; village in town of Brewster	Yarmouth.
West Bridgewater; town in Plymouth County; area, 17 square miles	{ Abington. Dedham.
West Brimfield; station in town of Brimfield, on Boston and Albany R. R.	Palmer.
West Brookfield; town in Worcester County; area, 20 square miles	{ Barre. Brookfield.
West Brookfield; principal village in town of same name	Brookfield.
West Chelmsford; village in town of Chelmsford, on Stony Brook R. R.	Lowell.
West Chop; light-house on north coast of Tisbury, Marthas Vineyard	Marthas Vineyard.
West Cummington; village in northwest part of Cummington	Chesterfield.
West Dedham; village in town of Dedham	Dedham.
West Dennis; village in town of Dennis	Yarmouth.
West Dudley; village in town of Dudley, on New York and New England R. R.	Webster.
West Duxbury; village in west part of Duxbury	Abington.
West Falmouth; village and railway station, in western part of Falmouth	Falmouth.
West Farms; village in southwestern part of Northampton	Northampton.
West Farms; village in Westfield	Granville.
West Fitchburg; village in Fitchburg, on Fitchburg R. R.	Fitchburg.
West Gloucester; village in western part of Gloucester	Gloucester.
West Gloucester; station (railway) near central part of Gloucester	Gloucester.
West Granville; village in town of Granville	Granville.
West Groton; village in Groton, on Fitchburg R. R.	Groton.
West Hanover; village in west part of Hanover	Abington.
West Harwich; village in town of Harwich	Yarmouth.
West Hatfield; village and railway station, in southwestern part of Hatfield	Northampton.
West Hawley; village in town of Hawley	Hawley.
West Hingham; village in Western part of Hingham	Abington.
West Hollow; brook in Leyden and in State of Vermont	Greenfield.
West Leominster; station on Old Colony R. R., Fitchburg branch, in Leominster	Fitchburg.
West Leyden; village in town of Leyden	Greenfield.
West Manchester; village and railway station, in southwestern part of Manchester	Salem.
West Mansfield; village in town of Mansfield, on Boston and Providence R. R.	Taunton.
West Meadow; brook in Brockton and West Bridgewater	Dedham.

	Atlas sheets.
West Meadow; hill in Haverhill; elevation, 337 feet	Haverhill.
West Medford; village in town of Medford, on Boston and Lowell R. R.	Boston.
West Medway; village in town of Medway, on New York and New England R. R., Woonsocket division	Franklin.
West Millbury; village in town of Millbury	Webster.
West New Boston; village on Buck River, in the eastern part of Sandisfield	Sandisfield.
West Newbury; town in Essex County; area, 15 square miles.	Newburyport.
West Newbury; village in town of same name	Newburyport.
West Newton; village in town of Newton, on Boston and Albany R. R.	Boston.
West Northfield; village in town of Northfield, on Connecticut River R. R	Warwick.
West Orange; village in town of Orange on Fitchburg R. R ..	Warwick.
West Otis; village in southwestern part of Otis	Sandisfield.
West Parish; village in Westfield	Granville.
West Peabody; railroad junction in northwestern part of Peabody	Salem.
West Quincy; village in town of Quincy, on Old Colony R. R., Granite branch	Dedham.
West Rocky Gutter; brook in Middleboro, 2½ miles long; tributary to Double Brook	Middleboro.
West Roxbury; village in city of Boston, on Boston and Providence R. R	Boston.
West Rutland; village in town of Rutland	Worcester.
West Sandwich; village in Bourne	Plymouth.
West Scituate; village in west part of South Scituate	Abington.
West Springfield; town in Hampden County; area, 15 square miles	Springfield.
West Springfield; village in town of same name, on Boston and Albany R. R	Springfield.
West Sterling; villege in Sterling	Worcester.
West Stockbridge; village in town of same name	Pittsfield.
West Stockbridge; town in Berkshire County; area, 20 square miles	Pittsfield.
West Stockbridge; mountain in Stockbridge; altitude, 1,850 feet	Pittsfield.
West Stockbridge Center; village in the town of West Stockbridge	Pittsfield.
West Sutton; village in town of Sutton	Webster.
West Tisbury; village in town of Tisbury, Marthas Vineyard.	Marthas Vineyard.
West Townsend; village in Townsend, on Fitchburg R. R., Peterboro and Shirley branch	Groton.
West Upton; village in town of Upton	Blackstone.
West Wachusett; brook in Princeton, 2 miles long	Worcester.
West Ware; village in town of Ware, on Boston and Albany R. R., Athol branch	Belchertown.
West Warren; village in western part of Warren	Brookfield.
West Waushacoum; pond in Sterling	Worcester.
West Whately; village in western part of Whately, on West Brook	Northampton.
West Worthington; village in northwest part of Worthington.	Chesterfield.
West Wrentham; village in town of Wrentham	Franklin.

A GEOGRAPHIC DICTIONARY OF MASSACHUSETTS. 121

	Atlas sheets.
West Yarmouth; village in town of Yarmouth	Yarmouth.
Westboro; town in Worcester County; area, 17 square miles	Marlboro.
Westboro; village in town of same name, on Boston and Albany R. R.	Marlboro.
Westbrook; village in northern part of Hatfield, on Mill River.	Northampton.
Westfield; town in Hampden County; area, 41 square miles	{ Springfield. Granville.
Westfield; village in town of same name, on New Haven and Northampton R. R.	{ Granville. Springfield.
Westfield; river, right-hand branch of Connecticut River, in western part of the State	{ Granville. Becket. Chesterfield. Westfield. Greylock. Springfield.
Westfield Little; river in Blandford, Russell, and Westfield. 10 miles long; tributary to Westfield River	{ Springfield. Granville.
Westford; town in Middlesex County; area, 32 square miles	Lowell.
Westford; village in town of same name	Lowell.
Westford; station on Nashua, Acton and Boston R. R., in Westford Station	Lowell.
Westminster; town in Worcester County; area, 37 square miles	Fitchburg.
Westminster; village in town of same name	Fitchburg.
Westminster; station in Westminster, on Fitchburg R. R.	Fitchburg.
Weston; town in Middlesex County; area, 17 square miles	Framingham.
Weston; village in town of same name	Framingham.
Weston; station on Massachusetts Central R.R., in Weston	Framingham.
Westport; town in Bristol County; area, 52 square miles	Fall River.
Westport; harbor at mouth of Westport River, Westport	Fall River.
Westport Harbor; village in southwestern part of Westport	Fall River.
Westport Mills; village on line between Westport and Dartmouth	Fall River.
Westport Point; village in southern part of Westport	Fall River.
Westhampton; town in Hampshire County; area, 28 square miles	Chesterfield.
Westvale; village in town of Concord, on Fitchburg R. R.	Framingham.
Westville; village in Taunton	Taunton.
Westville; village in Sturbridge	Brookfield.
Weweantic; river in Carver and Wareham	{ Middleboro. Plymouth. Falmouth.
Weymouth; town in Norfolk County; area, 19 square miles	Abington.
Weymouth; harbor on northeast coast of Weymouth	Abington.
Weymouth Back; river forming northeast boundary of Weymouth	{ Boston Bay. Abington.
Weymouth Fore; river on east coast of Quincy	{ Abington. Boston Bay.
Weymouth Landing; village in Weymouth Fore River, Weymouth	Abington.
Whale; cove in eastern part of Rockport	Gloucester.
Whately; town in southern part of Franklin County, on Connecticut River; area, 22 square miles	Northampton.
Whately Center; village in central part of Whately	Northampton.

		Atlas sheets.
Wheeler; brook in Blandford, tributary to Pebble Brook		Granville.
Wheeler; hill in Berlin		Marlboro.
Wheeler; point of land in Gloucester between Mill River and Squam River		Gloucester.
Wheelock; hill on boundary between Charlton and Brookfield.		Brookfield.
Wheelockville; village in town of Uxbridge, on Providence and Worcester R. R.		Blackstone.
Whetstone; brook in Wendell, 5 miles long; tributary to Miller River		Warwick.
Whipple; hill in central part of Danvers; elevation, 160 feet.		Salem.
Whispering; hill in Woburn; elevation, 260 feet		Boston.
Whitbeck; mountain on line between Mount Washington and Egremont; altitude, 1,840 feet		Sheffield.
Whitcomb; mountain in eastern part of Florida; altitude, 2,300 feet		Greylock.
White; brook in Agawam, one-half mile long; tributary to Westfield River		Springfield.
White; hill in western part of Essex; elevation, 160 feet		Salem.
White; pond in Hudson		Framingham.
White; pond in southern part of Plymouth		Plymouth.
White; pond in Dedham		Dedham.
White; pond on boundary between Lancaster and Leominster.		Groton.
White; pond on western boundary of Harwich		Yarmouth.
White; pond in Concord		Framingham.
White; pond in Athol		Warwick.
White Head; on western side of Cohasset Harbor, Cohasset..		Abington.
White Island; pond in southern part of Plymouth		Plymouth.
White Lily; pond in northeastern part of Otis		Sandisfield.
White Loaf; mount in Southampton; altitude, 460 feet		Springfield.
White Oak; island in Middleboro, between Bartlett Brook and Taunton River; altitude, 100 to 120 feet		Middleboro.
White Neck; peninsula between Weymouth Fore River and Mill Cove, in northwest part of Weymouth		Abington.
Whitehall; village in Rutland		Worcester.
Whitehall; pond in Hopkinton		Blackstone.
Whiteman; brook in Ashburnham, tributary to Stodge Meadow pond; one-half mile long		Fitchburg.
Whiteman; brook in Ashburnham		Fitchburg.
Whitemore; hill in town of Lancaster; elevation, 435 feet		Marlboro.
Whiteville; village in Mansfield.		Dedham.
Whitin; pond in Northbridge, Sutton, and Uxbridge		Blackstone.
Whiting; pond in Wrentham		Franklin.
Whitinville; village in town of Northbridge		Blackstone.
Whitman; town in Plymouth County; area, 7 square miles		Abington.
Whitman; pond in Weymouth		Abington.
Whitman; river in Westminster and Ashburnham, 6 miles long.		Fitchburg.
Whitmanville; village in Westminster		Fitchburg.
Whitmarsh; brook in northwest part of Worthington		Chesterfield.
Whitney; station in Sherborn, on Boston and Albany R. R., Milford branch		Franklin.
Whittenton; village in Taunton, on main line Old Colony R. R.		Taunton.
Whittier; hill in Amesbury; elevation, 200 feet		Newburyport.
Whortleberry; hill in Dracut; elevation, 400 feet		Lowell.
Whortleberry; hill in West Brookfield; elevation, 968 feet		Barre.

	Atlas sheets.
Whortleberry; pond in Weymouth	Abington.
Wickaboag; pond in West Brookfield, flowing into Quaboag River	Brookfield.
Wickaboag; pond in West Brookfield	Barre.
Wicket; island situated near center of Onset Bay, about one-half mile southeast of village of Onset	Falmouth.
Wickett; brook in Wendell, 5 miles long; tributary to Miller River	Warwick.
Wickett; pond in Wendell	Warwick.
Wiggin; pond in Plymouth	Plymouth.
Wigwam; brook in Mendon, tributary to Blackstone River	Blackstone.
Wigwam; hill in town of Mendon; elevation, 540 feet	Blackstone.
Wigwam; hill in town of Wilbraham; elevation, 860 feet	Palmer.
Wigwam; hill in West Brookfield; elevation, 920 feet	Barre.
Wigwam; pond in Dedham	Dedham.
Wilbraham; town in Hampden County; area, 23 square miles.	Palmer.
Wilbraham; village in town of same name	Palmer.
Wilcox; mountain peak in northwestern part of Monterey; altitude, 2,155 feet	Sheffield.
Wild; harbor, arm of Buzzards Bay indenting coast of Falmouth, south of Nye Neck	Falmouth.
Wild Cat; brook in south part of South Scituate	Abington.
Wild Cat; hill in Ashland; elevation, 400 feet	Framingham.
Wild Cat; hill in south part of South Scituate	Abington.
Wild Cat; mountain in Bernardston; altitude, 1,059 feet	Greenfield.
Wilder; brook in Gardner, 3 miles long	Winchendon.
Wilder; river in Charlemont and Heath, 3 miles long; flows into Deerfield River	Hawley.
Wilkinsonville; village in Sutton	Blackstone.
Will; hill in Middleton; elevation, 220 feet	Lawrence.
Willard; brook in Ashby and Townsend, 6 miles long	Fitchburg.
William; hill in Charlton; elevation, 960 feet	Webster.
William; pond in Marlboro	Marlboro.
William; river in western part of Berkshire County, flowing south through Richmond and West Stockbridge into Housatonic River in Great Barrington.	{ Pittsfield. Sheffield.
Williamsburg; village in central part of Williamsburg on Mill River	Northampton.
Williamsburg; town in northern part of Hampshire County; area, 26 square miles.	{ Northampton. Chesterfield.
Williamstown; town in extreme northwestern part of Berkshire County; area, 51 square miles.	{ Berlin. Greylock.
Williamstown; village in northern part of town of same name	Greylock.
Williamsville; village in West Stockbridge	Pittsfield.
Williamsville; village in town of Hubbardston	Barre.
Willimansett; village in Chicopee on Connecticut River R. R.	Springfield.
Willis; hill in Middleboro; elevation, 200 feet	Middleboro.
Willis; hill in Montague	Greenfield.
Willis; hill in Sudbury	Framingham.
Willis; pond in Sudbury	Framingham.
Willis; reservoir in Douglas	Webster.
Willow; brook tributary to Mystic River	Boston.

	Atlas sheets.
Willow; point in Great Quittacas Pond	Middleboro.
Wilmington; town in Middlesex County; area, 18 square miles	Lawrence.
Wilmington Center; village in town of Wilmington on Lawrence Branch of Boston and Lowell R. R.	Lawrence.
Wilmington Junction; railway junction on Salem and Lowell R. R. and Boston and Maine R. R., Wilmington	Lawrence.
Wilmington; station on main line of Boston and Maine R. R., in Wilmington	Lawrence.
Wilmington; station on Boston and Lowell R. R., in Wilmington	Lawrence.
Wilson; brook in Warwick	Warwick.
Winchell; mountain in Granville; altitude, 1,362 feet	Granville.
Winchendon; town in Worcester County; area, 45 square miles	Winchendon.
Winchendon; village in town of same name on Boston and Albany R. R., Ware River branch	Winchendon.
Winchendon Center; village in town of Winchendon	Winchendon.
Winchester; town in Middlesex County; area, 6 square miles	Boston.
Winchester; principal village in town of same name on Boston and Lowell R. R.	Boston.
Windmill; point of land on northwest coast of Hull	Boston Bay.
Windsor; town in northeastern part of Berkshire County; area, 37 square miles.	Hawley Chesterfield. Becket. Greylock.
Windsor; pond in town of same name	Hawley.
Windsor Hill; village in central part of Windsor	Greylock.
Wine; brook in Phillipston, 2 miles long	Winchendon.
Wing; cove of Buzzards Bay, on southeastern coast of Marion.	Falmouth.
Wings Neck; light-house on southwestern extremity of Wenaumet Neck, in Bourne; fixed white, fifth order; lantern 44 feet above sea level and visible 12 miles	Falmouth.
Winimusset; brook in New Braintree, 1¼ miles long; tributary to Ware River	Barre.
Winneconnet; village in Norton	Taunton.
Winneconnet; pond in Norton	Taunton.
Winning; pond in Billerica	Lowell.
Winter; hill in Dracut; elevation, 240 feet	Lowell.
Winter; pond in Winchester	Boston.
Winthrop; town in Suffolk County; area, 2 square miles	Boston Bay.
Winthrop; fort on Governors Island, in Boston Harbor	Boston.
Winthrop; pond in Holliston	Franklin.
Winthrop Head; cliff or headland on southeast coast of Winthrop	Boston Bay.
Wipple; station in Palmer, on Ware River branch of Boston and Albany R. R.	Palmer.
Wire; village in Spencer	Worcester.
Witch; brook in Townsend, 2 miles long; tributary to Squannacook River	Groton.
Woburn; city in Middlesex County; area, 14 square miles	Boston. Lawrence.
Woburn; principal village in town of same name, on Woburn branch of Boston and Lowell R. R.	Boston.

A GEOGRAPHIC DICTIONARY OF MASSACHUSETTS. 125

	Atlas sheets.
Woepecket; island in Buzzards Bay, about 1 mile northwest of Naushon Island	Falmouth.
Wolf; brook in Townsend	Groton.
Wolf; hill in Southbridge; elevation, 700 feet	Granville.
Wolf; swamp in Townsend	Groton.
Wolf Plain; brook in Rehoboth	Providence.
Wolfpen; hill in Southboro	Marlboro.
Wollaston Heights; village in Quincy, on Old Colony R. R.	Boston.
Wood; brook in Middleboro, 1½ miles long, tributary to Tespaquin Pond	Middleboro.
Wood; hill in Andover; elevation, 340 feet	Lawrence.
Wood; hill in Douglas and Webster; elevation, 939 feet	Webster.
Wood; pond in Ludlow	Palmer.
Wood; pond in Middleboro	Middleboro.
Wood End; village upon Long Point, Provincetown	Provincetown.
Wood End; light-house in Wood End in Provincetown	Provincetown.
Woodbridge; island in Merrimac	Newburyport.
Woodbury; point on southern coast of Beverly, east of Beverly Cove	Salem.
Woodbury; station in western part of Essex, on Boston and Maine R. R.	Salem.
Woodchuck; hill in North Andover; elevation, 320 feet	Lawrence.
Woodruff; mountain in central part of New Marlboro; altitude, 1,740 feet	Sandisfield.
Woods Holl; village in southwestern part of Falmouth	Falmouth.
Woodville; village in Hopkinton	Blackstone.
Woodsville; village in town of Shirley	Groton.
Worcester; city in Worcester County: area, 32 square miles	Worcester. Webster.
Workman; brook in Coleraine, 2 miles long, tributary to Green River	Greenfield.
World's End; head of land 80 feet high on southern side of entrance to Weir River on north coast of Hingham	Boston Bay.
Worthington; town in Hampshire County; area, 33 square miles	Chesterfield.
Worthington; brook in Agawam, 1 mile long	Springfield.
Worthington Center; village in central part of Worthington	Chesterfield.
Worthington Corners; village in north central part of Worthington	Chesterfield.
Wreck; cove on west side of Monomoy Island	Chatham.
Wrentham; town in Norfolk County; area, 35 square miles	Franklin.
Wrentham; village in town of same name	Franklin.
Wright; brook in Billerica, 2 miles long, tributary to Shawshine River	Lawrence.
Wright; brook in northern part of Mount Washington	Sheffield.
Wright; ponds in Ashby	Fitchburg.
Wright; river tributary to Mill River in eastern part of Williamsburg	Northampton.
Wyman; hill in northern part of Manchester; elevation, 160 feet	Salem.
Wyman; hill in northeast part of Braintree	Abington.
Wyoma; lake in central part of Lynn	Boston Bay.
Wyoma; village in central part of Lynn	Boston Bay.

                                                                Atlas sheets.
Wyoming; village in Melrose on Boston and Maine R. R., west
   division .... Boston.
Yarmouth; town in Barnstable County; area, 26 square miles. { Yarmouth.
                                                                { Barnstable.
Yarmouth; village in town of same name..................... Yarmouth.
Yarmouth; camp-meeting grounds in west part of Yarmouth.. Barnstable.
Yarmouth Port; village in northwest part of Yarmouth ...... Barnstable.
Yokun; river in Lenox... Pittsfield.
Yokun Seat; hill in Lenox; elevation, 2,080 feet.............. Pittsfield.
Youth; pond in Methuen .... Lawrence.
Zachary; pond in Upton .... Blackstone.
Zion; hill in Winchester; elvation, 300 feet................... Boston.
Zoar; village in town of Charlemont........................... Hawley.

○

www.ingramcontent.com/pod-product-compliance
Lightning Source LLC
Chambersburg PA
CBHW071454160426
43195CB00013B/2110